BEYOND RELATIVITY

TRANSCENDING THE SPLIT BETWEEN KNOWER & KNOWN

ART TICKNOR

TAT FOUNDATION PRESS

TAT Foundation Press, *www.tatfoundation.org*

Cover design by Bob Fergeson, based on an original concept by Nina Enger.
Cover photo: "Reflective Morn" by Bob Fergeson, *www.NostalgiaWest.com*

Cover fonts: Palatino Linotype, Trajan Pro
Text fonts: Palatino Linotype, Amazone BT, Printers Ornaments One, Life BT

Library of Congress Control Number: 2013934559

Ticknor, Art.
    Beyond Relativity : transcending the split between know-er and known / written by Art Ticknor.
    p. cm.
    Includes index.
    ISBN 978-0-9799630-9-4

1. Spirituality. 2. Self-Realization. 3. Philosophy. I. Title.

Table of Contents

LAUNCHING THE VECTOR
Ready ... Aim 1
Ch. 1. Dissatisfaction 3
Ch. 2. The Catalyst 21
Ch. 3. Determination 33

RISING ACTION & DARK DAYS
Ch. 4. Signposts of Progress 54
Ch. 5. Determination Tested 74
Ch. 6. Crisis of Hope 95
Ch. 7. Stuck in Despair 119
Ch. 8. Struggling to Move 145
Ch. 9. The Knot Untied 168

THE VECTOR MOVES ON ITS OWN MOMENTUM
Ch. 10. Action for Others 216
Ch. 11. Conviction State Revealed 250
Ch. 12. The Last Straw 289

Appendix I: Common-Sense Meditation 325
Appendix II: The Diamond Sutra, Simplified 333
Appendix III: Douglas Harding & Richard Rose 346
About the Author 354
From Readers of Solid Ground of Being 358
Graphics Credits 362
Index 364
The Bottom Line 367
When You're Ready 368

The formula: Look until you see.
The caveat: You may have to go through zero to reach infinity.

Launching the Vector

Ready ...

L oving that which *seems* produces confusion and misery. Loving that which *is* produces clarity and the end of suffering.

What *is,* is your true self, your true state of being. Ultimate truth is the same as knowing the self. But how can the self be known? It requires transcending the split between knower and known, which requires going beyond relativity.

An intentional pursuit of self-knowing, or defining the self, is the real meaning of a religious or spiritual path. The terms *religious*—from the Latin verb "to bind back"—and *spiritual*—based on the Latin verb "to breathe," but generally associated with the belief in the existence of an individual entity that survives death, have connotations that can be off-putting and misleading. A more neutral term for the pursuit would be self-discovery or self-definition.

There's no more justification for *believing* in ultimate or absolute truth than there is for disbelieving. An honest seeker for the truth of self suspends disbelief and questions beliefs. We need to become disillusioned of faulty beliefs about what we are, which involves a struggle against the current that's sweeping our organism from birth to death. If we succeed, we will have cast off all limitations and constrictions, returning to the state of unconditioned, complete and perfect being.

This book is organized into three sections dealing chronologically with the path of self-discovery: from the conscious outset, through the cycle of hope and despair, to the end of suffering—the end of suffering from existential uncertainty, from the sense of separation, vulnerability and mortality. Beyond relativity to That Which Is, to Eternality.

Aim ...

*T*he Outer World as we experience it is a projection of the mind about which we know nothing directly ... only indirectly through the sensory apparatus. The Middle World, the dimension of knowing, is where perceptions and conceptions, thoughts and feelings, are experienced. In the Middle World, knower and known are split ... and the knower is never the known. Only at the center of our being, which is beyond time and beyond space, do we transcend the split and find the end of isolation from the self that we've longed for.

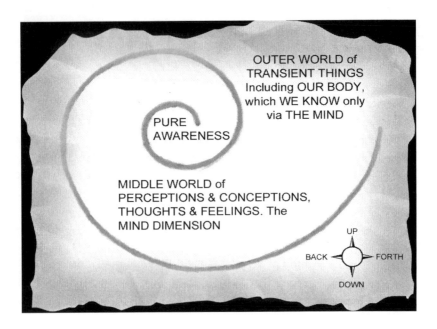

PURE AWARENESS

OUTER WORLD of TRANSIENT THINGS Including OUR BODY, which WE KNOW only via THE MIND

MIDDLE WORLD of PERCEPTIONS & CONCEPTIONS, THOUGHTS & FEELINGS. The MIND DIMENSION

UP

BACK — FORTH

DOWN

1. Dissatisfaction

*T*here's no set practice, route, or number of steps that you can follow to find your self—*the* self. Each individuality or personality is built up based on possible predispositions and life experience, and finding the self is a subtractive or reversal process.

Fortunately we don't have to undo all the learning, all the conditioning, and all our genetic dispositions in order to return to knowing our true state of being. But there is an unfolding, a process of disillusionment, that occurs as we see through our faulty beliefs about what we are. And like the dairyman notes of his cows, there are many paths back to the barn.

I've looked back at my particular path of unfolding by going through 26 years of journals kept between 1978 and 2004, and I've extracted some details for the beginning section of each of the following chapters. The message I hope that comes through: If this fellow can make the trip, anybody can do it.

What you're looking for is closer than you can imagine … closer than your breath, closer than thought or feeling. But if you think you know how close you are, or that you can gauge your progress, you may be fooling yourself. A better way to say that is that an outer part of you may be fooling a more interior part.

The critical factor that led to my success was perseverance. Persevering is difficult during periods where you're not inspired, and even more difficult during periods where you lose hope. But there is always a way … and it's often elusive in its simplicity. For example, my friend and mentor Richard Rose once advised: If you can't inspire yourself, find someone else to inspire.

WHAT CAUSES ACTION is irritation. We move toward acquiring what we desire and away from what we fear. The search for self is prompted largely by the dissatisfaction that goes with believing we are something that was born and is going to die—a thing apart, incomplete, vulnerable, and uncertain. There's a feeling that something's missing, that there's a hole in the center of our being. Coexistent with that deep want is the desire to fill it. But try as we might, we find that nothing is completely and permanently sufficient.

We may go to extraordinary lengths to convince ourselves that the longing is no big deal, or that there's no way to really satisfy it, but we have to try to keep ourselves as distracted as possible to avoid feeling the deep longing, or as medicated as possible to numb the feeling.

Like all pain, the pain of dissatisfaction and unfulfilled longing is trying to tell us something … that there's a problem that needs attention. Trying to mask the symptom doesn't really help in the long run. Pain is a motivator, and the pain of existential dissatisfaction is trying to motivate us to look for wholeness, for completion.

MY MOTHER TOLD me, when I was a grown man with a family of my own, that I had uttered my first complete sentence standing at the screen door in our kitchen, looking toward the back yard: "I want out!" I carry a picture of that scene in my memory now, but I have no idea if it's an actual childhood memory or one that was conjured up as an adult. In any case, and in retrospect, that demand became my silent mantra as an adult. Maybe even before that.

I did a fair amount of skiing when I was growing up near the Vermont border in upstate New York. There were occasional times when I would get a sense of great freedom while skiing down a hill. An even greater sense of freedom occurred in infrequent flying dreams. The night I met Richard Rose, at age 33, I experienced "walking on air." To me, freedom was associated with not being attached to the earth. It was a particular feeling. And the problem was that it was 1) infrequent, and 2) transient.

I HAD A SHELTERED, physically comfortable childhood and parents who provided a stable and secure environment. But I had an increasingly miserable time from school age on, feeling anxious and uncomfortable in my own skin.

Despite gliding through high school with good grades, I flunked out of my first year in college, not having a clue about how to study effectively. Toward the end of that summer my girlfriend announced that she was pregnant—and I was delighted! I felt like I'd found a direction for my life for the first time.

Several months after our son was born, I experienced what I considered the first spiritual elevation of my life. Without any warning, one day while looking at my son the words formed in my mind: "Here's someone I'd like to see ahead of myself at the trough of life's goodies." In other words, I'd fallen in love with someone other than myself. And the revelation simultaneously showed me the "before" condition: "I've been the most selfish person on the planet." I was 19 years old then and felt like I'd been blessed far beyond anything I deserved.

A FEW YEARS LATER, when I was nearing the completion of an undergraduate degree in math, I got hit with a mental bucket of cold water: I admitted to myself that I had no great talent for math and that to continue on with my sleepy plan to go to grad school and stay in academia wouldn't be honest to future students or myself. "I'll have to get a job and go to work eight hours a day five days a week for the rest of my life" struck me as a horrendously boring prospect.

But I took my responsibility to my wife and son seriously and turned my head away from the disappointment. At that time large corporations were starting to install computers to manage their finances, and I stumbled into the nascent field of computer programming for data processing. After a few years of working for my first employer I was distressed at not yet running the company or at least being one of the top executives— my belief in unlimited capability not yet having hit the wall of objective evaluation—and I signed on with a smaller company that was more dynamic in its use of technology.

Before I was 30 years old I was in charge of data processing for the second employer, managing a department of more than 30 people and a multimillion-dollar budget. I had a nice home, a wife and family of three children all of whom I loved dearly— but there was some missing purpose or meaning in my life.

I suffered through periodic bouts of intense dissatisfaction and frustrating attempts to identify what would ease the anguish, but for everything I contemplated I could mentally fast-forward to its attainment and realize, "No, that won't do it." I thought of those agonizing periods at the time as identify crises, although I had no idea why that label occurred to me. But in retrospect, it's exactly what was happening.

In order to ease the pain, I began self-medicating with alcohol, trying to keep a mild buzz on after work and on weekends—a symptom of covert depression, I suppose. I could see no exit from my prison.

I still have the piece of paper where I wrote, on April 1, 1977, "What I want out of life":

1. Self-realization (Watt, Leary, ...)

2. Self-employed
3. Very informal life style (clothes, house, ...)
4. Compatible friends
5. Provide great atmosphere for kids, other people to develop
6. Integrated neighborhood
7. Private room
8. Experience commune living
9. Travel

I also have the following notes I wrote for myself on 6/14/77 on the topic: "What have I learned from the first 32 years of my life, and where am I going from here?" including:

Things I've learned about myself:

1. I'm basically a loner—not by choice, but by nature; I would like to have friends very much, but a combination of shyness and over-criticality of others keeps friendship from developing.
2. There's a big gap between my self-image and the person I think I should be; this is what causes my shyness with others—not wanting them to see the real me (fear of exposure).
3. The only things I'm really interested in are:
    a) Building a beautiful personal environment (architecture, landscape design, interior design).
    b) Learning more about my self and actualizing my potentials.
4. I have a deep desire to experiment with human relations; whenever I read something like Rimmer's novels about premarital living groups or books about communal living, I want to experiment with the ideas immediately.
5. I have a romantic, unreal streak. When I think how out-of-touch I was as a child, I'm constantly surprised at how practical and realistic our kids are—very little fantasy compared to what I think my early years were like.
6. I have positive vibes toward ecstatic experiences (e.g.,

Leary and LSD, Yogananda and religious ecstasy) but have very little respect for institutionalized approaches.

7. I get great pleasure from holding our children when they are small (before they're say 8 to 10) and would always like to have a small child in the house.

Things I've learned about other people:
1. Other people are a mystery to me.
2. I want other people to like me.
I try to treat other people with respect and not make demands on them.

Things I've learned about life in general:
1. From a practical standpoint, I believe that my individual life is of finite duration and has no inherent purpose (other than being part of the scheme of species survival)
2. I like the idea that the individual may be an eye on the universe—that in reality there is no separate self, that we're just manifestations of the universal and infinite whole.

Where am I going from here?
1. Since I'm "going" somewhere effortlessly, why not just relax and enjoy it? (Flow with the Tao.)
2. In my own low-investment way:
    a) Pursue Eastern philosophies and the art of meditation/consciousness expansion.
    b) Find work that is satisfying.

ONE RAINY SUNDAY AFTERNOON in the spring of 1977 my wife and I had taken the kids to a local library, and she spotted a poster she thought I'd be interested in. It was about meetings of a Zen group at Ohio State University. I'd been reading Alan Watts, who popularized Zen in the US, and although I didn't understand what Zen was really about, something in me was fascinated by it. So I decided to check out the group at OSU.

I had done some graduate work in computer science there but was not in school at the time so wasn't in tune with the academic calendar, which ran on quarters. When I went to a meeting, it was during a quarter break and the meetings weren't in session. I think I forgot about it for a while then went again … with the same results. I called the university and talked with the faculty adviser, who said he didn't really know much more about the meetings than I did. I don't recall the details of my procrastination and forgetting, but something in me wouldn't let up. It was nearly a year after seeing the poster when I finally attended a meeting of the Pyramid Zen group.

Based on my impression from reading Watts, I was expecting something like people in black robes sitting silently and staring at burning candles. What I found was a group of a dozen or so people sitting in a circle of chairs, talking … talking … talking. My reaction: "These people don't have a clue what Zen's all about." But after getting over my initial snit, I realized that they were talking about things I'd never heard anyone talk about (and hadn't come across in my decades of obsessive reading) and that I was deeply interested in.

THAT WAS IN 1978, when I was 33 years old. The Zen self-inquiry group had formed a few years earlier after students had heard a talk by Richard Rose. I became a regular participant, even spending several nights a week talking with some of the folks who were seriously pursuing a path to Truth or Reality and had rented a house in the campus area that they treated as an *ashram*, albeit one without a resident *guru*.

Living on Borrowed Time

*T*here's the *small* problem of life and the *big* problem of life.

No one knows if they'll live to see another day. Is there a penalty for dying ignorant of what you really are? That's the big problem of life.

Then there's the relatively small problem of the quality of today's life. You're on the roller coaster ride of experience … not knowing why you're experiencing or what experience really is, experiencing less perceived control over experience the longer you live, afraid to look behind you (sensing the hound of heaven's incessant footsteps behind you), moving, always moving physically or mentally (afraid of staying still, of silence), procrastinating, always procrastinating.

There's no solid ground under your feet. Your feet are a projected belief … that can walk on 1,800-degree coals and not be burned. Is your entire life a hypnotic projection? What do you have that won't be taken away? At gut level, what do you want out of life? Why are you here?

Are you what you experience? Does experience define you? Are you relying on experience for your salvation or rescue? What if all experience is the flickering of shadows on the cave wall of mind? What if the dream of life ends before you awake? Where will that leave experience-defined you?

To & Fro

To and fro
Heel and toe
The older I get
The slower I go.

What Is Your Relationship to Awareness?

I posed the above question to some friends, and the following interaction ensued with one of them.

In a pretty obvious intellectual and even experiential way, I know that only awareness is aware and absolutely could not be reporting to anything that is an object in/of it. IT IS PRIMARY! Of course it follows that since there is awareness RIGHT HERE I am awareness. For some reason, that doesn't solve the apparent situation of the awareness here being something individual that is vulnerable and will go away. It seems like the awareness here is dependent on the experience called Wyatt.

My Objective: Determine with certainty my true relationship to the mind and body (relative to the assumed position of somehow being dependent on the mind and body).

Regarding "… relative to the assumed position of somehow being dependent on the mind and body," what specifically do you currently believe—that you're *primarily a consciousness* that only operates when the body-brain is in certain states? If that's it, then by your definition you don't exist when that body-brain is not in those states? Or do you believe that you're *primarily a body*—a complex protoplasmic creature with a complex biological neural network that has various active states?

I'd say the assumed position is that I'm primarily "a consciousness" that only operates when the body-brain is in certain states. I wouldn't object to the assertion that I come in and out of existence with certain body-brain states. This existence began when this body-brain functioning started and will end when the body-brain functioning ends.

Do you actually believe you don't exist when the body is in non-dreaming sleep but that you actually do exist when the body is in the dreaming state?

I would say that what I take myself to be is not existing during non-dreaming sleep. Of course, non-dreaming sleep can only be imagined in retrospect while the consciousness I take myself to be is active. The consciousness I take myself to be can only imagine its own inactivity as an idea and can never experience it. This does beg the question whether that actually ever is unconsciousness.

I suspect you're mixing your intellectual speculation with your emotional belief. You really don't believe you exist when the body's in dreamless sleep?

Good call on this one. I most definitely do believe that I am still in existence during dreamless sleep even if it is in retrospect. Also, I have to confess that I somehow believe that I-Wyatt will not die. Intellectually, I know that all body/minds die, but there is a belief that this somehow does not apply to me.

Wyatt, if there's a "real" you that doesn't die, it would have to be a "you" that wasn't born and that is "here" right "now." And it would know itself right now.

"I am the real you that doesn't die, that wasn't born, that is here right now, and that knows myself right now." What am I?

Unhappiness

*U*nhappiness is so far away
It's difficult even to recall;
I did a lot of running
And yet I didn't run at all.

❧

A Mood Is a Message

So Art, what does one do when confronted with a powerful mood like sadness? What I typically do is sit with it. The urge to break it down logically and analyze the mood pops up constantly, but I attempt to turn my head. After a while, I start to feel better and the mood has passed. But something tells me those are golden opportunities, but I'm not sure of the best way in which to react.

*A*s with dream interpretation, we can ask ourselves what message the mood may be trying to get across. An elated mood generally tells us things are going great, while a sad mood reminds us there's a problem. Feeling diminished alerts us to the problem, which is connected with the belief that we're something that can be enhanced but also diminished … with an expected finale of total diminishment. "Is it true?" we can ask ourselves. "What am I (that can be diminished)?" And thus the focus can shift from the mood-message to self-inquiry, to looking for what we are.

To know ourselves, we have to find that core of ourselves which knows itself.

❧

Afraid to Commit

*R*egarding: *"The bottom line, I think, is to 1) notice what we're looking at, and 2) turn our head away from it if it's not what we're looking for."*

This idea with meditation makes sense and is clear. The issue I seem to run into is determining what to look for. If I try to simplify, I might pick something like a resolution to a specific conflict, though when thinking about it that does feel too low—I should be aiming to observe the conflict and the process to try to resolve it. My question seems to be how do I resolve that conflict between wanting to take this simple approach to meditation, but not being able to settle on one thing to look for because of competing interests?

The mind wants to look for what it worships, what it idolizes. I think it's the same for everybody—i.e., worshipping the self—but you'd have to ask yourself if that's true in your case. And I don't think it really makes much difference if the closest someone can get is to describe what he loves as beauty, truth, or some other ideal. Looking for ultimate truth, beauty, self, etc., will lead us to the same place. The ultimate beauty will not fade, ever. The ultimate truth will be beyond all limitations. The ultimate self will be beyond all limitations and never fade.

I have the feeling that your question of what to look for is a form of procrastination … wanting to think about something rather than look for it. We don't "know" what we want to find, because we can't conceive of that which is beyond limitation and doesn't fade. You may have to pursue 1,000 things foolishly before the mind builds some discrimination and begins to narrow the search down to a few possibilities and then to one possibility. Don't fall into the trap of never starting the search because you can't determine what the object of your search looks like.

Two Awarenesses?

*Y*ou have talked about the consciousness of self versus the Awareness of Self several times. I'm telling you, I have been struggling with that whole concept for years. I can't get it resolved and it's driving me crazy. I think this mind is not able to resolve it—I* *will actually have to experience it to know. Anyway, for now—it's one heck of a koan.*

The self-consciousness vs. awareness issue turns out to be a confusion of the mind, as you say. We're conditioned to look at "our awareness" as something that arises from the body. But if we consider the possibility that awareness is primary, and the body comes out of it, that may expand our self-inquiry.

So we start with the hypothesis that awareness is primary ... That Which Is. If it's primary, it doesn't need any help from the body to be what it is—i.e., aware. If awareness is primary and needs no help being aware, where does that leave H. [the correspondent] or Art? We say, wait a second; I'm an individual that's aware that I'm aware. So there's impersonal awareness and there's my personal, individual awareness ... two awarenesses. In fact that's how it actually looks within the mind's view. But the more we introspect the mind looking for "me," the more the attributes of that "me" drop off. We end up with a conviction of being a separate awareness with no other attributes than awareness. Where's the personality or individuality? We'd have to see the limitations or edges of our "personal" awareness, which we don't find.

Maybe what we are is awareness—the primary awareness. Could that primary awareness be the one and only awareness? Could that primary awareness be self-aware? The truth is obvious and in plain view, but the resistance of our conviction of being an individual awareness has to be burned out or blown out in order to admit to ourselves the truth that we see. That occurs by looking and questioning—i.e., self-inquiry.

Love & Friendship

O *ur family moved my dad to a smaller facility, a home with 6 people. He seems to be doing better in that type of environment. But he's getting weaker. I don't think he has much time left.*

As for me, the disease is progressing rather quickly. I have little upper body strength, but can still walk and drive. My mental abilities are diminishing as well. I can't work any more. I'm receiving disability payments though.

It sounds as if you've found some equanimity regarding your deteriorating condition. Everyone is in a similar deteriorating condition most of their lives. The slower it manifests, the more time we have to adjust to it and rationalize it. So in a way, the faster it occurs, the better chance we have to watch it with dispassionate interest and turn our attention to the big question.

What you are is eternal. You will be fully back there when S. [this friend of several decades, a fellow seeker I'd lived with and ran a business with many years earlier] dies. From a standpoint of life, it would be nice for that to occur before the body dies, sooner rather than later, but it only affects the picture-show ... not the reality that creates and witnesses it.

Love and friendship in life are dim echoes of our true state of being but point to it with great poignance.

❧

Separation

uring the last isolation [i.e., solitary retreat] I came to the logical conclusion that there can be no separation between subject and object. But I'm not convinced and would like to know if there is something I'm missing?

The subject is not an object. And because it isn't an object it can't have a place in space. And without a place in space it can't be separated from the object—only objects can be separated from each other.

If the above is correct it has a lot of implications, but the emotional belief in being a separate observer seems to win out.

I wonder if you're trying to build a theory—the theory of how things really are, TOHTRA. That's okay, but any theory has to be validated by observation. Since you claim you don't observe the observer, there's still work to be done to validate or invalidate the theory. The facts you observe include a conviction that you're a separate observer. Look at what's looking to find support for that conviction. What are the attributes of what's looking? If it's separate, what are its distinguishing attributes?

Thinking is secondary to observing. Observing is not dependent on thinking ... it goes on with or without thinking's interference.

It's no mistake that Richard Rose described the goal as observing the observer. Another way to put it is to become aware of that which is self-aware.

Always Right Behind You

*W*hat you really are
    Is always right behind the mind-you.
The mind-you is always running away
From Me, the Real You,
Like a person jogging on an exercise treadmill.

The mind-you rests
When the treadmill of consciousness
Shuts off, in what the mind-you
Thinks of as dreamless sleep.
Otherwise, the mind-you is afraid
To stop running, intuiting that
The treadmill would then take you back
And over the edge.

When you're tired of seeming
And ready to return consciously to Being
(So that the mind-you will know
What and where you've always been),
All you need to do is just stop
Running away from Me.

Afflictions to the Sense of Self

*H*ow can we get behind the sense of self, which always
    seems to be behind our view, to see what we really are?
Some of the most relevant life-experiences for that purpose are
what Richard Rose termed *afflictions to the individuality sense.*

"I felt like I was kicked in the stomach," or "I was stabbed
in the heart," or "it feels like the world is against me" may describe how afflictions to the sense of self hit us. They're unpleasant surprises that we aren't adequately prepared to deflect from

getting under our defenses. Perceived failures, rejections, disappointments, lack of consideration, lack of due respect, feeling we love someone more than they love us, desertions, departures, deaths of loved ones … all these are examples of possible afflictions to the self, and I imagine you can call up others.

The mind reacts to recover from these deflations. If we become conscious of the reaction pattern, we get some distance or detachment from it, and the mind may "skip a beat"—like a glitch in the matrix[1] that momentarily breaks the mind's hypnosis.

Question: What was a sharp affliction to your sense of self? How did your mind attempt to recover from the hit? Anger, resentment, hurt feelings, other? How do you generally react to negative emotions in your dealings with friends? Family? Casual acquaintances? Strangers?

❧

Self-Definition

*R*ichard Rose used the term *self-definition* to describe the spiritual path. And one of his most pithy dictums was: "definition requires comparison." Discovering the true self— what we are at the core of our being—removes our existential suffering. We define[2] the self by seeing clearly what we're not (i.e., retreat from untruth, from faulty beliefs about what we are). This retreat is a relative process—moving from less likely to more likely beliefs—until we transcend the mind dimension at the very end of the path.

---

1   http://en.wikipedia.org/wiki/Glitch
2   *Define*, a: to determine or identify the essential qualities or meaning of; b: to discover and set forth the meaning of.

2. *The Catalyst*

$\mathcal{I}$ n the previous chapter, I left off my tale of dissatisfaction at the time in the late winter of 1978 when I had encountered and started becoming active in the Zen self-inquiry group at Ohio State University. In addition to attending the weekly meetings and spending time with group members at their ashram, I started reading books by Paul Brunton, P.D. Ouspensky, Jiddu Krishnamurti and others, including a self-published book by Richard Rose—the guiding light of the OSU group and a handful of similar groups at other universities—titled *The Albigen Papers*.

My reactions to reading Rose's book were two: first, I thought he had the finest sense of humor I'd ever come across; but second, he came across as having great conviction (okay, I thought: "this guy thinks he knows everything")—and I was absolutely certain that it was impossible to know anything for sure. I didn't catch the contradiction of my certainty about uncertainty at the time.

It turned out that Rose held four weekend get-togethers each year at his farm in the northern panhandle of West Virginia. When the April weekend was approaching, the folks in the Columbus group asked me if I'd like to go over with them, but I was content functioning in the OSU group and wasn't interested.

Near the end of March, after I'd been attending the OSU group meetings for five weeks, Richard Rose showed up unexpectedly for a meeting. When I walked into the meeting room in the student union and saw him, I immediately deduced who he was from descriptions I'd heard. And I introduced myself, told him I knew I was there for a selfish purpose, and asked him why he did what he did. (I'd heard how he gave public talks without charging for them and how he let people stay on his farm asking only that they pay for their share of the utilities. So

I figured there must be some ulterior motive. Skeptical, aren't I.) I didn't mean it to be rude but saw in retrospect that he could easily have taken it that way.

Rose had attained his sixty-first birthday earlier that month. He was a short man, built at that time somewhat like a fireplug, or the *pyknic* type in Ernst Kretschmer's classifications of body types, as Rose described himself. He had a fringe of white hair and sparkling blue eyes.

He responded to my probe by saying: "First of all, what you're doing isn't selfish." And then—was it my imagination, or did his eyes sparkle a little more?—he added: "I do what I'm doing because I can't help myself. It's an obsession."

That knocked the chip off my shoulder, but in a disarming way. "This fellow's okay," I realized.

Rose talked and answered questions during the meeting, and at some point the sound of a brass gong, like the large circular ones I associate with Zen monasteries, reverberated in my mind. I was amazed, not having ever suspected that something like that could happen. The words that then formed in my mind were: "This man is telling the Truth; I've never heard it before, but something in me recognizes it!"

After the meeting, we went to the McDonald's restaurant in the basement of the student union and listened to Rose some more. I could see that other people sitting near us were fascinated by what he was saying, too. As I left the restaurant, I was shocked to realize that all the data coming into my consciousness told me that my feet were absolutely not touching the ground as I walked! (This from a guy whom Rose later teased as having a nothing-but-the-facts mentality like Joe Friday, the fictional detective on the "Dragnet" radio and TV series.) It dawned on me that the phrase "walking on air" wasn't merely a loose metaphor but that other people must have experienced the exact phenomenon that I was experiencing.

A couple days later I asked myself what it was that Rose had said that produced the euphoria I'd experienced. When I thought back on it, I realized the message that had hit me was: "All the answers are within."

I HAD SCANNED THE HORIZON FOR YEARS and years, searching for the missing purpose or meaning that would make my life complete. (I was looking for what would make me complete but didn't know that.) I had become increasingly discouraged since I was already blessed with all the gifts I thought should be enough to make me happy, yet with everything I conceived of to pursue, I could see they still wouldn't fill the void.

Then, blessing of blessings, I met a man who opened my mind to an entire direction it hadn't intuited. He pointed me in the direction and gave my mind the words it needed to find the feeling to follow back to its source — to my source.

When the mind is ready to hear the truth but not yet able to accept the truth, the Truth manifests in an external form — as when Krishna appeared to Arjuna in the *Bhagavad Gita*. Richard Rose was the *guru* who appeared, the external manifestation of Truth that pointed the way home.

Are You the Thinker?

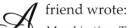 friend wrote:
My objective: To discover if I am the thinker.

The words "depleted" and "lost" describe my current feelings. To get away from these feelings I've been distracting myself with surfing, hobbies, menial chores, and by breaking celibacy. It doesn't surprise me that I'm feeling tired after my recent surge of activity, but I wasn't expecting to be so lost. Usually I have a strong intuition about what direction to go and I pour my energy into that. Right now, every course of action seems like an OK idea, but nothing grabs my attention. That last shock I experienced—waking up with the feeling of specialness missing—seems to have kicked my compass overboard. Actually it's worse than that; I'm beginning to think my steering wheel isn't connected to anything. Conceptually I can grasp that I'm not in control of anything, but my gut isn't there yet. My gut feels a little sick about it. Without the sense of control how can there be motivation or enthusiasm? Looks like the next crisis is shaping up already. I think fear might be around the corner for me.

I believe that I am in control. That belief is what is being threatened by the event last Friday (the sudden change in my pride-state). I didn't plan it or expect it—I was asleep when it happened. I have to face this threat, don't I?

In order to understand our psychology, it's often instructive to look at extreme cases. For example, chronic worrying is not a logical investment of our mental CPU cycles, so there must be an emotional belief behind it. A chronic worrier is less likely to tell himself that he can't help it, that it's an addiction, than to *feel* that it is effective. The logic to support the belief goes something like this: "If I don't worry, terrible things will happen." The supporting evidence isn't hard to find: "I couldn't sleep a wink last night worrying about whether I was going to get fired today. I didn't get fired. Therefore, worrying is effective."

It's disturbing to you that you awoke from sleep into a new conviction-state. Why? Because you believe that you effect changes in your convictions by thinking yourself into them? Yet you experienced an in-your-face example that contradicts your theory. And if you're not creating your beliefs through conceptual thinking, what else might you be taking credit for that's not true? What about moods, for example?

Are motivation and enthusiasm something that you've created for yourself in the past?

❧

Waiting for Revelation

When we're drawing conclusions, we're falling asleep. Questions are what prod us to try to awake. The best question is a powerful feeling of dissatisfaction or incompleteness. It doesn't need to be cultivated. If we set aside a period each day to find some mental space or clarity, the best way to kick it off may be to feel that feeling.

We're basically waiting for revelation. We need to accustom the mind to waiting/watching under tension. The revelation will likely come when we're not expecting it … and most likely after a period of intensity.

❧

Lo-Cal Snacks

When all movement (i.e., mind) is seen as a thing apart, you'll be looking from home base. What will you be standing on?

*F*or the self-inquirer: If it's possible for the self to know itself, then you're looking for that which is self-aware. Where are You going to find That?

A prayer of the seeker's heart: I'm lonely, desolate. I have a dim memory of what perfect love felt like, and I want that back, permanently. Where art Thou, Eternal Beloved? Why hast Thou deserted me? Thy absence seems like endless torture … endless burning … endless drowning. O, Love, end this unbearable misery.

I am the real you that doesn't die, that wasn't born, that is here right now, and that knows myself right now. What am I?

*M*editation: the mind becoming conscious of what you are always doing.

Two of Me?

*T*here is something I would like to ask you about Art if you don't mind, because last week something I heard you say comes the closest to describing what I felt. About a month ago I had something happen that felt like the very first time I had any kind of understanding (if it even was anything) that was somehow well beyond intellectual understanding, actually I didn't and still don't "understand" it. I had just woke up, but was still laying in bed, when I got this crazy feeling, very difficult to attach words to it, lasted for maybe a few seconds, but was the first time I had experienced anything like it, something you said in one of your talks described it for me better than anything I'd heard or read, about there being 2 of something. This was really brief but so intense, I almost had this quick visual of 2 arrows pointing at each other or something, I don't really even know, like something watching itself, felt like a gigantic paradox, in that moment I was scrambling, it was a feeling of holy crap, wait a minute what the hell is this??!! It didn't feel scary, i had a feeling of wanting to run with it, or to it, but getting stuck, I don't have the right words for it, I have no idea what I was thinking before it happened, I was barely awake. What do you make of that? Is that the "highlight of my year" or me fooling myself? The thing that makes me think it was maybe something real is that I wasn't doing any kind of visualization or anything, I wasn't trying, it just happened. About 2 mornings later I had a similar thing happen, just as brief and maybe slightly less intense, same thing though, felt like I just got stuck, then it was gone. Hasn't happened since. Haven't mentioned it to anyone 'til now. So if there is a Universal awareness in everything, what is the second something, if we're all from the same *source, how can there be a second something, is it awareness aware of itself? And if so that would mean it's the same awareness in you that is aware of itself, meaning that there is absolutely nothing personal going on here in my space or anyone's, I can't even comprehend that, although that makes more sense to me. Or is there something personal in me that is capable of being aware of the universal awareness. Is my line of reasoning going in the right direction? To me it makes no sense logically that there's something personal in me, but how can there be a feeling of 2???!!! Ever since that morning I have this desperate feeling that I'm looking in the wrong way, like some shift in my point of view has to happen, and I can't see it. Maybe that shift happened for that brief moment, I don't know? You know those pictures that are made up of dots and when you stare at them long enough and in the right way, you see a sailboat or whatever, I feel like I'm staring at one of those but the damn thing is still just dots!!! Any thought on this would be greatly appreciated.*

The "two arrows pointing at each other" realization as you were waking up could be a productive thorn if it sticks around and you can't dislodge (forget) it.

Any of the Douglas Harding exercises in two-way looking could add to the consternation.

It could be a highlight of your year or of your life to date :-)

"So if there is a Universal awareness in everything, what is the second something, if we're all from the same source, how can there be a second something, is it awareness aware of itself?"—That kind of thinking doesn't get at the problem. Don't start off with a postulation. Work from what you can observe. (And hold the stuff you read, hear, postulate, etc., in the back of your head as possibilities only.) If you watch the mind, you (may) become aware that it feels like you are what's observing the wall, the fingers on the keyboard, or whatever. "I'm what's back there looking out at the world." So that's the arrow pointing outward. "But wait a second ... how am I aware of that outward-looking me? Ha! I am aware of that outward-looking me!" That's the arrow pointing inward. If I watch closely, I (may) see that it's like the thumb and forefinger rubbing together. Which one is feeling the other? If I look carefully, I (may) "see" that it depends on where the attention focuses ... that if the attention's on the thumb, then the thumb's feeling the forefinger, and vice versa. Similarly, you (may) "see" that the attention can only be on the outward-looking awareness or the inward-looking awareness at any time, with the aware-me of the moment being somewhere behind my view. And since we're identified with that-which-is-looking (when we wake up a bit from being hypnotized by what we're observing), at any instant we are either the outward-looking awareness or the inward-looking awareness. So if we're careful not to lump them together and say: "Oh, yeah, I'm both," we (may) see that we believe ourselves to be two distinct awarenesses. Yet we have a conviction that we're not two things but a singularity of some sort. This recognition of our dichotomy, our twoness, is a terrible contradiction of our basic conviction. "What the hell is this??!!" indeed.

None of these observations have anything to do with the possibility of a universal awareness, which is another issue altogether. That's a conundrum that you can speculate on but I don't see how that speculation would lead us back up the ray of creation to our source. (I may be wrong :-) It could definite-ly shake up your thinking and keep you off balance, which could be an incentive to look for certainty. But you can't find it through speculation and deductive reasoning.

"But how can there be a feeling of 2???!!!"—indeed. Regardless of how, it's an observable fact. And if you keep watching the mind, trying to find yourself, trying to observe the observer, it will eventually lead to seeing a contradiction or lie you're telling yourself about what you are. And then, if you can't turn your head away from that contradiction, something has to give.

❧

HDTV

*D*efinitions:
    Personality—a mask for individuality to wear.
Individuality—a faulty self-belief.

You're watching the story of [its name goes here] unfold in front of the mind's eye, with its torso, arms and legs hanging out of you, and its head that only appears in mirrors and photograph-ic images.

Its story is so fascinating that you're identified with this character, as you may temporarily identify with the lead char-acter in any interesting cinema or TV drama, forgetting yourself as you truly are.

❧

Struggling to Open

I still can't grasp why God's alleged will for us seems to be at cross purpose with nature's. Reunion with the Source vs. the

allowance/creation of an ego to further individual delusion and collec-
tive procreation?

God's will is whatever happens. It's the collapsing of the probability wave in quantum physics. Reunion with the Source may
not be God's will for all creatures. Not all buds on an apple
tree flower … not all flowers set fruit … some of the fruit feeds
deer, some feeds bears, some feeds humans, some feeds worms,
moths and maggots, some fertilizes the ground, some produces
seeds that germinate into new trees. The apple tree, the apple,
the flower, the seed, the moth, the maggot, the worm, the bear
and the deer may not feel separate from their source. The pre-
self-conscious child may not feel separate from its source. The
ego is, by definition, the feeling of being something separate.
Our bodies are going to fertilize the earth, may even feed a
bear, may participate in creating new bodies, may help take
care of other bodies. They will undoubtedly serve nature's purpose in whatever way god wills. If god also wills for some or
all of those bodies to graduate from self-consciousness to Self-
consciousness, I don't see that as being at cross-purpose to nature. It may or may not serve the cosmos in some way, but I'm
rather sure it doesn't interfere with cosmic functioning.

*This brings up a lot in me. Mostly rage, frustration, and self-loathing.
I am not willing to accept that (that I'm an unflowered bud) about
myself, when it may actually be the case that, the way it stands now,
my destiny is to live a mundane life—to not Awaken.*

*This, in turn, brings up the fact that there is a conviction state
somewhere far back, that drives everything, that I will "have" a
Realization—it'll just be a matter of time. I'm not sure how much of
it is a genuine intuition and how much of it is simply a subtle rationalization that holds the illusion intact. For now I'll assume it's a pipe
dream that holds the identity intact.*

The truer feeling about what is actually happening is that I am a horribly compromised individual (a set of contradictory and confused impulses) and that the way things are now, I am not destined to awaken. It's like I'm resisting the voice: "Yes, it's totally possible to simply just be a guy who has a job, who loses his hair, who gets married, and all in all has an ordinary life, with no shot at awakening."

I know I don't need to believe or be convinced of either outcome, but I need to look at what I'm avoiding, which the apple tree metaphor helped out with.

Is there value in a seeker accepting the fact that he may be a flowerless bud?

You've nailed the EXACT obstacle. You're NOT the bud you're watching. You are NEVER that which is seen.

Acceptance relates to the past and present, not some imaginary future. In all honesty, how can you pretend to know one way or the other what's in store for that lovable bud that you're watching and identified with (in love with because, in fact, you are its creator). If the flower bud is self-conscious, it may feel that it's struggling to open. How poignant would that be, looking at what you've created and knowing that it's struggling to find Your Love, which has never left it.

3. Determination

*O*ne of the activities that Richard Rose had suggested to us at the meeting where I first met him, near the end of March in 1978, was to set a one-hour meditation period every day. [See the "Decalogue" item in chapter five for a summary of some of his other suggestions.] I had read Rose's "Meditation and Visualization" essay[1] before meeting him, so I had some ideas about what to do, and I began a meditation practice on April 3rd that year. Less than a week after that I decided to give up alcohol. I wanted freedom from a habit I felt was controlling me, and I wanted to put the freed-up energy toward meditation.

By the end of April I was participating in the Zen group activities two nights a week and meditating the other five nights. I had fallen off the no-alcohol wagon one night at a restaurant and one Saturday at home. In early May I journaled about a growing desire to discover the Truth. I was also struggling unsuccessfully to start remembering dreams, which Rose recommended as a source of material to help study the mind.

Richard Rose gave another public talk at Ohio State U. in mid May. He described life as a play, with love as its theme. He felt that the greatest lovers are quiet workers for others. But he advised that we forget about the lover while trying to cultivate observation of the thinking mind.

Shortly after the talk I began meditating on the two mornings when nighttime meditation wasn't practical, and I also had my first vivid dream recall. In the dream Mr. Rose was saying that I needed to get away from distractions; he suggested that I come over to the farm and spend some time by myself there.

In June I wrote in my journal: "I think I've been searching for a path all my life, and knowing that I've finally found it is starting to sink in...."

---

1   Now in the *Meditation* booklet of Richard Rose.

In the early 1970s Richard Rose had set up a foundation to encourage people who were searching for truth to work together in non-dogmatic friendship. The TAT Foundation held four gatherings each year at Rose's farm in rural Moundsville, WV. As I mentioned previously, my newfound friends in the OSU self-inquiry group had invited me to go to the April meeting, but I wasn't interested. Reviewing my journal, I see that there was a fear component of the decision that I'd forgotten. Anyway, I did go to the July meeting and returned with the inspiration to start taking on some responsibilities for the functioning of the OSU group.

By the end of July I was participating in group activities three nights a week, meditating for a half hour on those three mornings and for an hour on the other four evenings. In early August I noted in the journal that I'd taken a day off from work to spend with my 7-year-old daughter, Meg, and that I'd had wine with the meal when we'd then taken the family out for dinner that evening—"the first alcohol in a long time"—so apparently I'd been doing okay on that front.

Toward the end of September I'd made the following journal entry:

> Afraid to be hard on myself ... want things to be easy, comfortable ... no pain ... no risks ... no commitment. Is my spiritual path important enough to make a commitment to? In a positive sense, no—don't know what I'm after; in a negative sense, yes—nothing else matters.

That may give you an idea of how my mentality was focused on an intellectual perspective, and I'd say that was the most obvious thrust of my search—trying to understand the truth. But underneath that, I was feeling my way. Most, maybe all, progress on the path of self-knowing comes through intuitive discernment.

IN EARLY OCTOBER of 1978 I documented my first stab at verbalizing a commitment regarding the spiritual search: "Work with others now, and devote my life to helping others if I'm successful." I also noted that "there seems to have been a voice in me which has been saying for a long time: Define me, find me."

In mid-October I did a five-day solitary retreat at Rose's farm. My friends in the OSU group were skeptical that I'd do it, but I had written to Mr. Rose stating my intention, which made it a commitment in my mind.

I fasted (water only) for the duration—another first for me—and experienced a *satori* or epiphany that accompanies a jump to a more anterior view of the mind's operation, which I'll go into in more detail in the next chapter. But what turned out to be a more disruptive product of the retreat was the second conscious incursion of intuition to break through my analytical armor (the first one being the gong-ringing that occurred when first meeting Mr. Rose). It announced itself by a light bulb lighting up in my head—an event I thought only happened in comic books or cartoons—and the words that followed were: "My only chance for mental clarity is through a prolonged period of celibacy." I recognized it as intuition since it came with great conviction and my mind had absolutely no argument with it.

Celibacy was the term that Richard Rose used to mean no intentional sex-action. I'd forgotten until I saw it in one of my journal entries for that November that I'd been intentionally celibate for a month before the retreat ... but I did recall my reaction of amazement when I realized I'd been celibate for thirty days, since it was beyond anything I'd ever imagined. Rose had warned that indefinitely continued celibacy could be problematic and that if a man hadn't reached self-realization by forty, his next best chance was as he was dying.

I was exhilarated by the prospect of remaining celibate until then—a mere six years since I'd just had my thirty-fourth birthday—and looked forward to sharing my inspiration with my wife after the retreat. I thought she'd share my enthusiasm (silly me) and be happy to go along with it.

I wrote to Mr. Rose when I returned home, telling him about the retreat (he lived in town during the school year, and I hadn't seen him) and asking some questions, including whether I was too old to be successful in my search and whether my wife's disapproval of my continued chastity should veto it. I opened his response with some trepidation. I didn't have a very good opinion of my abilities and expected him to be even less optimistic. But a wave of euphoria swept over me when I read the second sentence, which he had underlined: "I think you'll make it."

His response to my first question was: "No one is too old." Regarding chastity he replied: "Either partner should be free spiritually so that sex does not take priority. Friendship need never be broken—and should not." He concluded the letter with the following answer to a question I'd asked about mental clarity: "This clarity will increase whenever the distractions are all removed at once. The thing is to make such a retreat once or twice a year."

PROGRESS SELDOM GOES in a straight line, and that seems especially true with an abstract goal such as going within to find the truth of our being. It's wise to expect that we'll encounter adversity on the spiritual path. Some will undoubtedly come from the outside world, but the more subtle adversity will come from within.

Early in November I noted in my journal that since I'd returned from the solitary retreat there had been a little voice saying, "Meditation is boring. You don't really have anything to meditate on. You don't really know what you're doing. Why bother?" About two weeks later I recorded that I'd had a very productive meditation that night ... and wondered why. A few days later my complaint was: "I'm doing the search because it's the only thing that makes sense—but my heart's not in it; there's no sense of urgency." Something in me persisted, though.

Toward the end of the month I was watching the following thought process during meditation:

What should I do?

What are my options?

1. Give up the path of self-definition.
2. Give up part of the path (group work; celibacy).
3. Get my wife interested in self-definition.
4. Don't give up.

What are the likely consequences of each option?

1. Self-destruction.
2. Loss of spiritual freedom, leading to #1.
3. Best option; low probability.
4. Risk loss of wife, family, job, etc.

A few days into December I recorded my first verbalized resolution: "I am determined to witness whatever is doing the looking. Nothing will get in the way." During that day's meditation I reiterated my determination: "I will witness the thought observer if it's the last thing I do; nothing will stop me—no fear, no laziness, no sidetracking desires." And during the following day's meditation, I reaffirmed my determination to observe the observer, which meant the same thing to me as knowing the true self.

The feeling of determination stayed with me for at least a week. Then I wrote in a journal entry: "Last week's *infusion of determination* is gone; now replacing it with an intellectual affirmation." As wonderful as they can be, feelings come and go. I hear all the time from seekers who say they can't do anything when they're not inspired, that they're waiting for inspiration. I was fortunate enough that the intellect seemed to be able to get additional mileage from inspiration, which visited me rarely. In fact, the pattern I came to see over the years was that about the only time I experienced inspiration was during solitary retreats—and then I would find inspiration bubbling through my neural system like champagne.

SEVERAL DAYS LATER I witnessed and documented the following realization: "My whole mentality and intuition point to this work as what I must do. I take the responsibility and make the commitment to follow this to the end—"

Looking back, I see that when we make really honest commitments to ourselves we aren't bending our arms to try to make ourselves do something we don't want to do. On the contrary, we are recognizing what we really want to do, what's most important to us, and admitting it to ourselves.

And the following day I found myself making a life prediction:

◊   Marriage and job fall apart
◊   End up in West Virginia, possibly after a stint leading the Columbus Zen group
◊   Years of solitary retreats interspersed with work and much trauma
◊   Work with others (talks, etc.)
◊   Reach enlightenment in early forties

◊   Spend the rest of my life helping others on the path

In subsequent chapters you'll see whether there was any ac-
curacy in those predictions.

IN THE MIDDLE OF DECEMBER, on the same day that I made the
above prediction, I learned to my surprise that the young fellow
who was leading the Columbus group, and who had become
one of my two closest friends in the group, was quitting the
group and the spiritual path. I felt hurt that he was deserting
the group and me; felt sorry for him that he'd become discouraged and lost the path; felt anger toward him for past affronts
(afflictions to my overly sensitive ego); and a slight concern that
it could happen to me. Several days later I made the following
journal entry:

> I'm determined that what's happening to Bill won't happen
> to me; I'm committed to see this through, even if it takes my
> entire life. I should expect to go through periods where it will
> seem stupid, useless, crazy, etc. Must be prepared.

I ended the journal entry for that night with this emotional
recognition or prayer: "Father, your son is lost and wants to
come home—"

The Liquidity Trap of Self-Ignorance

*O*n his *Return of Depression Economics and the Crisis of 2008,*
Nobel award winning economist Paul Krugman related
a story published in 1978 by a couple who were members of a
baby-sitting co-op in Washington, D.C.[2] The association issued
coupons entitling the bearer to one hour of baby-sitting, and

___
2   "Monetary Theory and the Great Capitol Baby-sitting Co-op
Crisis," by Joan and Richard Sweeney.

baby-sitters would receive the appropriate number of coupons from the baby-sittees. The system ensured that over time each couple would provide as many hours of baby-sitting as it received.

The situation developed, however, where couples who felt their reserves of coupons were insufficient were anxious to baby-sit but reluctant to go out. Opportunities to baby-sit therefore became scarce, making couples even more reluctant to use their coupons. The co-op went into a recession. Krugman explained that's basically what caused Japan's economy to stall for over a decade—a lack of demand for the available productive capacity.

Some couples in the baby-sitting co-op would have been willing to go out, but nobody would lend them coupons. There were the same number of coupons as previously but there just weren't many in circulation, which is what economists call a liquidity trap.

The baby-sitting recession developed largely because people wanted to save the credits they earned from winter baby-sitting to use in the summer, when they wanted to go out more. But in the aggregate that doesn't work and produces a winter slump. What was needed was to "get the price right": points earned in the winter would have to be devalued if held until summer—an expected inflation or anticipated loss of value. If the slump becomes deep enough and lasts long enough, it moves from recession to depression status.

Okay, but how does all that apply to self-inquiry? Let's say the desire to know the self is like one of the co-op couples. It makes some headway (saves up some coupons) then runs into obstacles: other players (competing fears and desires in the internal co-op) are trying to do the same, and stasis develops.

There may be a seasonality slump in self-inquiry that a new season will take care of by bringing a resurgence of going-out (or in this case, going-within) desire. But what if we don't want to lose the time, don't want to chance an automatic recovery, or the recession morphs into a season-defying depression? What would it take to get the price right so that the going-within desire produces action?

Remember we're talking about a co-operative operation. The aggregate of fears and desires will have to come into alignment with the going-within desire or not impede its action. Some of those other players may support the going-within desire by lending it coupons … not out of altruistic motives but because they see it won't hurt their getting what they want and may even help. The going-within desire will have to carve out time to pursue its goal and not be overly distracted during that time by the other players.

To bring this analogy down to a practical level, what can we do to end a recession or depression affecting the going-within desire? Demand for productive capacity (i.e., action) depends on desire, and desire depends on a feeling of want—that something important is missing or lacking. The first game-changer is to feel that want, not run away from it. Feeling a feeling is a rather instantaneous activity. It doesn't require effort. Effort goes into trying to repress feelings so they stay below an apparent level. Feeling a feeling is more of a slowing down, relaxing. (Are you too busy to take a few seconds to feel what you're feeling?)

Feeling a want and its attendant desire automatically leads to action unless the co-op isn't cooperating. The other fears and desires may interfere directly, at a feeling level. A fear may occupy center stage like Chicken Little and convince the co-op that the sky will fall ("I'll go crazy" or "my life will be ruined," for example) if the going-within desire gets its way. Or a more subtle coalition of members may convince the co-op that going-within is okay but not just now ("I'm busy right now," "I'm too tired," "I can do it better later," and so on). How is this inevitable adversity sidestepped? The co-op may have to form a committee of determination that recognizes the interference patterns and decides not to be overly influenced by them when they occur.

If you find yourself feeling overwhelmed by a conviction of helplessness, consider the possibility that your intuition is picking up an important life-lesson. As happened with a West Virginia man who couldn't stop eating and got to a weight of 600 pounds despite trying everything in his power to reverse the trend, when you get backed into the corner of honestly admitting your helplessness to solve a problem on your own or with all the resources you've enlisted, your only option is to hope that there is some unseen/unknown higher power that can help … and to implore that possibility for help. The WV man said he found himself praying. Within 11 months he had lost 300 pounds and was still losing weight when interviewed by a local TV station. When I honestly admitted to myself that I was backed into a corner and prayed to a higher power or inner self for help, I found that help was always available and capable of blasting away any adversity. Praying for help opens the heart-mind.[3]

Lastly, get out of the way. That happened for Jill Bolte Taylor, the brain researcher, when a hemorrhage shut down most of her left-hemisphere's operation. When it started coming back, slowly, after surgical intervention, she saw that the "self-story" concocted by the left hemisphere—who she was, what her credentials for self-importance were, her judgments and resentments of other people when they didn't enhance her self-image, and so on—had previously determined her actions … and that its automatic reaction mode in response to feelings didn't have to be followed blindly.

If life doesn't provide you the lesson in such a dramatic way, you can try to test the water by doing something for someone else without any expectation of reward (anonymously if possible and without telling anyone).

✀

Blindsight & Group Efforts

S elf-inquiry for the purpose of self-realization, of becoming with full awareness what you already are, is an extreme sport. The contest takes place within the mind, where the pretenders to the throne of Self—the various desires and fears, the prides and paranoias—vie for supremacy. Eventually a sole contender emerges: ego, "I am-ness," the individuality-sense. That "one" is extremely elusive, however, remaining always just out of view.

A group of people coming together forms a temporary organism. An organism has a purpose or objective, which can be

---

3   Especially if we pray with the caveat: "If it's in the cards," or "Thy will, not my will, be done." If we think we know what's best and get upset with not getting what we want when we want it, we haven't honestly admitted our helplessness and just want to game the system.

explicit or adventitious. For example, a business organism may be created to produce profits above wages for its owners. If the workers become owners, then the goal becomes a mutual goal, assuming that the employees are working to make as much money as possible in return for their labor.

What about an organism of spiritual seekers? Ideally its goal would be to help the members, the participating human organisms, reach their deepest goal. The deepest goal of the human organism is, in my opinion, to find permanent wholeness or completion, which can only be found through recognition of its oneness with That Which Is.

What is your conscious goal for wanting to participate in a temporary organism of spiritual seekers? "I don't know" may be true from an objective viewpoint, but the spiritual seeker is mired in a subjective view, where "I don't know" reflects a lack of introspection or lack of honestly admitting one's motivations. Our motivations aren't generally pretty, but they become refined as we progress within.

Do you have a conscious life-goal? What are you trying to achieve if it's not in the context of an overall life-objective? Are your actions in response to a deep desire or want? Could satisfaction of that deep desire or want become your conscious life-goal?

Getting down to business in self-inquiry begins with a solitary daily practice that occurs in silence. It includes reading of material that's related to your life-goal; thinking about what you've read, what you've heard, and otherwise experienced; and meditating on your goal. Many people read and think about their life and where it's going, but a directed meditation practice is, I suspect, rare.

Self-realization may occur during a period of intense introspection or during a period of relative relaxation that follows. The first *satori* or partial opening of the mind (resulting in a profound but lesser realization) that I experienced was at the end of a day at work following a weeklong group retreat. My eventual breakthrough occurred 25 years later when I was sitting, doing nothing, on the final evening of a weeklong solitary retreat. The mind-lock will open when you're not expecting it. If it occurs during a retreat, then you're done with the seeking phase of your life. If not, what can you take with you that will strengthen your inner-directed vector?

If you've participated in group retreats before, it's valuable to look at what you took away—gained or lost—from them and how the experience affected your ongoing work. Back in the 1960s and 70s, encounter groups were popular forms of group retreats that encouraged increasing awareness of oneself in the moment through intensive discussion, close relationships between group members, and the expression of feelings. Participants often went away from the encounter weekends feeling better about themselves.

Most of us seek True Happiness through incremental happiness and seek True Knowing through incremental knowledge.

That approach works to some degree or extent, and may be a necessary prelude, but the process of self-knowing is one of seeing through illusory beliefs about the self … in other words, a process of disillusionment. When those illusion balloons burst, there's often a sense of relief but also of deflation. Regardless of whether a group retreat is inflating or deflating, the spiritual seeker wants it to strengthen his inner-directed vector, and the serious seeker, I believe, wants it to strengthen his solitary daily practice.

If you are thinking about or planning on a group retreat, you may want to ask yourself some questions along these lines:

- What is your conscious goal for wanting to participate in a temporary organism for spiritual seekers?
- Do you have a conscious life-goal? What are you trying to achieve if it's not in the context of an overall life-objective?
- What do you want to work on during the retreat? What do you feel unable to do on your own that you want help with? What help do you want from fellow participants? What help from any coaches or teachers who are participating?
- Do you have a daily practice that you want feedback on? Do you want help establishing a daily practice?
- What difficulties do you predict will occur for you during the retreat?

In *Stumbling on Happiness,* Daniel Gilbert described the phenomenon of blindsight, where patients with certain kinds of brain lesions have no awareness of seeing, and they report truthfully that they are completely blind. Brain scans show diminished activity in the areas associated with *awareness* of visual experience, yet they show normal activity in the areas associated with vision. When researchers flash a light on a particular spot on the wall and ask the patients if they see it, the patients reply "of course not." But when the researcher asks the patients to take a wild guess and say anything randomly or point at the likely spot, they guess correctly far more often than random chance would indicate. He tells us it's like their eyes are projecting the movie on the theater screen in their head, but the audience is in the lobby getting popcorn.

What are you seeing that you're not consciously aware of?

❉

Looking & Questioning

*T*he infant human and maybe all animals other than man look at "the world" without a self-concept to refract the light. The infant or animal learns without reflection to avoid touching a hot stove or getting too close to a fire.

The older child gains guile, looking at the world through the prism of I-amness. It pursues its desires and tries to avoid its fears by projecting memory into the future and making decisions accordingly.

The shock of mortality hits some people as children, some as teens, some in later decades—maybe a bell-shaped distribution. This shock may open a new line of questioning: Where did I come from (before birth), and where am I going (after death)?

Growing dissatisfaction with one's life, sometimes registering as a feeling of emptiness or incompleteness, drives some people into further questioning: Is there some purpose to life? Is my life-experience a classroom? If so, what's the lesson it's trying to show me? Are dreams part of the teaching material? If so, what are they trying to get across?

A "rude" shock such as suddenly realizing (when driving the car, for example) that all activity is occurring automatically and that "you" aren't doing it, or a mere turning of the inner head and seeing that the self you believed yourself to be is nothing but a mental construct, a phantom, brings some people to the ultimate question of existence: Then who or what am I, really?

There is living without questioning, which is equivalent to sleep-walking, but life doesn't typically allow that to go on indefinitely. Disappointments, failures, rejections, sickness, loss—these and other afflictions try to wake us up. There's a progression of questioning as the sleepwalker, blind to the Light despite having his eyes open, struggles to see.

What is your question?

Sitting in Rapport with Yourself

"Rose did say that a person should sit for rapport with themselves. This was different from meditation because the mind would eventually go blank in meditation and it'd turn into dreaming."[4]

Have you tried to sit in rapport with yourself? Would you recommend this too? How would I go about sitting in rapport with myself?

---

4   From the August 2005 "TAT Forum" article by Shawn Nevins [excellent reading material]

[My response to the above inquiry:] Why, that wily coyote! Sitting in rapport with yourself requires admitting there are two of you, doesn't it? I never thought about doing it intentionally, but it will happen when you introspect the mind. Rapport is a synchronization of mental activity ... where you're sharing thoughts and feelings with the "other person." It's not like mind reading, where you pick up another person's thoughts or feelings like a spy or peeping Tom. Rose's recommended approach to studying the mind was by 1) remembering your objective, and then 2) turning your head away from thoughts that aren't relevant to that inquiry. So it's basically a process of watching the mental mouse hole to see what comes next.

❧

We Succeed by Failing

I guess by what you said in the Closer than Close video I should just sit with my spin cycle—disengage it as much as possible (without turning it into another more concealed spin cycle!) and let it burn out my transistors! Is that it??

Advice on what anyone should do is problematic. We succeed at spiritual work by failing. Someone who's been down a road may be able to warn you about not wiping out on a blind curve, etc., but "do this" advice might delay progress. Since progress depends on disillusionment, the best advice would be wrong advice :-)

Your particular resistance may be designed to blow out rather than do a slow burn. I sort of doubt it, but I don't know. I believe that the searcher has to reach a point where he honestly feels he's tried every door but, unlike Sartre's conclusion [*No Exit*], he doesn't convince himself that there isn't a doorway.

For me, I saw the triangulation process at work that Benoit and Rose described.[5] So I suspect that everyone proceeds through a similar head- or heart-battering over a contradiction that yields the next, more abstract internal battering ... until a final opposition comes that burns or blows out the resistance. My next-to-last opposition was the contrast between the Richard Rose and Douglas Harding paradigms. I could see through the one that everything was outside the undefined me, but through the other I could see that everything was inside me. And they appeared to be equally valid.

My final opposition was when I saw that awareness was self-aware ... and yet I was convinced that I was a separate awareness aware of that self-aware awareness. It wasn't an intellectual knowing or even an emotional knowing but a dead-ahead showdown in the middle of the street at high noon.

❧

Silence & Stillness

There's a silence that is the absence of sound ... and there's a silence that witnesses sound and the absence of sound. We could name it Silence.

There's a stillness that is the opposite of movement ... and there's a stillness that encompasses both movement and non-movement. We could call it Stillness.

Our true self knows itself through witnessing sound and the absence of sound ... through encompassing movement and non-movement.

Silence and Stillness are unknowing.

---

5   See the essay on Triangulation in chapter 5.

The Middle Way

*T*he middle way is not half way between right and wrong, up and down, movement and no movement, life and death. The middle way is between and beyond. The middle way encompasses life and death ... is neither, and both.

Pardon Me, But...

*P*ardon me, but if someone says: "This technique will take you to nirvana ... it worked for me," how do they know? It may actually have impeded their progress, or it may have been completely irrelevant. How do they know? Cause and effect may be attempts of the mind to impose order on chaos. How do they know?

If a particular path or technique appeals to you more than any other, follow it with your whole heart. It may help, or it may impede. How will you know?

You'll know nothing for sure until you know the knower. And then all you'll know for sure is what you are. But believe me, it will be enough.

But don't believe me, don't take my word for it. The honest teacher says: "Doubt what I say. Find out for yourself."

A Special Case?

"*W*hy don't you ever ask him any questions?" somebody asked, referring to the third person in the conversation. (I'm a known question-asker, often trying to prod conscious seekers by undermining their unconscious pretense of knowing.)

"He's a special case," I responded. "He's already enlightened … he just doesn't know it."

Of course I said this only to discombobulate the third person, the subject and object of the exchange.

There is some truth to the fact that every seeker is already enlightened … but no truth to the frequently accompanying assertion that there's nothing to be done in order to realize it.

❧

Umbilical Cord

I continue to wish and pray that I can find some sense of this umbilical cord. In a way that I can grab on to it. This would give me so much more hope, which would hopefully displace some of my negativity.

[The above comment was referring to a statement from *Mister Rose: The Video*: "The whole path to truth is through the umbilical cord. A mental umbilical cord. Links you to the Brahman. We are the Atman."]

I came into conscious contact with the umbilical cord as a result of a question sticking in my mind: "What is the source of my awareness?" The answer came in the form of a simple vision. It's something we see by direct looking, although we don't know how to do it. So it will appear by seeming accident … but the mind's active inquiry may be a causal agent. If we allow the mind to pursue a question that it really wants to know the answer to—which may entail acting on a feeling of the circumstances the mind needs in order to have an interval with nothing else to do—it will eventually find what its looking for.

In my case, it occurred during a solitary retreat.

Rising Action & Dark Days

4. Signposts of Progress

I was fortunate in that what I now view as signposts of progress occurred early in my search. They were typically so different from my ordinary mental experience that I didn't describe them in much if any detail in my journals, apparently convinced that I would never forget them.

The first such inner event occurred in the spring of 1978 when I began participating in the self-inquiry group at Ohio State University. I recall the meeting monitor having asked me what I was thinking about on the way to the meeting. My response was that I wasn't thinking about anything, merely looking at the leaves budding out on the trees. When I came out of that evening's meeting, I found myself stopped in my tracks: I realized that I was watching my thoughts as they occurred—something I didn't know was even possible.

I considered those irregularities in the typical flow of my internal scenery as discontinuities. Later, when I saw The Matrix film, the term "glitch in the matrix" also seemed to fit. In addition to the "light bulb" experience that occurred during my first solitary retreat in October 1978 (described in the chapter three introduction), there was another discontinuity during that retreat. And like the watching-my-thoughts experience, it was also a stopped-in-my-tracks event.

It had been cold and rainy for several days, and I was staying in a little trailer that had no heat or electricity. One morning the clouds had cleared enough for the sunshine to be reaching the earth, and I was walking along a gravel road with a stream running nearby. The road was shaded by large trees, but I noticed a rock on the edge of the stream with the sun shining on it and thought how nice it would be to sit on the rock and warm up in the sun.

Then I noticed a "No Trespassing" sign nailed to a tree. And my mind started spinning on the possible danger of being shot by a disgruntled property owner (this was rural West Virginia after all) versus the pleasure of sitting in the sun. I had stopped moving along the road, all my attention focused on seeing the argument playing out in slow motion—something I'd never witnessed before. I saw various desire and fear "voices" or arguments lined up for and against trespassing in order to get to the rock. They were grouped into two tug-of-war teams, and the side that made the most noise won the argument!

Just observing the decision-making operation in great detail that one time left me convinced that, one, it was a very primitive process, and that, two, I wasn't in charge of it. It was like a program running on its own, with a cast of fear and desire "characters" that I hadn't created or written the scripts for. A veritable "dynasty of fear in a playhouse of desire," as Mr. Rose described life, in *Carillon*.

The daily meditation and other practices we cultivate on a regular basis keep our hats in the ring for those magical times when the distractions are all removed at once.

IN FEBRUARY OF THE FOLLOWING YEAR, 1979, my wife and I had taken our children ice-skating at an indoor rink near our home. And I overheard her comment to a friend of hers who had come with us about how my skating had changed. I had noticed it with amazement, too, but wouldn't have known if it was just my imagination. I had done quite a bit of recreational skating growing up in a small town in upstate New York, and my ankles had always been somewhat weak. As an adult I had only skated a few times each winter, and my ankles had always felt noticeably wobbly to me. But this time, that was not the case. What had changed? The only thing I could think of was that I'd been celibate since September. A period of celibacy had strengthened the weak ankles I'd had since childhood—both physically and psychologically.

That wasn't the only effect the celibacy was having. My wife was increasingly unsettled by it, and she had recently returned from spending two weeks with her parents at their winter home in Florida, leaving the children with me. When she'd returned, she said she wanted to separate. I told her I didn't think it was in the best interest of the kids but that I'd support whatever she wanted to do. Nothing more was said about it for nine months.

The night of the skating outing I saw in a dream that I'd been operating from a passive state of mind for most of my life—passivity anchored in a conviction of fatalism—but was getting flashes of some better, clearer conviction state. A month or so later my mother asked me what I was learning about myself, and I told her I saw that I had a passive personality, which was a surprise to me. We had never had any discussions about psychology or personality, so it surprised me even more when she agreed as if it were the most obvious thing!

Another surprise was when I found myself meditating spontaneously, for the first time, in March. That didn't occur very often over the years, and it always felt like a great gift.

I BEGAN A SECOND SOLITARY RETREAT in April, marking the start of the second year of my new life. I fasted (water only) for the week, again not wanting to bother with food. On the last day of the retreat, I wrote in the journal that it had been more productive than the first one, although I don't recall any progress "signs" other than a determination to establish a regular morning meditation on weekdays. I had also made some predictions about my life:

1. My marriage would fall apart during that summer.
2. I would change jobs during the year, and I would be fired from the new job within two years, which would be followed by difficulty keeping jobs.
3. I would complete the search in 1984, at age 40, after which there would be a sorting-out period, starting my own business, and working with others for the rest of my life. (Turns out there was more than a modicum of optimism in this one.)

The next noteworthy item in my journals was from that September. My daughters and I had driven to central Pennsylvania to meet my parents half way, at relatives, to celebrate my father's 77th birthday. On the drive back, I had the feeling that I could make a mature assessment of my spiritual objective and hurdles and then come up with an adult plan of attack. That was my second experience of the feeling, which had first occurred during my son's football game shortly before that. I think it was a good direction, but I can't say that I ever accomplished it.

Shortly after that, in early October, I had my first experience of my "inner head" turning around and looking into the void. I had been reading *The Conquest of Illusion* by J.J. van der Leeuw at the time and suspect it provided the trigger.

In October I also did my third solitary retreat, again fasting for a week. I noted a dread of meditation building before the retreat began and that I wasn't looking forward to it as I had the previous one. I didn't journal and don't recall anything significant occurring during the retreat. But in memory, the solitary retreats were always high points of my life.

One day in mid-November I got a call from the receptionist at work, telling me that someone was in the lobby to see me. When I got there, it was a sheriff's deputy, with a summons to appear in divorce court. I'd had no warning that this was in the works.

DURING THE LAST WEEK OF DECEMBER 1979 I participated in an intensive at Richard Rose's farm. One of the other participants had an experience the week afterward and had been spouting quatrains of poetry nonstop for 24 hours before some of us gathered in West Virginia that following weekend. I felt sympathetic toward him when he became depressed because the other folks didn't buy his claim of being enlightened, and I suggested we go for a walk. On that walk I experienced conscious rapport with another person for the first time. It was as if two minds were experiencing the same thoughts and feelings—and it contradicted what I'd previously believed to be the boundary of my mind and between individuals.

The following Friday, after the regular work day was over, I had been talking with my secretary about science and how I couldn't wait 50,000 years to find out the purpose of life. She asked me if I knew the purpose, and that touched off an analysis of various possibilities, leading me to a state of "creative confusion" I hadn't experienced before. At 5:45 something began to happen. I made a note: "Oh my God, I almost went." I remember taking a 3-ring binder from my desk and putting it on my knees, swiveling my desk chair facing away from the door, and waiting for the last folks to leave their offices. Then, at 6:00, I locked my door, turned off the lights, and relaxed.

I had the feeling of going upward, although I was conscious of remaining in my chair, and was seeing things from a higher perspective. Many worded thoughts rushed through my mind trying to interpret and pigeonhole what I was seeing. The title or caption I put on the view was the conviction that "SOMETHING IS"—and I noted the awe that went along with it, since my mind couldn't conceive of how that could be. For something to exist, it would have to come from somewhere, and tracing it back, there would have had to be a first something. But where could that first thing possibly have come from? It would have to have come from nothing.

I felt myself or my view descending back to where I was in my chair, and then it started to ascend again. I found myself saying goodbye to everyone I loved and prayed the ascent would continue. I didn't want to come back. This time I saw that what's false is as valid as what's true and later captioned the view as "EVERYTHING IS JUST THE WAY IT IS."

I again found myself descending to where I had been consciously sitting the whole time. I didn't lament the return, telling myself that I must not have been ready to go farther.

When I saw Richard Rose that weekend, I told him about the experience. He listened, seemed to agree with the views I described, and said, "You've had a minor *satori* ... but don't fall into the trap of thinking there's nothing to be done." To myself I said, "I can't believe he'd think I would draw that conclusion." Years later, reviewing the journal entry and other notes I'd made at the time, I saw that I had written that very conclusion, word for word, at the time! There's no better way than reviewing a journal to see how easily we can fool ourselves.

THAT SAME WEEKEND I had the first vision in my life. It was as if I walked into a three-dimensional painting and was able to walk down the paths of two possible futures, depending on which fork in the road I took. It became evident to me that one of the paths would leave me in a much better position to protect my children, although it would require personal sacrifice. There was no argument in my mind about which path to take.

Opening Your Heart

Q: *I feel like I get more out of meditation if I'm in a "softer"*
state of mind, similar to the state of mind you noticed me in
(and pointed out) during the last day [of a weeklong group retreat].
Knowing what you know of me, what can I do to get into this state of
mind more often, especially before meditation? It seems like a vulner-
able state I want to avoid at most times, but there are times I'm willing
to get into it if it means I'll make progress.

I think you've hit the nail on the head: vulnerability ... and specifically the belief that we're vulnerable to (able to be wounded by) feelings. The sensitive intellect is largely a response to
emotional vulnerability, a defense mechanism to try to ward off
feelings that threaten to overwhelm the ego. Why haven't you
jumped into self-definition, which intellectually you see as the
only hope of salvation? Could it be fear by the ego, with its rational defense structure, of being overwhelmed? Overwhelmed
by what? Certainly not by thought? But by feeling, by the irrational?

"We try to be so rock-ribbed, we poor mortals!" as Alfred
Pulyan wrote to Richard Rose. What is the nature of your prayer
before meditating? Is it rational or irrational? Do you lay your
heart open to the Lord? Do you feel the pain of humanity as it
calls out for comfort (literally, strength through unison)? Is this
what you're trying to get from relationships? It's a great burden
to project on another human being.

Softening requires relaxation, like opening the fist.
Meditating to become conscious of what we really are requires
acknowledging our existential angst, feeling the pain of existence. When it becomes intuitively obvious to us that whatever
created us (the Creative Principal is a good, neutral phrase used
by Hubert Benoit in *The Supreme Doctrine*) hasn't abandoned us

but is, in fact, the inner self that we're searching for, then we can honestly open ourselves to ask the inner self for help.

Of course we first have to get to the point where we admit the need for help. Once that occurs, then our pre-meditation softening or opening up proceeds along the lines of allowing ourselves to feel the existential angst and then feeling our connection to the inner source or self.

"Do I truthfully want Truth at all costs? (L's reflection to me that it seems I'm just wanting Realization because I think I'm supposed to hit me as being true.)"

Don't be distracted by words. Find the words that match your feeling. I had put together a meeting poster a while back and was looking for a graphic to go with it. The one I found is a panel with Chinese calligraphy for Truth-Beauty-Freedom-Love. I believe we're all looking for the same thing, but different words describe what we're looking for to different mentalities. There is something you want at any cost ... you'll find the word or words that describe it to you. My initial description of my deepest desire borrowed Richard Rose's words (to become the Truth at any cost) and over the years a couple subtitles appeared. One was based on a phrase from Ramana Maharshi: to obey the Lord in thought, word and deed. One phrasing may have described the conceptual side while the other was more emotional. The umbilical cord connecting us to our source vibrates, and the music that vibration produces reaches us in silence.

"I still do not 'get' that I'm not the Do-er, much less the observer."

This is like effort: feeling that we're the doer or that action takes effort depends on how much of the mind's operation has come into conscious view. When my kids were little, they loved being pushed on swings before they learned to pump the swing themselves. If anybody had asked me if I was the one doing the pushing, I would have laughed at the absurdity of the question. My body was producing the movement that pushed the swing ... I was identified with the body ... and therefore I-the-body was the doer. And so on up the line to thinking, decision-making, etc. When we intuit that what we're looking for lies within, then we struggle to go within. It seems like it takes endless effort. Occasionally an accident occurs and we take a step back or within ... or we cross a dividing line without realizing that a discontinuity has occurred.

You are what observes, what experiences, what's aware. You can't conceive of that not being an individual something (body, mind, spirit, soul, whatever). What resolves the existential angst of that position is becoming consciously aware of what you are (observing the Observer in Rose's wording). The path is one of looking until that occurs—i.e., the split between knower and known is transcended.

Looking All the Way Through

*F*oyan (1067-1120), recognized as one of the great masters of the Song Dynasty revival of Zen in China, asked an audience: "Are you in harmony with truth or not? Here you cannot be mistaken; investigate all the way through."[1]

What exactly does it mean to investigate all the way through?

Nobody can tell you how to do it. You have to keep putting effort into trying to know the self, trying to find the truth, trying to observe the observer until all the tumblers fall into place and the lock opens.

The progression in my case went like this: I began implementing Richard Rose's teaching, as outlined in his *Psychology of the Observer* and other writings—especially based on personal interaction with him—beginning in 1978. The objective was to define the self by using the following approach or paradigm: The dividing line between inside/outside is the line between viewer/viewed, and anything in the view is outside the self. By this method I pared down my self-definition to that of a featureless separate observer or awareness.

In October 2003 I visited Douglas Harding at the recommendation of a friend and fellow Rose student who had successfully reached self-realization. Douglas did his "tube" experiment with me, and I saw clearly that I was the space for all things. In other words, everything in the view was inside the self. This left me in a state where my mind was able to flip back and forth between the two contradictory paradigms or ways of viewing the world and my assumed relationship to it, both of which seemed equally valid: 1) all things are outside the self; and 2) all things are inside the self. A contradiction like that is like a lit fuse in the mind.

I visited Harding again in February 2004 and bought his *Little Book of Life and Death* when I returned home. When I read the Prologue, it brought on the desire to get more serious than ever before. I hoped the feeling would hold until a solitary retreat I had scheduled for May.

---

1   *Instant Zen: Waking Up in the Present,* translated by Thomas Cleary, is a book of Foyan's teachings.

On the last day of that May retreat, a Sunday, it had been overcast most of the day, but the sun came out late in the afternoon, raising my hope that I could see the sunset over Lake Erie—which I had left as a treat for the last night.

That evening I noted in my journal that Sunday had been an unplanned transition day from the relaxed but intense focus of Friday and Saturday, when I had been rigorously going through the "exercises in immortality" in the Harding book, to the expected end of the retreat on Monday. I also noted that I had been feeling "antsy" all day—very unusual for me—up through and including the 8 PM walk to the lake.

At 9 PM I journaled the following:

Have been sitting not doing anything since I got back [to the cabin] around 8:30. Great! [This is something I have never been able to do as long as I can remember, always having to have some distraction to occupy the time.] Found myself looking into what I look out from spontaneously, as has happened a couple times earlier today. Just occurred again as I finished tea, moved from the kitchen table and sat in a chair in the LR. This might have been a deeper glance, for it became obvious that what I'm looking out of is Self-aware—that there's no "little person" sitting in a chair [inside my head] watching a movie screen. [My previous concept of an observer.] The screen is self-aware. There can only be one observer—and that's IT....

When I attempt to look, the question: "What am I looking out from?" pops into my head, and that seems to be the "open sesame."

Then at 10:12:

This creature moves from the chair to the kitchen table, to record what has occurred over the past hour. His hand writes, not knowing how it knows. His memory is somewhat sketchy, so he will see how much of what occurred comes back. I say "he," but he is really Me. Well, as real as a shadow gets. I have created this one—a tableau of events, a story—and projected it so that he thinks he's alive....

Previous *satoris* or discontinuities had always felt as if there was farther to go but that the mind was somehow not ready.

I finally "saw" the truth—that what we're looking out from is self-aware. That seeing was not of internal imagery but an intuitive seeing, which I don't know how to describe. It's "seeing" in the sense of something having become obvious, but by a direct knowing as opposed to conceptual understanding.

And a component of this direct seeing was an admission or acceptance of the implications. That acceptance could be described as a letting go or a dying of the individuality sense, which is what occurs when you look all the way through.

The Way Out Is the Way In

*W*hen I turn my awareness / consciousness on itself, it disap- pears in the first millisecond. So my awareness / conscious- ness seems to be nothing more than part of my mind. Yet it is the only tool that I have to search for what is beyond my mind. So I will be never able to experience (be aware of) what is beyond. It feels like checkmate. Is there more that I can do?

An analogy, looking at the problem from "down here": You're attached to a virtual-reality machine, watching a fascinat- ing movie. In the movie you experience a range of emotions suggested (in terms of Santanelli's *Law of Suggestion*) by the movie. Hypnotic sleep, in other words. In order for there to be objects of conscious, there has to be a subject of consciousness, and a relative identity has developed for that subject based on the virtual-reality experience. "My name is Jerry, I live in Amsterdam," etc. The conviction of vulnerability—a background program that kicks in based on what you're experiencing—leads you to try to find a solution to self-vulnerability. Somewhere in what you've experienced, the suggestion caught your attention that finding out what you are will solve the problem. You can't conceive of that finding to be other than more subject-object experience. Regardless of what you-the-subject witness, it's always an object and therefore not you-the-subject. The solution: you have to "go there" to recognize your true self. You can't find it in the virtual reality. You have to wake up from the hypnotic sleep. That waking up may result from sufficient shocks in the virtual reality experience, and it may be helped along by witnessing the struggle that's always occurring in the "inside" experience—the conflicting fear and desire reactions, how they get sorted out, and the higher-level conflict between the body urges and the voice of intuition.

The way out is the way in. It comes with detachment from the hypnotic attraction of the view. Here's an example of one of those delusion-bubbles bursting when I was a kid, probably around age 6 or 7. I was playing with a friend in our dining room, building a fort with Lincoln Logs and staging a battle between the Army and the Indians. My mother came in from the kitchen and said to my friend: "You'll have to go home now, we're getting ready for dinner." I was shocked that she could be so rude to my friend, and the rapport that I'd had with her, along with a conviction of her angelic nature, was gone—like the popping of a soap bubble.

I don't want to be lazy, so here is what I am thinking about: Spending time daily to look into what cannot be seen. Staying in the "between-ness state" where I don't express nor suppress, but just stay in the fire in the hope that 'the other side' will transform it. Pick up praying again. Stop thinking about the dilemma in my Q and start doing something, anything.

The impression I have, from what you've described, is that your life is a concatenation of somewhat frenetic activity … as if you're trying to keep ahead of the Hound of Heaven.

Perhaps I'm just lacking a little bit in faith, or weary. Anyway, I'd like to ask you a question, but have a difficult time finding one that is pure and essential. Or maybe I'm just tired of fighting, and want to surrender to what is (without having to ask myself what is stopping me from doing so).

You can pray for surrender, but you can't "do" it. Since you aver that you don't know What Is, you're not in a position to "do" surrender or obeisance to it. When you honestly reach the view that you've tried every door, looked under every stone, etc., you'll have no option but surrender.

Quoting you: "The bottom line, I think, is to 1) notice what we're looking at, and 2) turn our head away from it if it's not what we're looking for. That determination obviously becomes subjective. So it becomes a question of looking at something sufficiently until we see whether it is what we're looking for or at least relevant to what we're looking for. There will be a discontinuity when we graduate from subject-object seeing to knowing what we are by becoming one with it. You'll know it's a new kind of knowing."

The above rang a bell. It sounds to me like the core of the Search in a few sentences. Yet I'm afraid I'm in a dead end with this, like I stated in my Q above.

Being afraid that you're at a dead end sounds like me, when I was a kid and my parents took my brother and me to New York City for a vacation. We'd walk maybe half of one of those interminably long Manhattan blocks, and I'd become sure I couldn't possibly walk any farther, so I'd insist that they stop torturing me and get a cab :-) If you're in the middle of the block and can't get someone to carry you or hire a conveyance, the options are to lie down and wait for help or death, whichever comes first, or to keep walking.

More Lo-Cal Snacks

*T*he trap we're seemingly caught in is a hypnotic attachment to the outer world of things and the middle world of thoughts/feelings.

Worried about losing the self? You can't leave yourself behind when your attention retreats from the outer and middle worlds. Your self is that attentive awareness.

*E*nlightenment: the mind becoming conscious of what you are.[2]

---

2   What-you-are is what's aware. What's aware is awareness. Awareness is self-aware, which becomes intuitively obvious to the mind at some point in the search for self. Being self-aware, awareness has always "known" itself. The problem is only in the realm of the mind, the realm of experience. All experience is limited by the mind's limitation (i.e., the split between knower and known). Awareness "sees" itself through the mirroring of the mind. The mind's knowing that it's conscious—the result of the mirroring, or of two-way looking as Douglas Harding termed it—may be the clue that leads us back to the source.

*W*hen God euthanizes you while leaving you alive, God wakes up.

*H*ow do you know if you're moving in the right direction? Watch your mood.

*I*f you want to get a feeling for what keeps your identification with the ego-construct solidly intact, one of the things you can do is ask yourself what you'd feel lost without. I recognized one time, quite a way along my search, that the Philosophical Self-Inquiry group meetings in Pittsburgh and my interaction with friends at TAT were among the obvious underpinnings in my case. I'm not recommending trying to dislodge whatever you may see as sticking points—they may actually be helpful in getting you to the end of the line. But the recognition ("If these things were taken away, I'd be lost") may help loosen the tie that binds.

*W*ould a moment of Pure Love that immolates you in its flame of joy be more desirable than an eternity of safety?

Purity of Intent

I wonder if purity of intent is something that is cultivated or the person had all along or changes from person to person.

I think you'll find that purity of intent increases as self diminishes. Eventually you reach a point where you become what

Richard Rose called an egoless vector: you see there's nothing in it (i.e., in self-realization) for the self you believe yourself to be, but you keep acting (retreating from untruth) based on momentum that has built up over time.

One of the popular bromides among tired seekers is that you should stop seeking since seeking is itself the cause of discontent. That panacea fits neatly with the platitude that you're already self-realized, and all you need to do is recognize that fact. Paradoxically, both statements have some truth. You'll find that in the final hour you'll give up seeking, and when you die while living you'll see that the Self has always known itself. But neither of the statements points to a *way*.

We keep seeking until we've tried every metaphorical door that may open to reveal Truth or Self, and we die to seeking—and find what we've been searching for—only when we've tried all the doors.

Salt Doll

*W*ould you choose not to have been created if you had the power to do so? [I asked.]

I wouldn't dare try to mess with the Creator's plan. But somehow, this doesn't mean I can stop wishing that I were never created and never found myself in this mess. [A friend replied.]

You wish you hadn't been created, yet you so badly don't want to die. Imagine a pre-butterfly caterpillar in the pupal stage who wishes he'd never been created yet doesn't want to "die" in his current form. He *will* die in his current form, either ending his existence or completing his metamorphosis into a butterfly.

I just looked up "pupa" on Wikipedia and found that it's the Latin word for *doll.* And that reminds me of the metaphor that Ramana Maharshi used on occasions, likening the self to a salt doll. If the salt doll has mind-life breathed into it, and if that mind allows self-consciousness, that consciousness will be identified with the salt doll. (This is my rambling; don't blame Ramana for it.) If that doll is thrown into the ocean, it will merge into the ocean and that consciousness will lose its identity with the doll form—and its restriction to form or individuality. Enlightenment or self-realization is like what would happen if that consciousness identified with the salt-doll form became free of that identification and merged back into the ocean of aware All-and-nothing-ness before the salt doll died.

❧

Casting Off Illusion

The tiger's in a cage...
An opportunity arises, and he jumps
Headlong into freedom,
Only to find himself trapped again
    By limitation.

The tiger or the mouse
Discovers there's always been
A means of egress behind him,
Back through the projection of self and other
    Into true Freedom.

5. Determination Tested

*T*his section of my search chronology covers the first half of the 1980s. I had moved to Los Angeles in early 1980 and lived there until mid-1981. I had friends there, fellow seekers, and enjoyed their companionship greatly, but I was rather indifferent to whether I lived or died during my first year in LA. My previous state of mind had been yanked out from under me, and it took a while before a new one formed.

Highlights of the year included seeing and hearing Jiddu Krishnamurti during three weekend talks in Ojai that May and hiking in the San Gabriel mountains north of LA with friends on many weekends.

In June I noted that I wasn't feeling a strong conviction about my goal of finding out who I was, but my intuition said it was the right thing to do, and my intellect said there was nothing better to do. I found myself praying for a burning desire for truth at the beginning of meditations in July. I don't recall those prayers ever having been answered.

In October I participated in a weekend intensive with friends, during which I renewed a commitment to help others and made a commitment to end rationalization (i.e., faulty justification of behavior). I saw that my focus had been on changing physical habits for the previous couple years, and I was ready to start on mental habits, which I suddenly felt was possible.

At the end of October I had experienced curiosity about what I was for the first time. That occurred during a nighttime walk, and it struck me something like a mathematical puzzle.

The year ended with seeing my children for the first time since January, followed by a New Year's Eve get-together with friends at Richard Rose's farm in WV.

I GAVE NOTICE THAT I WAS LEAVING THE JOB in Los Angeles I'd been working at for a little less than a year in January of 1981, and I started selling or consigning TAT books and journals to bookstores in LA, eventually traveling north to Santa Barbara and south to San Diego to do so.

At the end of January I reaffirmed my commitment to find the Truth regardless of what it took and renewed the committed to help others in the process. Celibacy continued. It gives a hint of the impression I had of my meditation practice when I noted one "good" meditation in March as compared to the drowsiness I was typically fighting.

I had been studying dreams for at least a year by then and was disappointed that none had seemed significant. There wasn't much in the way of successes during this period to reinforce my spiritual practice.

The following notes came from a phone conversation with Richard Rose in mid-March:

- Don't try to meditate on a topic; you'll interrupt the flow of conversation in your mind.
- Go along with the dialogue; just don't be sidetracked by reverie (food, sex, business schemes, etc.).
- Understand yourself better by watching reruns of past traumas when these come up.
- Meditation will provide inspirations.
- Do what's in front of you, and watch for opportunities to do what you want to do.
- You will find a way to do that which you want to do.

Three days later I was feeling "off balance" after trying to implement his advice, and I was dreading meditation.

Three weeks later I felt I was finally getting the hang of the beginning steps of meditation after three years of effort. (I suspect this might be a typical cycle with any contemplative practice.)

In mid-April I noted an insight: "I have been praying in the wrong direction; 'outside' is confusion and delusion; God must be 'inside.'" On awaking the following morning: "I of the waking state is not Self-aware. This I is not me; it is a foreign creature." And later that day I read something in the *Bhagavad Gita* that I thought described that same insight: "He who has conquered himself by the Self, he is the friend of himself; but he whose self is unconquered, his self acts as his own enemy like an eternal foe."

I left California in mid-May of 1981, heading east, stopping in cities along the way to sell TAT books. I visited my children in Columbus, stopped in WV to see Richard Rose, stopped in Pennsylvania to see favorite relatives, and spent several weeks with my parents in upstate New York, including several fly fishing and golf excursions with my father.

In mid-June I left the northeast for Tampa, Florida, with stops at cities along the way to sell books. I went there to see about establishing a wholesale food business that could support an ashram. By the end of July the produce business I'd attempted to establish was struggling, and my meditation practice had fallen by the wayside.

In early November I noted that I'd taken a day off from the produce business three weeks earlier and hadn't resumed it. I didn't understand why. It seemed like a paralysis of will. The only positive note was that I'd reestablished my meditation practice during those three weeks.

In early December I attended a talk by Ram Dass—Dr. Richard Alpert, an eminent Harvard psychologist in the 1960s and buddy of Dr. Timothy O'Leary of LSD fame. I remember being impressed that he admitted, despite his vast popularity as a guru in the 1970s, that he wasn't enlightened.

I ended 1981 by picking up my son Chris in Columbus, staying overnight with him at Richard Rose's house, and then spending Christmas with Chris in New York with my parents.

1982 BEGAN WITH A GROUP INTENSIVE for the month of January with Richard on his farm.[1] After that I returned to Florida and spent February setting up talks for Rose in Orlando, Lakeland, Tampa, St. Petersburg, Clearwater and Sarasota. The turnouts were disappointing; it probably would have been better to focus on one or two locations.

I felt like I made poor use of the following months on my goal of going within. I mainly focused on trying to find work, and I noticed a recurrence of narcissism that had been largely absent since January of 1980.

Nothing was developing along the job line in Tampa, so I eventually checked out-of-town newspapers in the library—the pre-Internet method—and saw that it looked like there were opportunities in Atlanta. I packed my sparse belongings, moved to Atlanta in August of 1982, and found a job immediately. In fact, on the first phone call I made from an ad in the Atlanta newspaper, I talked with the treasurer of a small software company about a position that the president was looking to fill— and before I even went in for an interview and talked with the president, I *knew* that I had the job. Nothing like that had ever happened to me before.

I'd spent time with my kids the previous December and then saw them again in April of 1983. The job in Atlanta entailed a lot of traveling, which I enjoyed, culminating in a trip to England, Ireland, Holland and Norway in May, after which I transferred to the company's San Antonio office, where the software developers worked.

In August I noted in the journal that I'd been reverting to a mundane state there—drinking socially and finding my head turning to women. I'd grown a beard shortly before my trip to Europe and wondered if that had been a sign of impending *cherchez-la-femme* activity.

---

1   See "Notes from a 1982 Winter Intensive" in chapter 11.

A FRIEND ASKED ME not long ago if I'd gone through many periods of depression during my years of searching, and I told him no, that the only depression I experienced was one that settled on me in January of 1989. (More on that later.) But reviewing the journal during this period, I saw that I'd been "sleeping eight to ten hours a night during my recent depression." That shows how the mind misremembers the past—and the value of keeping a journal in order to get a more objective look back.

August of 1983 was also the date when I found a used copy of Franklin Merrell-Wolff's *Pathways Through to Space*, which I'd been hunting for several years, and began reading it. My reaction at the time was that I knew it was important, but I didn't know why. When I first began reading *Pathways*, I came across a passage where Wolff talked about the merits of mathematical abstraction in problem solving. And that reminded me that on the night before purchasing the book I awoke with a memory of how I used to do math problems (my undergraduate major was theoretical math) and saw the possibility of applying that type of problem solving to the solution of self-definition—a strange coincidence or a premonition?

The highlight of September 1983 seems to have been the arrival of a book I ordered, *The Zen Teaching of Huang Po: On the Transmission of Mind,* translated by John Blofeld. I noted in the journal that the previous day, September 17, marked five years since celibacy began. What I didn't note, probably because I thought it was permanently etched in my mind, was that I had lost celibacy in the spring of 1983 (that was in Atlanta, before moving to San Antonio in late May; I had received a letter from Richard Rose shortly before that, telling me to be careful, but it didn't dawn on me that he was talking about celibacy) although it had taken several months before I actually admitted it to myself. And I recalled my amazement when, on my October 17 birthday in 1978, I realized I'd been celibate for an entire month—something I hadn't imagined as even possible.

In the next journal entry, dated November 22, I wrote:

> I sense a type of destiny, possibly my death—although I don't feel it's time. If I die, I'll regret not saying goodbye to [my parents and children]. I wish them to know the beauty I've experienced and hope they get closer to the Light than I have.
> I feel that I'm deep asleep—and if I can't make any progress in awakening, I have no desire to hang on.

The following journal entry was on December 10, where I described a trip I'd made to Hawaii over the Thanksgiving holiday. It reminded me of the warmth and friendliness of many of the Hawaiians, like the young bus driver in Honolulu who had stopped the bus and caught a bee to show some kids on the bus. (Wish I'd included more details on that.) Several tourists asked me directions on how to get to places in Oahu … I must have looked like I knew my way around, which I didn't. One was a fellow from Australia who was on his way around the world with his wife and kids. It turned out they would be visiting his brother in San Antonio, who owned a seafood restaurant around the corner from where I lived.

Another coincidence occurred when waiting to board my return flight at the Honolulu airport. I struck up a conversation with a young Hawaiian guy who turned out to be flying on standby, so we said goodbye when boarding started. He ended up on the seat next to me on a plane that had 350-plus seats, and during the flight he told me his life story. He was the only one of his friends to escape the poverty they had grown up in (common among the ethnic Hawaiians, he said). He had joined the Marines and stuck it out through boot camp, the first ethnic Hawaiian that his drill instructors had seen who didn't quit on them. He was now working for World Airways, the carrier we were flying on, had a wife and new son in Oakland, and was newly relocated to Honolulu. His wife, who was Japanese American, didn't want to leave her family there, so he was commuting back and forth. He told me his name, Bill Mitchell (William Robert) and his son's name, William Joseph. He invited me to look him up if I got back to Hawaii, and he gave me his address there so he could show me around, have me meet his friends and stay with his family. [I'd forgotten about meeting you by the time I reviewed the journal for this book, Bill. But I remember now the strong rapport between us and will try to look you up if I ever do get back to Hawaii. What fond memories that journal entry brings back....]

That was the last entry in that volume, leaving the remaining two thirds of the notebook blank. The next volume, which began as a dream notebook, starts with an entry for March 23, 1985. A little more than a year is missing from my records. Maybe another volume will show up. But for now, I'll just reconstruct the main events.

A company in Fort Lee, New Jersey had purchased the company I'd been working for in Atlanta and San Antonio in the fall of 1983, and soon afterward I was working under the direction of a manager in New Jersey. In the spring of 1984 I warned the manager that I planned to take a month's vacation in the fall to spend in the woods of West Virginia.

When the time of my vacation neared, the manager asked me to keep working on a project that was in development, but I was firm in my determination. The parent company was having financial difficulties and had already been through one downsizing. Another occurred later in the year, and when a third took place early in 1985, I was among the displaced.

I left San Antonio for Miami, stopping to visit a friend, Steve, in Tampa on the way. I'm guessing that I arrived in Miami shortly before I started the dream notebook toward the end of March and that I devoted April to job hunting. I recall walking into a conference room for an initial interview at Metro Dade County (now called Miami-Dade County) at their suburban technology center. It was a panel interview by maybe half a dozen people including the manager of the job I was interviewing for. And as soon as I walked into the room I *knew* I had the job. The interview was cordial and ended with the usual "we'll be in touch with you" without giving any indication of which way the interviewers were leaning. Sure enough—as with the job in Atlanta—I was offered the position and was happy to accept it.

Looking back, I could see that once I made self-definition my #1 priority, everything else took care of itself.

I wrote on June 16 that I felt a strong need to find or create an environment for quiet introspection … a writing table, peaceful walks. On August 31 I began a solitary retreat for two weeks on the Rose farm—in a one-room cabin with a bed, a table, and two chairs as furniture, amid a large tract of undisturbed woods. On the night of September 4 I had the most memorable dream of my life:

I was waiting with many children and adults to meet Jesus. He arrives on a bus. I see him lying on a seat (the side of the bus being transparent), and it appears as if he might be dead. But he's just resting. I get on the bus, help him off with his cloak, which is a deep purple with a diaphanous orange lining. [Color was rare in my dreams, so I already had a sense that this was an important one.] He and I get off the bus and go into a building, alone together. He surprises me by saying my name, then we sit and he talks to me very gently and sweetly. [The exact words as I remember them: "Arthur ... everything is going to be okay."] I'm overwhelmed and start to weep. He smiles and says: "Now Arthur, Arthur" in a faint accent. He has a jeweled pendent hanging from the inside of one eye along his nose, very pale skin, not a particularly handsome face, light reddish, frizzy hair ... not at all like any picture I had of him.

I awoke from the dream weeping, and every time I recalled the dream over the following days, possibly weeks, I began weeping again. If you knew me, you'd know I'm not a weeper, and I had no explanation for myself to explain the reaction.

Strangely, after the entry for a dream on the night of September 26, the next entry was for the night of December 15th. September 27, by the way, was my father's birthday. So I'll fill in the gap based on memory. I recall clearly that I made frequent trips between the suburban tech center to the Dade County downtown headquarters in that period, often riding the elevated Metrorail. Coming home in the late afternoon there were magnificent sunsets that seemed to wrap around the entire horizon.

One evening on the homeward ride I distinctly recall feeling hot and nauseous. The train was air conditioned and not overly crowded. It may have lasted fifteen or twenty minutes then disappeared entirely. About a week later the same thing occurred again. The next day I got a phone call telling me that my father had died the preceding day, November 25. I didn't even know he'd been sick, but I found later that he'd had two heart attacks—at times that corresponded exactly to the two nausea experiences on the Metrorail—and died as a result of the second one.

I later searched back through the journal to look for the date of the Jesus-on-the-bus dream and found that it was eighty-three days before my father's death (at age eighty-three). My best guess is that it was an emotional preparation of sorts, using a symbolic image of the only childhood figure who had a more authoritative status than my father to tell me that everything was going to be okay. I was surprised to realize, since I hadn't felt close to my father since childhood, that it felt as if one of the two foundations of my life was gone.

Richard Rose came to Miami for some public talks that December (1985). I had subleased a condo prior to his visit, and shortly after he arrived, his wife let him know that he'd gotten a postcard from one of the TAT members, Sam (Sandy) B. He hadn't heard from Sandy in a while, and it turned out that he was living in Miami Beach. Richard called him, Sandy came over the next day, and a couple weeks later we became room-mates in the condo. This connection led to a lasting friendship and even a business partnership for a year or so before Sandy decided to return to school to study architectural engineering.

Hear, Say

*T*here's something wrong with your story:
You say you came into the world when you were born.
But you don't remember the preceding or timely events.
You remember coming into this room, though....

❧

Being Is

In response to a question by a correspondent about a one-time experience of self-realization versus a deep and abiding awakening:

*W*hen you return to the source, you're beyond the body and beyond the mind. When you become aware of your source, you realize you've never been anywhere else. The body and mind are "out there" ... objects of awareness. Whatever occurs "out there" doesn't affect you one iota. If awareness isn't projected back into the bodymind, it dies. If it is, then the bodymind is reanimated and appears largely the same to other animations as before your self-realization. But you know what you are. If the awakening isn't deep and abiding, it's not the final self-realization. Awakening is NOT experience. It's beyond experience (which the mind can't conceive of). The only way for the bodymind to consciously reflect awareness is for it to be in one of the conscious states. Experience depends on the bodymind functioning. Being (abiding in what you are) does not depend on the bodymind.

Existence is transient.
Being is.
Existence is apparent.
Being is.
Existence is problematic.
Being is.

The vast majority of people who claim to be enlightened may not have died while living & are, at best, deluded. Are you looking in the wrong place for answers? They can't be found by reading about someone's purported realization. They can't be found by trying to comprehend someone's purported realization. They can only be found by "going" within ... retraversing the projected ray of awareness back to its source. That's the work that everyone tries to avoid doing. It requires self-observation and self-questioning. It threatens to rock the boat big-time.

You can't become absolutely certain that self-realization is possible or that it will settle your soul, so to speak, before realizing your true identity. Absoluteness depends on recognizing your essential nature. The nostalgia voice or the longing for Home within us hints that we came from Perfection, and our deepest longing is to return to Perfection. Our mentality has to somehow pick up the conviction that such going within holds the best hope of finding true satisfaction.

The Marshmallow Test

*J*onah Lehrer describes an interesting study of 4-year-olds done by a Stanford psychologist in *How We Decide*. The test was to sort out the kids who liked marshmallows (almost all of them) & put a marshmallow in front of them. They were told they could eat the marshmallow at any time, but if they waited for a few minutes while the psychologist ran an errand, they could have 2 marshmallows when he returned. Almost all of them opted to wait for the 2 marshmallows. As he left the room, he told them if one of them rang a bell, he'd come back and that bell-ringer could eat his marshmallow at that time (but wouldn't get the 2nd marshmallow). A few of the kids were able to hold out for up to 15 minutes, although many lasted less than a minute before ringing the bell & others just ate their marshmallow without even ringing the bell as soon as the psychologist left the room. He did a follow-up years later, when the kids were high school seniors, and was amazed to find that the marshmallow test was a great predictor of their behavior as young adults—grades, alcohol and drug use, stress reactions. It even predicted their SAT scores much more accurately than IQ tests given to them at age 4. Those four-year-olds able to resist the temptation were able to shift their attention away from the marshmallow pleasure ... some put their hands over their eyes, others kicked their desk, walked around the room, and so on. They turned their inner heads! That head-turning activity is largely in the prefrontal cortex, which is the last part of the brain to mature. Lehrer concludes that's why teens are so likely to engage in risky behavior ... they don't yet have the mental muscle to restrain themselves, to turn their heads.

Calm contemplation about the biggest internal opposition that you're aware of—for example, staying in school or leaving school, getting married or remaining single, consciousness of awareness, life and death—requires that kind of mental muscle, and your life-experience may be setting up the right conditions for you. The feeling I have is that the mental muscle is somehow connected with being able to look at the void of awareness without flinching ... which may be necessary in order to resolve the fundamental question of self-consciousness and the problem of death.

How can you set the stage for periods of calm introspection rather than engaging in distractions or worrying about mundane concerns?

❧

Ladderwork

S *o, ladderwork works in many ways then? This would be a way of teaching in a manner, to those on rungs below me...?*

I have become aware of another awareness lingering in the background but only seem to be able to remain on the edge. I want to be able to dive in, yet can't. Any thoughts on this you might pass on to me?

Ladderwork involves working with people on our rung of the ladder plus those on the rung above and the rung below us. When we help our rung-fellows climb up, they help push us up. Think of the ladder as a triangular one, like a mountain, with the preponderance of people on the rungs near the base ... all struggling, most unconsciously, to climb the mountain. As we get toward the higher rungs, the struggle becomes semi-conscious at times. Richard Rose used to talk about what happened to Jesus as an example of someone who reached down too low on the ladder ... also as an example of how he talked to hundreds or thousands of people but most didn't really hear his message: They couldn't be helped by someone too far up the ladder.

The awareness of another awareness in the background can take you all the way home. Douglas Harding's experiments in two-way looking are predicated on the assumption that intentional looking will yield repeated glimpses of the background awareness until the view becomes permanent. I think it worked for Harding but took 44 years after his initial realization. I think someone who followed his path exclusively would need to be motivated by trust in a strong intuition. I prefer Rose's suggestion of looking until the observer is known. He intentionally didn't offer a technique, figuring that would slow down the seeker who'd been bitten by the truth bug.

When my inner head was held on looking at awareness, it became intuitively obvious to me that awareness was self-aware ... and that it didn't need any help being so. In other words, I saw that awareness and self-awareness are one and the same. And then I realized that the final conviction remaining of what I believed myself to be was a separate awareness that was aware of self-awareness. My mind admitted that there was a lie in one side or the other of those views and kept looking at awareness until the truth became known ... until I recognized what I was at the core of being.

❧

Decalogue

I had attended 5 meetings of the Pyramid Zen Society at Ohio State University when Richard Rose showed up unexpectedly. The group had formed a few years earlier after students heard a talk by Rose, who lived about 130 miles east of the college. He talked and answered questions during most of the meeting. I felt terrific synchrony or rapport with him. Much of what he said rang "true" —i.e., when I heard them verbalized, I recognized them as things I knew nonverbally. Here are 10 items I later transferred from notes I made during the meeting to a journal I was keeping at the time:

1. You have to set priorities based on what's important to you.
2. If you're interested in spiritual search, it will be fun (not a chore).
3. You can't force yourself along the path.
4. Set a 1-hour meditation period every day. Many, many things will come up to compete with it. It will take about a month to get to the point where you can do some effective introspection toward the end of the hour—another five months to get in the groove.
5. Memories of interaction with parents and siblings are good material for meditation. Realize that you weren't always in the right.
6. Anything within the past 2-3 years is probably too recent.
7. Dreams are a good source of material for meditation. Write them down.
8. The biological role / natural purpose of the female is to bear children and be submissive to the male. The role of the male is to protect the female and children.
9. Sociologists and psychologists are building a paradigm full of lies. Most psychologists since (and including) Freud (but excluding Jung) have been packagers/marketers.

10. All you need to do is to listen to the conflicting voices within yourself.

Triangulation
Conciliatory Path to Self-Knowing through Insight

There are times when the mind gets glimpses from a higher perspective than it's generally aware of—like getting an instantaneous view of the earth from a space station. I think of these occurrences as *satori* or *eureka!* experiences.

A friend reported an example of these glimpses where she saw or intuited that all things "have equal—something—weight or validity or whatever." (She added, "Poor wording for something that went deep.") Now that may sound like nonsense—after all, some things are true while others are false, some bright while others are dark, pleasant versus unpleasant, and so on. Picturing a line, we can place things along the line according to how they compare in relationship to some set of opposites:

FALSE ⟵⟶ TRUE

Less true things | More true things

How would we get a view, though, that shows us all things are equally valid in the sense of being true or false? It's like an incomprehensible report from a creature in 3-D space to a creature in 2-D space, as described so simply and brilliantly in Edwin Abbott's *Flatland.*

From the higher perspective, the mind looks down on true-false as the base of a triangle seen from its apex:

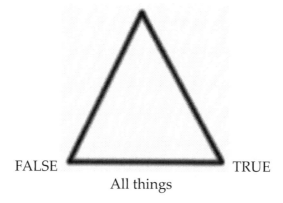

FALSE   TRUE

All things

If one is searching for absolute truth or validity, such a glimpse gives us an important clue. The mind gets a higher perspective by a conciliation of, or triangulation above, opposites.

If one is searching for the ultimate validity of things, then the next triangulation might be over a baseline of things versus no-thing. If one is searching for the ultimate self, conciliation of self versus other could lead to conciliation of oneness versus zero-ness—the equivalent of things versus no-thing, or of life versus death.

The materialist is likely to believe that such triangulation is an endless process, whereas the idealist may believe otherwise. The intuitional mind admits the possibility of a final triangulation to Complete Validity—and its attainment as the *ne plus ultra* of existence.

"What I am is Awareness" is a phrase I frequently remind myself of, whenever I think of it—I don't need a refrigerator sticky for it, mind knows it is true, and I am only reminding myself that all that comfort and discomfort are in an unreal being, a projection as you call it, or a collection of memories as I would call it.

hat's good ... also the clue as to where to find the umbilical cord that takes you home. From the mind's view there are two awarenesses ... the one we're looking out from and the one that's conscious of the outward-looking one. Intuitively, though, you don't feel like two "things" or two different awarenesses, do you? But the mind sees two awarenesses within (plus the billions of other awarenesses outside). What's the truth? How can you triangulate over this awareness-looking-out and awareness-looking-back split?

You've seen or intuited that all things have equal validity. "All things" can be split into endless camps of opposites: heavy things, light things; bright things, dark things; true things, false things, and so on. "All things" form the baseline of a triangle, with the description of opposites at either end. Triangulation refers to a view from the top point or apex of the triangle.

"All conscious beings" could represent the baseline of a triangle. But it's difficult to conceive of what the view from the apex of that triangle might be (since you believe you're one of those conscious beings at the base). You could consider the opposite ends of the baseline to be "my consciousness" and "my son's consciousness," for example. Again it would be hard to conceive of the view that reconciles those opposites.

When we come to that most relevant pair of opposites, "my outward-looking consciousness" and "my backward-looking consciousness" the triangulation or transcendence may happen when we see or intuit the self-aware nature of the outward-looking consciousness. If we see that the outward-looking consciousness is self-aware, where does that leave the belief in a separate self that's aware of it?

A Workshop Session

Synopsis: To know the self, we need to go beyond relative knowing. To do so requires finding the conciliatory position beyond all opposites. The workshop includes exercises and discussion aimed toward that objective.

1. "What is love?" Round-robin definitions—to bring feelings to the surface

- o   Something you've experienced?
- o   Something you've read/heard about?
- o   Compared to what (i.e., opposite)?

2. Look inside: What are you feeling?
- o   Watch for 3 minutes using a vipassana "noting" technique or equivalent (looking vs. thinking about)
- o   Report on what you've seen/felt

3. Look inside for a belief "close to your heart" that you feel sure about

- o   What is the feeling of it?
- o   Look for the argument against it.
- o   Is there a conciliatory position above the opposites?

The mind tries to solve a problem by moving toward the opposite. But we ride the pendulum back and forth between too much and not enough. The solution occurs by seeming accident when we find ourselves observing at the still point from which the pendulum depends. That is the conciliatory position above the domain of opposition. The first such jump within the mind occurs when we get freed from the morass of identifying with emotions, which swing back and forth from positive to negative.

When that occurs, we gradually become aware that we're on another pendulum, which swings back and forth between refereeing the continual war of desires and fears and feeling the intuitional messages coming into the mind, which Blavatsky termed the voice of silence. The conciliatory position above that pendulum swing is the point from which we can observe the workings of the mind with the mind.

Beyond that, a "third eye" becomes conscious of awareness, and the mind gets caught in a loop of watching itself watching itself. This final opposition cannot be transcended in the mind. And if the mind continues this conscious tail-chasing to the point of surrender, we find ourselves back Home—viewing the mind from its source and knowing that we're beyond the limitations of manifestation, beyond life and death … and always have been.

❧

Group Retreat

$\mathcal{L}$ ike a bus ride …
Waiting for the bus, it finally appears.
We're carried along faster & farther than our own energy would carry us.
It offers certain comforts, maybe also some interpersonal frictions,
But the ride ends, becomes a memory.
It may be the last bus ride.
All experience disappoints, leaves us unfulfilled.

6. Crisis of Hope

$\mathcal{I}$n February of 1986 I visited my mother in upstate New York, where she and my father had lived for more than fifty years. Later that month I noted that I had the first overtly sexual reveries in seven or eight years and was not able to turn my head away from them immediately.

At the April TAT meeting Rose delivered one of his not-missing-a-beat quips. Someone had asked him: "Isn't the purpose of art to make people happy?" And he responded: "Yes, but he has to learn to make himself happy first."

In May I had dreams of being in an orphanage and of being in a family situation where I wasn't Art Ticknor and the family wasn't the Ticknor family. These may have been the first of several examples scattered over succeeding years where my self-definition loosened in dreams before doing so in the waking state.

Toward the end of June I noted a higher misery level in the preceding six months than at any time since meeting Richard Rose. I also journaled about becoming close friends with a young work colleague recently out of college and newly married. Jill and I spent a day at the beach at her suggestion, and she told me about her addiction to cocaine. I'd also become friends with a young Cuban American colleague at work, and Ray and I had many enjoyable times together during my early years in Miami, including my first and only trip to the Miami jai alai *fronton*. I haven't stayed in contact with either of these friends and wonder how they're faring.

In August of 1986 I spent a weekend in Maryland with my friend Bob C, planning a trial business project with him. I had reviewed my personal goals on the plane ride, describing them as:

- To live an unselfish life, and

- To retreat from untruth.

I'd noted that it was relatively easy to see selfishness and relatively hard to see untruthfulness.

In September I did a weeklong solitary retreat at the Rose farm from the 27th through October 3rd. I don't know if the start date was planned that way, but it would have been my father's 84th birthday. I'd spent the two days prior to that with Richard and noted that he'd said: "You're trying to do things by formula, and there isn't one." On September 30th I wrote:

> I've tried for over 8 years to go within—with no apparent success. More of the same is not likely to accomplish anything. I will try relying on my Source to show me the way.

I speculated that rigidity/inflexibility of thinking was my *chief feature,* a Gurdjieffian term for what's blocking freedom, and recalled Rose's smile when I told him I was seeing that pattern. He said he'd seen that for a long time and that it had advantages as well as disadvantages. I summarized the retreat on the morning of October 4:

> This is it. Leaving isolation today. Feel it has been productive if, for nothing else, to see how I'm ruled by distraction. Instead of thinking about myself last night ... my thoughts were obsessed with plans for building a [retreat] cabin.... As I prayed for guidance, my head came to the idea that I was almost 42—and have been a fool in terms of not getting serious about self-definition.

On October 16th I picked up my older daughter Jen at her college in Tarrytown, just north of New York City, and we spent the weekend with my mother. On the last day of October I was looking back over my life and saw high points followed by periods of deterioration:

- The bliss of pre-school years, pre-self consciousness. Deterioration through the first year of college.

- Bliss of marriage and births of three children. Seven years of dissatisfaction before meeting Richard Rose.
- Ecstasy associated with encountering Rose. Followed by years of higher highs and lower lows, gradually deteriorating to then (October 1986).

I returned north for the TAT meeting weekend of November 9-12, and then there was a break in the journal until early January.

I WAS BACK NORTH in early March of 1987 to pick up Jen at college and spend a weekend with her at my mother's house in upstate New York. During that weekend I noted a comment by Rose from a transcript of a radio interview at Kent State University:[1] "If you don't have trouble, you're not going to think." I called him on March 14th, his seventieth birthday. I was never comfortable talking with him over the phone. ("When I'm near thee, I love thee. When I'm far from thee, I fear thee," as I had written in my journal earlier that month.)

Rose flew to Miami in early April to take care of some family trouble his son had run into in Daytona, and I drove him back to West Virginia. I then went on to NY to see my mother and back to Columbus to spend a couple days with the kids before the mid-April TAT meeting.

A journal note from June: "I realize now that I have a split vector—I want to be loved, and I want to become the Truth." I didn't see at the time that they were both responses to the deep longing; one aimed outward, the other inward.

Three of us drove from Miami to WV for the July TAT meeting weekend. During this period I typically made five car trips a year to West Virginia to attend the four TAT meetings and the TAT New Year's Eve party at the Rose farm. Sometimes there was an additional trip for a summer intensive, and I would usually fly up for a solitary retreat.

---

1   In his *Direct-Mind Experience*

Later in July I'd noted in the journal: "haven't been sitting [i.e., meditating] for a long time now." That contrasted with a note from the end of May that I'd been meditating every day for a long time without the frustration that was usually associated with the practice.

Celibacy had reestablished itself in March, and I felt that mental clarity had been increasing since the end of April. The day after returning from the August intensive weekend at the Rose farm I realized that I was like Pinocchio, an inanimate object with life breathed into it by the creator's love.

I recorded a dream from the night of November 4th which had no pictures, only the voice of Richard Rose in a tone of disappointment: "... I assume each year that one of these days we're going to have the toughest talk in the city ... sure you've got a fat head, but...." and a final one in the notebook from the following night, where my father, my son Chris and I were driving a jeep up a steep bank, in a stream running down the hill ... my father stays behind so that Chris and I can make it ... I see him and shout, "C'mon, Dad, c'mon," but he just waves.

In early December I noted a decision that had formed over the previous few days: "After my mother passes on ... I will go somewhere (preferably the farm, if it won't cause problems) and fast until death occurs."

A 1987 RETROSPECTIVE I wrote in early January began with the statement that the year was characterized by three events:

1. Realization (in April) that the love I felt for someone whom I wanted to share my life with was not returned, resulting in three months of depression.
2. Reemergence of sexual reveries after seven or eight years of absence.
3. Decision on action for ending my life.

I noted that the love was still strong but that I was trying like hell to suppress it and the hurt of rejection, and that one of my

regrets when I left all this would be the pain I've caused because of the demands this desire for love has made on others.
I wished that I had no attachments ... no one to cause pain to.

The retrospective ended with a quote from Pindar: "Man's
life is a day. What is he, what is he not? Man is the dream of a
shadow."

In the middle of the month I expressed in writing a feeling I
had toward Richard Rose, possibly presaging a trauma that was
coming in the future:

> Thou art my God.
> When thou smileth, the sun doth shine;
> And when thou frowneth, the night settleth in.

Hubert Benoit[2] described how we compensate for the dis-
crepancy between feeling that we're the center of the universe
and the life-experience that effectively contradicts that belief.
The form of compensation that best fit my mentality was one he
termed idolatry. When I was little, I strove to please my parent-

---

2   *The Supreme Doctrine: Psychological Studies in Zen Thought*

idols. When I was in school, the idols—the compensatory im-age—gradually changed to teachers. When I married and had a family, my happiness derived from seeing my wife and kids smile. Later on, Richard Rose became my idol—not the person, but his teaching and dedication to helping others in what we both felt to be life's greatest pursuit.

OTHER THAN A PERIOD IN 1981-82, when I moved to Tampa to investigate starting a produce-distribution business between there and the northern panhandle of West Virginia that would provide work opportunities for a few people as the base for a Florida ashram, I had worked in computer-related activities all my adult life. Then in mid-1986 I quit my regular job, did a little consulting work with a friend and fellow TAT member, Bob C., who specialized in computer systems for the printing industry, and launched a home remodeling business at the end of that year with another friend and TAT member, Sandy B., who had become a housemate the previous year. Neither of us had any experience in that field, but we found plenty of work and amazed ourselves at how beautifully our jobs turned out. We worked steadily for a year, then Sandy decided to go back to school for a degree in architectural engineering, and I began a one-man business of ceramic tiling work at the beginning of 1988.

I did mostly residential work, and I encouraged the home-owners to work along with me if they wanted to. I reduced the labor charge by 33% if one homeowner worked with me or by 50% if two did, and homeowners worked along with me in about half of the projects. Other contractors I talked with couldn't believe the approach I was taking, imagining all sorts of problems. But I was extremely fortunate and enjoyed the co-operative effort. I also accumulated many stories about interest-ing people ... and many fond memories.

In the middle of November 1988 I took a month off to do a long solitary retreat at the Rose farm, and in January 1989 I moved my mother from upstate New York to Miami. But I'm getting ahead of myself a bit and will go back to my journal entries for 1988.

After my 1987 retrospective in January 1988, journal entries are sparse until late February, when I flew to Baltimore in conjunction with consulting work with Bob C. and then on to New York, to see my older daughter. We spent the day exploring Staten Island then drove to Corinth, about 200 miles north, so Jen could spend the weekend with her grandmother.

In May I was thinking about son Chris one night and how he just needed to lay out a strategy for what he wanted to accomplish … and realized the same applied to me: "have always yearned but never strategized," I wrote.

In July, back in Miami after the 4th of July TAT meeting in West Virginia, I noted my convictions about Richard Rose:

1. I believe that RR has found the answers.
2. Through him I found what I believe to be the only purpose of my life.
3. I feel like I've done everything I can to *become*, yet have made little progress due to my own inadequacies.
4. I feel like RR has abandoned me to my own hell.
5. I somehow blame him for not transforming me into a dynamic seeker.
6. I believe that RR lives his life to help others.

"WELL, HERE I AM, BACK IN ISOLATION. I'm looking forward to the next 4 weeks, hoping for clarity and inspiration. I plan to start off with 3-4 days of fasting. No plans beyond this." That's how I started the journal entry on the 27th of November. That was followed by two questions:

Q: What can I learn from the 10+ years since I met RR?
Q: What is the source of my awareness?

On the 29th I noted that the sun had already set at 3 PM(!) There was a wind-up clock that I started using and found that my watch was losing about an hour of day. I assumed that the battery needed to be replaced. A strange thing occurred, though: The day I flew back to Miami after the month-long retreat, the watch started keeping accurate time again.

"The first week of isolation seemed beautiful and peaceful," I wrote. "When I'm here, the conviction that I can't accomplish anything is lifted from me. (A different state of mind.)"

I had always felt guilty that I wasn't a great seeker like Rose. But I noted the following comment that he'd made in the Q&A session after a talk at Boston College: "I am not an individual who says suddenly, 'I'm going to get rid of these hang-ups and barnacles and be a free individual.' I had to be almost programmed to look for the truth."[3]

On December 9th I wrote that I'd finished rereading *Direct-Mind Experience* and that the parts that hit me most were the Boston College talk and the Psychology of Miracles talk, while the last two chapters, Notes on Between-ness and Points of Reference, felt overwhelming. "Makes me realize how little I've traveled and how far there is to go. Discouraging. Yet I'll keep praying. I know that anything is possible."

I also noted that my thoughts reflected my state(s) of mind, that my states of mind are based on convictions, and these convictions aren't necessarily correct. The following day I asked and answered the question: What are my convictions in the state of mind I've been in (i.e., before isolation)?

1. Inadequacy—can't do things by myself.
2. There's nothing worth living for (boredom).
3. Woe is me (self-sympathetic view;) nobody loves me.
4. Things will continue this way.
5. "Hopeless and helpless."

---

3   From the transcript in Rose's *Direct-Mind Experience.*

And a trend had been developing over those past few days. Particularly at dusk, I found myself "just sitting." That evening I'd pulled a chair up to the wood stove and was reviewing some past scenes, when: "suddenly I realized that this was the first time in my life that I've been relaxed/calm enough inside to just sit easily and think."

From the second day of the retreat on, I'd been writing comments about how beautiful the surroundings were … an obvious reflection of the isolation conviction state. On the 22nd for example, with just one full day remaining: "This place has to be the closest thing to paradise on earth." As always, the seconds in isolation seemed to drag, but the days had clicked off rapidly. "The time, as always happens here, has disappeared as if by magic."

THERE WERE NO JOURNAL ENTRIES from the last day of the solitary retreat, December 24th, until February 23rd of 1989. I had brought my 83-year-old mother to live in Miami on January 15th, and she was staying with me and my two housemates in our 4-bedroom house until her furnishings arrived and she could move into the house I had luckily found for her just across the street from me. On January 21st I sent a letter to Richard Rose updating him on my mother's move and details of my isolation retreat, asking for his reactions and guidance as I always did after solitary retreats. The result this time was different from the past, though. After some weeks went by without hearing from him, I assumed my letter must have gotten lost in the mail. So I printed a copy of it from my word processor and mailed it. More weeks went by without a response. Something clicked, and I concluded: Mister Rose has lost hope for me; therefore, my situation is hopeless. That conviction ushered in a period of hopelessness that lasted for nearly eight years, until late in 1996.

My friend Paul S. asked about my reaction many years later (9/13/10):

> *You attributed the onset of your depression to a belief that Rose saw your situation as hopeless. Did it ever occur to you to put the question directly to him all those years, or was it a matter of pride, fear...? Do you believe you had to assume this for things to work out the way they did. What if Rose had told you point blank you were hopeless, would you have altogether given up or fought to prove him wrong?*

My response:

Here was my bind concerning asking Rose if the shock was intentional: I didn't think he'd give me a straight answer ... or that I'd have any way to know if it was a straight answer. If he did it intentionally (which I still suspect), admitting it would have killed the effect. Also, the reason why we don't do something is often even vaguer than why we do something. Do you know what I mean? My guess is that Rose was trying to shake me from using him as my authority, sensing that he needed to break my dependence on him ... from trying to agree my way to truth.

No, I wouldn't have fought to prove him wrong. He was the compensatory image of my idolatry. I worshiped his teaching as the god whose number one idolater I wanted to be. He, or more specifically his teaching, including his actions, couldn't be wrong as long as they were the god I worshiped.

I did give up for that 7 years, but self-realization was still my highest value, so the best thing I could do in those circumstances was to try to support others who still had a chance ... thus moving to the farm to keep it open for other people's solitary retreats.

Paul's reply:

With your type of relationship to Rose, I can see why you were stymied, although you never know if verification could have shortened your struggle.

Observing the Observer

"*Observing the observer*" is a way to describe both the quest and the accomplishment of knowing the self. The phrase itself points out the paradoxical nature of self-inquiry. How does one go about such an endeavor? Richard Rose provided his thinking on the topic in his "Meditation Paper" booklet and in *Psychology of the Observer*. Following are excerpts from an email conversation with a friend:

For years I've been under the impression that watching yourself was the primary proactive activity and that the next level occurred spontaneously when kismet connected with a mind that had been trained to observe objectively. Trying to observe the observer, as stated in the Meditation Paper, results in endless dichotomizing the visualization ad infinitum. I may have misinterpreted and it seems that you still have to attempt to try to observe the watcher as an activity and not merely as a side effect.

Consciously watching thoughts, feelings, etc. is really watching the not-self. It's paring down the faulty definition of self, which (self) goes back relentlessly to being identified with what's on the screen—i.e., the view.

> *Your comment is congruent with my past understanding, which is: that the action of "disidentifying" with the view on a regular basis (more the better) and with intensity (created from energy conservation) and with novel approaches (to avoid plateaus) creates an environment in which the potential to flip to an anterior perspective is increased.*
>
> *However, what I have been hearing from you (not necessarily what you have been saying) is that we can't just keep trying to watch the not-self (e.g. dumping more things over on that side of the fence until one day we realize there's nothing more to throw and say wow this must be the real me, the guy tossing the junk out), but that we have to try, as in struggle, to watch the watcher.*
>
> *So the question becomes, is viewing the viewer a side effect from intense and repetitive exercises in self observation, or is it something that comes from intense and repetitive attempts, albeit seemingly futile and paradoxical, to actively view the viewer? If the latter, how do you know you are doing it correctly without falling into the act of imagination?*

I sense that there's a confusion that you're attempting to resolve so that the mind can go back to a state of less irritation. Should I do you a favor or do you a favor?

When something new appears to be part of the view, this is the paring down of what was previously considered to be the self. There are really two big globs of stuff we're talking about: me-as-thinker/feeler (i.e., identification with thoughts and feelings) and me-as-mental-process (i.e., decision-maker, introspector, etc.).

Intentional self-inquiry is a conscious attempt to get congruent with what life's trying to do for us. This could be described as going Home, knowing the Self, or you name it. So how do you go Home when you don't know where it is (and can't, since it's everywhere and nowhere)?

You won't know when there's nothing more that could come into view, but when you have removed all the features you can imagine, you'll be left with an apparently featureless (no arms, no legs, no thoughts, no feelings, etc.) observer-self as your self-definition. And, yes, you can say that this featureless observer-self must be the real me ... but can't you already do that? Does it solve the problem?

The solution only comes when you get beyond the mind. The ultimate problem is that 1) you already know what you are—"I'm what I'm looking out from," in Harding-speak, "and what I'm looking out from is what's aware. In other words, I'm what's aware." Right? So far, so good. But 2) "I'm also the featureless observer-self that's aware of what I'm looking out from, aware of awareness." Now watch the mind skate immediately off on a tangent.... This is the conundrum that the mind can't compute and can't afford to contemplate—i.e., not think about but look at. That would be observing the observer. What it sees (item #1) cannot be accepted ... or it would be the end of that oh-so-loved belief (item #2) in being a separate something.

There's no time or effort involved in accepting the truth. All the time and effort go into backing oneself into a corner—really, into eliminating all the BS that keeps us from admitting that we've always been backed into a corner. The rate of elimination varies inversely with our tolerance of procrastination and rationalization.

To become conscious of what you are, look at consciousness.

❧

Advice?

Q: *A while ago you mentioned that you were able to see some things that you thought would be valuable for people to do or not do in terms of finding an answer. What would your advice be for me?*

A: A friend in the UK wrote to me a few months back: "I would be grateful if you could tell me *exactly* what to do now and I will carry it out to the letter." I gave him a suggestion—one that could be carried out with very little effort—but he hasn't acted on it. He's not a man of his word, is he. One part of him was lying to another, more interior, part.

Reaction from Questioner:

Your response to me really hit home/cut deep. Thoughts about several things came up after reading it—it ratcheted up tension. One is that your response indicates that I am not a man of my word. I have thought around the edges of this before but never really stared it full in the face. I think I attributed it (lack of being a man of my word) to the bad state of mind I was in (considering that not me) or in small things would think it doesn't really matter. Especially if I am in a good state of mind, then it is all good (I am all good—special) so it can slide. But if I look at my life, I haven't been a man of my word, and that is hard to look at.

Another thing I thought about was the number of times I have asked you for help and then pretty much ignored any advice you gave, which this could be getting at. I have to admit I wasn't fully committed to doing whatever you suggested and could have been very wishy washy about it. Similar to this I thought about how you may be indicating you already gave me advice about exactly what to do and I ignored it—this particular thought struck deep as in my mind it tied to your advice of following my heart and my recent move. My feeling now is that I didn't follow my heart.

What you said at the end also struck me—that one part of him was lying to a more interior part. Part of not being a man of my word means I am lying to myself—yes that is pretty obvious (not meaning that in the tone of like well it is so obvious you didn't need to mention it but in the sense of my mind putting 2 and 2 together). It reminds me of Shawn's talking about being truthful in small things like being somewhere when I say I will and how if I don't think that is part of finding the Truth about myself then I am sadly mistaken. Perhaps the point of the lie is in asking for advice without the full intention to carry it out.

It is also possible that the deep sadness/regret I feel in regards to this is an overreaction in that I am not the lowest of the low—I am human and, in attempting to become more truthful, this can change.

I have actually been somewhat afraid to ask you the question of what you think I ought to do—I think because of a number of factors. Part of it was that I set you up as the spiritual authority in my mind (yeah well I did that and then didn't listen to your sugges-

tions—heh I can smile at that thought now) and that didn't work in part because I wasn't (still might not be) mature enough. I blamed you for a lot of my problems as opposed to looking at myself and as opposed to seeing you were trying to help me. I didn't want to slip back into that mode so I waited to ask the question until I thought I would be relatively safe from that happening. Heh it is funny how things can seem to be so clear for a while ... and then confusion and conflict jump in.

Reflection: The above correspondence occurred five years ago. I wonder what the friend's reaction will be if he reads this again.

✷

Love

A friend asked:
Just before [Richard] Rose's death, while meditating, I had a significant spiritual experience. I believe I found who I Really am. But I knew that I didn't have the final answer because I still had a longing.

Just recently, I recalled Rose talking about his LSD experience. He thought that he might be able to recreate his enlightenment experience by using the drug. He said that he "experienced ego death but no illumination." Maybe that was similar to the experience that I had. What do you think? And how do I go farther?

I think it's possible to get a glimpse of what we are without the mind's accepting the implications … which means there's still some less-than-true belief or conviction about what we are that hasn't been burned out or eroded away.

You can't "do" the final realization. It's a process of Love. You won't be satisfied until you find (become) total, unconditional love. It's truly a realization or recognition, not a doing … because what you're looking for is what you are. Become conscious of that which never changes. You and that are not two.

A nother friend asked:
Can you tell me more about Love? What role does it play, how can we find it and express it in the world?

Sure … your life experience is telling you endlessly about Love. The world is an expression of Love. If your will is consciously lined up with your source, then you're consciously expressing Love. (If not, your expressing it anyway :-)
Love is the answer to all questions, the satisfaction of all longing.
Love is impersonal. Love is beyond life … that which never changes.

Love is bigger than the universe, encompassing the universe.

Love has no dimension. It is smaller than the smallest point.

Love is the nothing from which all this emanates and into which it all returns.

The ocean of Love has no shores.

Love has color, loves color, but is colorless.

Love has multiplicity, loves multiplicity, but is not divided.

Love is the answer to all prayers, the asker of all prayers, and the content of all prayers.

Love is.

Only Love is.

Whatever is, is Love.

All that is said here is said about Love. All reference is to the subject, to You.

Love is the stillness between, behind and beyond all vibration.

Look for your Self between, behind and beyond.

Lo-Cal Snacks III

*P*ersonality is the mask hiding the delusion that obscures the truth.

*W*e can't control the behavior of those we love any more than we can directly control our own reactions. All the negative emotions that we feel can lead us to the unconditional love that underlies all experience, that witnesses all experience, and that engulfs every breath and every heartbeat. We don't see it until we see it, and then we realize that we've seen it all along. It's what we are, and it's the only seeing that sees itself.

*T*he only knowing-for-sure is knowing what you are. Knowing what you are is Absolute Truth. Will you be satisfied with anything less?

❧

*Y*ou have a stressful situation and get all wound up in it, but I know if you'll take or make time to step back from it and view it with some objectivity, you'll see that everything is perfect just as it is. From back there or up there, everything out here or down here is perfect just as it is. Including all our complaints. The cosmos is in perfect harmony and balance, but that occurs through the ups and downs of its parts. If we're identified with one of those parts, then we'll be up or down. Harmony and perfection occur only in wholeness.

❧

*T*rue Love, also known as Absolute Truth, adds nothing to you. It is not found by seeking for love or truth for your sake but by seeking truth for truth's sake.

❧

*T*he ultimate "sacrifice" is the prison of personality. Identification with fears and prides keeps our belief in personhood in place.

❧

*B*e careful of judging people solely by their words. If you're going to put your fate in the hands of a teacher or their teaching, it's important to get a feeling (intuition) for what the person knows about their essence. The intellect can be dazzled by intellectual brilliance & be inflated by identification. The intuition can likewise by dazzled by ego-enhancing feeling.

❧

*T*he intuitive mind is struggling to wake up to conscious awareness of its source.

*W*atching the story of your life, you're caught up in the lead character's trials and tribulations, forgetting you're what's watching ... not the movie being witnessed. That character is on a quest for happiness, for invulnerability, for complete satisfaction. That quest can only succeed in one way, and that's when the character recognizes his source ... or more accurately when the mind-machinery becomes consciously aware of its source.

State of Simply "Being"?

 o you feel you are in a state of simply "being"?

When I asked Douglas Harding if he felt like he'd had a long life—he was about 95 at the time—he paused then said: "Yes ... and no."

When you ask if I feel I'm in a state of simply "being," the only simple answer I can give you is the same one Harding gave me.

From the testimonies we've heard/read, some people go through a one-with-everything realization before possibly reaching a final breakthrough. For me, the primary realization was Nothingness ... with a secondary realization of Everythingness. Nothingness is simplicity. Everythingness is complexity.

From a feeling side, how does pure Awareness translate into Love?

Awareness could be characterized as Love since Nothingness loves its creations, Everythingness. Love in the most exalted form is identity. Nothingness = Everythingness.

Have you gained any more of a sense why God needed to branch out into individual rays?

As part of realizing the identity of Nothingness, the real I knows its wholeness. It has no before/after, no cause/effect, no splits, no whys or wherefores. Nor any wants or needs. Why it projects Everythingness is a speculation of the projection, of mind. The question arises because of the dualistic nature of manifestation, and there's no answer other than one that's concocted by the projection.

❧

"This Self Won't Die"?

I am working with triangulating between awareness and the belief I have in myself/desire that this self will not die.

The belief that "this self won't die" describes a feature you believe about yourself, like this shirt I'm wearing is blue. It doesn't get at what you believe that self to be. What is the self you believe won't die? Not theoretically, based on your reading, etc., but feeling-wise. We have to *look* to see what that self is that we believe ourself to be. In my case, I eventually saw that it was this "individual" awareness that can look inward and glimpse the awareness that looks outward.

But when something held my gaze on that outward-looking awareness, it became evident to me that it was self-aware. The words don't do the trick, but the point I'm trying to make is that regardless of whether we're getting there predominantly by thinking or by feeling, thinking/feeling are secondary.

What's primary is the inner looking (or listening, feeling, etc.) that drags us into accepting the truth of what we see.

The concept of what is aware being self-aware leaves me befuddled. It would seem that it is evident that whatever is aware is also self-aware, even when I believe awareness is between my ears. If there is a seeing that needs to happen here, I can't even envision it.... So I am just trying to feel or look at awareness.

When you try to feel or look at awareness, you have to try to feel or look back at yourself ... back at what's looking, don't you?

Yes. I think of it as awareness, consciousness, what I'm looking out from, what's looking—I don't differentiate when I'm trying to look, but then I'm not using words, I'm trying to feel or sense or something.

Oh. In other words, what I am is what is looking. And mind says, how do I know that's not just the body?

Okay, let's begin with: "I am what's looking." Somehow I know that I am that which is conscious or aware. And that awareness of myself as subject coincides with awareness of being in a familiar body about two thirds of each 24-four period. What I am may be that body or at least depend on that body, implying that it may end with the body's death or sooner. How can I find out for sure what I am?

The clue is that we *know* that we're conscious or aware. The mind somehow perceives awareness. It gets momentary glimpses of awareness by some ability to look back at itself. But when we try to do that intentionally—i.e., look back at what we're looking out from—the mind registers nothingness. It seems like what we are is always right behind us.

We are that which is aware—the subject that is aware of objects such as trees and people but also of thoughts and feelings. Yet we are also aware of that outward-looking subject.

When we rub our thumb and forefinger together, the finger feels the thumb when our attention is on/in the finger, or the thumb feels the finger when our attention is on/in the thumb. Similarly, we are that outward-looking subject when our attention is looking outward or the backward-looking subject when looking back at the outward-looking awareness. The attention can alternate rapidly back and forth but, if we observe closely, it's not in both locations at the same instant. Thus our observations tell us that there are two awarenesses that we are, alternately. The observations, however, don't agree with our conviction of being a singular, separate observer or awareness.

How do we solve this conundrum? We have to try to look at awareness, to "catch" the aware self, to somehow get behind our sense of self.

7. Stuck in Despair

*R*ichard Rose had an older brother whom he loved. He said James was a fatalist and very compassionate. During the 1930s, when he was working he would often give his paycheck to some family with kids who didn't have anything to eat. When WW II broke out, he joined the merchant marine, which was under attack by German submarines. James volunteered for the most dangerous job in the ship, working in the boiler room below deck … with little chance of survival if a torpedo hit the ship, which eventually happened. In Rose's *Carillon* there's a poignant poem he wrote after his brother died, titled simply "James." It starts off like this:

> When I'm alone with thee,
> When light and dark are gone,
> And earth's mad rush doth pause to let our minds converse,
> I hold the pendulum of time to still its tone,
> But scarcely see, for selfish tears thy shade disperse.

James died sometime before the war ended in the spring of 1945. Rose said his death showed him what a selfish person he was, in contrast with James. That's what falling in love sometimes shows us … and sometimes we don't recognize the love until the object is taken from us. The reaction results from the ego, the sense of self, having temporarily moved out of the spotlight of our attention and concern.

I have some young friends who are so caught up with their personal fears and unfulfilled desires that they get themselves tied in endless knots and tangles. The antidote is to "get outside their own heads." Life may bring them the experience to precipitate that, but paradoxically it can also occur from introspection—when we begin to just watch the mind rather than being caught up in its thrashing.

On February 23rd 1989 I wrote, "Fact: I am very unhappy. My life is flat and featureless. I feel like there is nothing to look forward to. In a way this state of mind parallels that of the 10 or so years before meeting RR." And a week later, "I am self-satisfied, as RR told me, in that I have no great curiosity about who I am, where I came from, or where I'm going. But I do long for a different state of being." There were just four entries in the journal for this period, the last one with the brief description of a dream on April 26th. No mention of the crisis of hope that was triggered in February and described in the introduction to the previous chapter; I suppose it was too unforgettable and too painful to need recording.

The next entry was in late January 1990. I noted that I'd made two commitments in the fall: to become a teacher, and to become a hypnotist. Rose thought that every seeker should study hypnotism in order to understand the mind's operation. I'd been working to establish a philosophical self-inquiry group at the U. of Miami for a while and more recently at Florida International U. I'd met a few people at each school and had worked on hypnosis with one student, but no group material-ized at either location. I'd resumed an almost-daily meditation practice (don't ask me why; it doesn't make sense based on my conviction of hopelessness) and wrote that: "The one great posi-tive note in my life is that celibacy was reestablished (Oct. 1988). As in the period from 1978-1983, it has been largely effortless, although I recently survived a several-day attack. However, I don't feel any smarter about how to maintain celibacy in the face of adversity."

A friend, Lee, forwarded the text of a recent letter from Rose, in which R had written: "Do all things for the sake of a higher power, and it will correctly guide your every step."

ANOTHER TRAUMA HIT during the April TAT meeting ... actually a great inspiration as well. The inspiration first: I was bringing a bowl of soup from the kitchen into the meeting room when someone I passed called to me. As I started to turn, I heard

Mister Rose say: "I'm right behind you," obviously to keep me from bumping my arm and spilling the soup. Then without missing a beat he said, *sotto voce,* "I'm always right behind you." I knew that the second statement was coming from a deeper place.

But when Rose inconspicuously invited some of the attendees to sit in rapport with him on Sunday afternoon and I wasn't invited, my ego was shaken. As I began the drive back to Miami, the trauma hit, and I thought: "If death comes now, it's alright; I'm ready."

I realized then the similarities among three experiences: the year after I left my family and didn't care whether I lived or died, the time when Mr. Rose turned his back on me at a public talk I set up for him in Miami, where for the next couple hours I wished I was dead, and this trauma, where the ego seemed willing to let go. [There was no mention in the journal of the hopelessness conviction; for some reason that hadn't had the same effect.] I saw the possibility that the last two traumas were done intentionally, saw why trauma might be necessary to loosen the ego's grasp and that it takes different forms of trauma for different personalities.

There were quite a few dream entries during May and mention of a June "Chautauqua" at the Rose farm followed by one entry in October and one in November, the latter three all focusing on the 12 years that had passed.

THEN THERE'S A GAP in the journal until January 1993. "Where have I been since the last entry (11/28/90)?" I asked myself. I'd heard that Don S, the last of the fellows living on the farm, had been asked to leave when Rose became suspicious that he was selling things that Rose owned. (It became evident later that this was the paranoia of early Alzheimer's disease.) I had called Rose and offered to move to the farm, to keep it open for people to use for personal retreats, and he said sure. I did that based on the desire to help others as I'd been helped, but I realized it would prolong my own misery by interfering with my plan to end my life after my mother's passing. I had sold the two houses in Miami, moved to the farm in July of 1991, and settled my mother in an apartment in town until I could find a suitable house for her.

I wrote that I longed for an isolation retreat but didn't feel I could leave my mother, whom I checked on daily, unattended. I had hoped to have her in a house with a live-in companion long before now, but it hadn't worked out. I didn't have a daily meditation practice at the time, but I noted that the extended period of celibacy, from October 1988, was still in effect.

There were few additional entries for 1993, the last one describing a dream near the end of October. Then one entry after the TAT meeting in April 1994. As I'd done for years, I manned the food counter to take orders from the attendees and supply their food from the kitchen that was (wo)manned by Cecy Rose. Mister Rose set a serious tone for the meeting on Saturday, sitting in front of the food counter with his back to me as he talked to the folks in the room. It reminded me of the shock after the 1988 isolation when there was no response to my correspondence. I felt that "god" had turned his back on me, and a conviction of hopelessness was reinforced.

Rose had said on Friday evening that the only way to change states of mind intentionally is when you get angry enough at the one you're in to fight it. My bind, I wrote, is that I'm a submitter to my states of mind rather than a fighter. I awoke during the night with the wish that I were dead, and—a new twist for me—that I had never been born.

THEN I LOCATED ANOTHER JOURNAL, this one beginning on New Year's Day 1992 and running through mid-October 1993, filling some vacant spaces.

We'd had the usual New Year's Eve party with RR at the farm, attended by guys and their families who lived in the area as well as seven guys from the Raleigh, NC Self Knowledge Symposium group. Bob C. was living in his cabin on the farm and running his IT business from there since the previous summer. Most of the entries for January were about the goat herd, the supervision of which I had inherited as de facto farm manager. The goats' job was to keep the multiflora roses from taking over the landscape. They took care of themselves three seasons of the year, then we took care of them during the winter.

They were giving birth to the new crop of goats during the coldest time of the year: "Rosie has 2 kids (tan male and black female). Premature kid found dead in the barn ... Sheba had a kid this morning (male, her first) ... Belle had a kid this morning; Brahma (Belle's daughter?) had a kid this afternoon," and so on. The births were interspersed with sickness: "Lulu having problems—back legs collapsing. Put her in a stall in the barn ... Lulu died today ... the year-old black and white Billy goat died today; he was moving slowly and making plaintive noises yesterday." The problem turned out to be caprine arthritis-encephalitis, a viral disease.

Richard, Cecy, and their daughter Tatia generally spent the weekends on the farm, but after the New Year's Eve weekend, they stayed in town the next two weeks—first due to Richard's getting the flu, then due to a snow storm.

There were people visiting the farm to see Rose most weekends and others coming to do solitary retreats. There was also a project going on to build a cabin for Dave G, which I seem to remember was in its early stages at that time.

Nine college guys and one gal came up from Raleigh the first weekend in March and stayed until Wednesday. Mr. Rose spent the weekend on the farm then came back out on both Monday and Tuesday to be available. One of the guys did a solitary retreat for three days. Another lasted only one day. Rose confronted another of the fellows about his negative attitude and didn't accept his TAT membership ($20).

The girl was there with her current boyfriend, but one of the local TAT members spent some time talking with her about personal relationships, how he was under pressure from his parents to get married, and asked her what her parents would do if she spent years on a spiritual path without producing babies, etc. Her head was spinning with conflicting desires.

Mr. Rose invited four of us locals and two visitors to celebrate his 75th birthday in town on March 14th. The other five of those and Rose left for Raleigh two days later, for a talk he was giving at the UNC Chapel Hill, while I stayed to keep an eye on things at the farm.

The ceiling in one of the cabins caught on fire while its occupant was out for a walk on March 24th. The room was filled with smoke when he returned, but fortunately one of the handy guys working on Dave G's cabin nearby dismantled the ceiling around the stovepipe, and saved the roof.

Rose gave a talk at the U. of Pittsburgh on March 26th and one at Duquesne on April 3rd. Good turnouts at both (120+ at Pitt, 70+ at Duquesne), but only a few showed up for subsequent meetings of the Pittsburgh self-inquiry group.

The April TAT meeting had a small attendance of local people (11), folks from Ohio (4), Pennsylvania (8), Maryland (3), North Carolina (10), and Colorado (1). I think Mr. Rose had started losing short-term memory by this time and was repeating himself frequently. Bob C. left that Sunday afternoon for his new home in Annapolis, having come to the realization while spending a year in his cabin that he'd devoted 20 years since meeting Rose (at age 18) to the spiritual search, and now it was time to get married and have a family.

When school was out for the summer of 1992, Raleigh folks started showing up for solitary retreats and short stays. Six of them (Billy, K.W., Georg, Danny, Shawn, and Augie) arrived for the summer. There were 35 attendees for the July TAT meeting and 28 for the Labor Day gathering. These numbers were maybe half or less of typical attendance in the 1980s.

On November 4th I began the entry with: "another hiatus of depression…" and noted that Bob F. arrived from Boulder the previous day for a month, including two weeks in solitary retreat. Rose gave a talk at the U. of Pittsburgh on the 12th, in the ballroom of the Student Union. About 80 attended, and he talked until around 10:30, mostly question-and-answer format. He had lost some of his mental sharpness, but his presence was still strong.

The Roses had Thanksgiving dinner in town, inviting five of us locals plus Bob F. and 19 others who were in town for the November TAT meeting. Mr. Rose said that the rapport that developed at the TAT meeting was the strongest one in quite a while.

Three people did solitary retreats between Christmas and New Year's Eve, at which time 10 of us gathered for the traditional party—a very small number.

Early January 1993 saw the return of K.W., staying in town with the Roses until their summer move to the farm. The new crop of goat kids began arriving near the end of the month.

Danny S. arrived in early March for a two-month stay. Sean McL. came near the end of the month for a month-long solitary retreat. Eric C. arrived in early April for a month-long stay. 49 people attended the April TAT meeting.

Three guys arrived from Raleigh on May 10th: Marcus for two months, Andrew for two weeks, and Chuck for three. Chuck left on the 12th when his bank transaction card didn't work here, Marcus on the 16th with intestinal trouble.

Two fellows did solitary retreats in June. Chuck C. fell off a roof in Pittsburgh, remaining unconscious in intensive care for more than a week. He had a slow recovery and never came back to the farm, where he'd been in the process of building a home.

Twenty-nine people attended the July TAT meeting. Bob F. returned to Boulder to tie up some loose ends. He had rented an apartment in Wheeling and would be coming back. Georg B. arrived on the 10th for a month or longer. Mr. Rose started laying bricks for the Community Building wing.

Shawn N. arrived August 1st for a two-month stay. Mike S. arrived from Raleigh on the 4th for two weeks; he left on the 5th. Bill McK. arrived on the 21st for a solitary retreat until the TAT meeting. Sean McL. arrived on the 30th for a couple months. K.W. left on September 1st. 32 people attended the Labor Day TAT meeting. Alex L. arrived on the 26th for an indefinite stay.

Dave G. brought 3 folks up from Raleigh for a work weekend in early October. They worked along with Bob F, Shawn, Alex and myself to replace rotted fence posts along the east property line. The following weekend a crew of 21 including

10 from Raleigh installed new fencing. Bart M. did a solitary retreat for a week in Dave G's cabin. And that was a slice of life on the Rose farm during the three years I lived there.

Q & A

I want to know what it FEELS like to know the truth/be enlightened/self realized (whatever).... what does it FEEL like for you???

Good! That's a good sign … you have to feel it for yourself; nobody else can feel it for you. It feels good! It gives perspective on all feelings.

What we're talking about is to be with full awareness what we already are. To do that, we back away from identification with objects of awareness and back into the aware subject.

What does getting serious mean? I'd rather just get serious now and get this over with. I'm completely committed.

Getting serious is recognizing that our innermost desire is to become the Truth. This recognition yields commitment to it as our #1 priority. The commitment is for a lifetime if necessary.

The commitment will turn us into an arrow aimed away from untruth.

The Truth is not individualized. Becoming one with Truth is dying before we die. Getting really serious is recognition of readiness for that dying to occur now.

*O*ne friend asked some other friends: *What's behind every-thing you see and experience?* One of them answered: *If you're asking what's behind the subject that sees and experiences, my response would be to say "I'm behind it, and I'm all there is—there's nothing else behind me."*

If "I'm behind it, and I'm all there is—there's nothing else behind me" ... what am I??

*C*alling on a higher power, or self within, makes sense. Can it/I hear me?

What you really are is what's aware. (That's obvious, isn't it?) What's aware is what hears every word that's spoken, sees every word that's read, hears every bird chirp, sees every thought, every feeling. You are the hunter, the bow, the arrow ... and the hunted.

*W*hat does it feel like to walk around in an awakened state (if that's what you would call it)?

The feeling that's important for the seeker to pay attention to is the feeling of longing / emptiness / dissatisfaction / isolation, or however it's interpreted by the mind. Once you know what you are & are walking around in an awakened state (or maybe realize that what's walking around is an animated cartoon character that was never alive :-) that deep misery is no longer there. The cartoon character may have a toothache, may experience rejection, death of loved ones, and so on, but you won't be lost in the view. And you'll know that his ups and downs, even his eventual death, won't affect you one iota. It's not an emotionless state, as many seekers fear. Emotions are felt deeper and unalloyed.

o you have a lot of thoughts? I'm asking because with me it feels dense up there, and sometimes I have the feeling that I'm missing out on something important. On the other hand I don't believe in repression. Meanwhile I'm mesmerized by my thoughts, time after time after time after time….

Sure … copious thoughts and feelings, a cornucopia of them. Thoughts … perception and all its reactions … are the experience we call life. The default mode of operation is being mesmerized by experience. The spiritual path is the struggle for the mind to wake up from the hypnosis. It's not a question of more thoughts, fewer thoughts, new thoughts, etc., but of who's experiencing the thoughts. The answer to that is not in thought/feeling. It's in the seer recognizing itself.

What Is Aware?

*M*aster: What is aware?
Aspirant: I am.
M: How do you know that?
A: I'm aware of it.

M: Is awareness a property of the body?
A: It seems to be.
M: Are you primarily awareness that has a body or a body that has awareness?
A: A body that has awareness.

M: Does awareness come and go?
A: Yes.
M: Can you personally testify to having been unaware, to having experienced unawareness?
A: Well … no. But I don't have any reason to doubt what other people tell me about seeing me asleep or unconscious.

M: Other people being objects in your awareness?
A: Well … yes.
M: And those other people have their own separate awareness?
A: Yes.
M: How do you know that?
A: Well … they tell me. It's obvious. I don't know.

M: Since you believe you're primarily a body, then I assume you believe that you're going to die?
A: Intellectually, I know that all body/minds die, but there is a belief that this somehow does not apply to me.
M: If there's a "real" you that doesn't die, it would have to be a "you" that wasn't born and that is "here" right "now." And it would know itself right now.

🌿

I am the real you that doesn't die, that wasn't born, that is here right now, and that knows myself right now. What am I?

❧

Self-Perspective

 A dear friend who had a recent realization wrote: *What is your current feeling about what you are? I feel that I am the creator of all. It's my world, created by me, but I have no control over it. I do not understand this. Something that has changed is that instead of me moving around in the world I now feel that the world moves around in me. I had done Douglas's experiment the night before the awakening but could not get it to stay. However, since then it has arisen naturally, especially when walking on the beach. I do not notice the immobility when around home.*

What I saw or felt when I was beyond the mind was that I was looking, as if with eyes closed, in the direction of where a belly-button would be if there was one and seeing that I was creating and watching creation there. I knew there was no "why" there, so ... like you say ... didn't know why I was doing it. I think Gurdjieff must have known something when he made the list of idiots and placed God at the top :-) BUT all seeing is with the mind ... and the closest the mind gets to understanding or comprehending the Truth is paradox.

"Inside" and "outside" are perspectives or paradigms of the mind. The conventional paradigm that most of us are conditioned into is that the world is outside us. Douglas Harding's mental experiments show us that the opposing paradigm, where the world is inside us, is an equally consistent and valid view.

Settled Your Soul?

A new friend wrote: *I've read your articles and descriptions of your experience, but it's different hearing it directly...so: Is the fact of your realization ever-present for you? Do you know what death is? Have you settled your soul?*

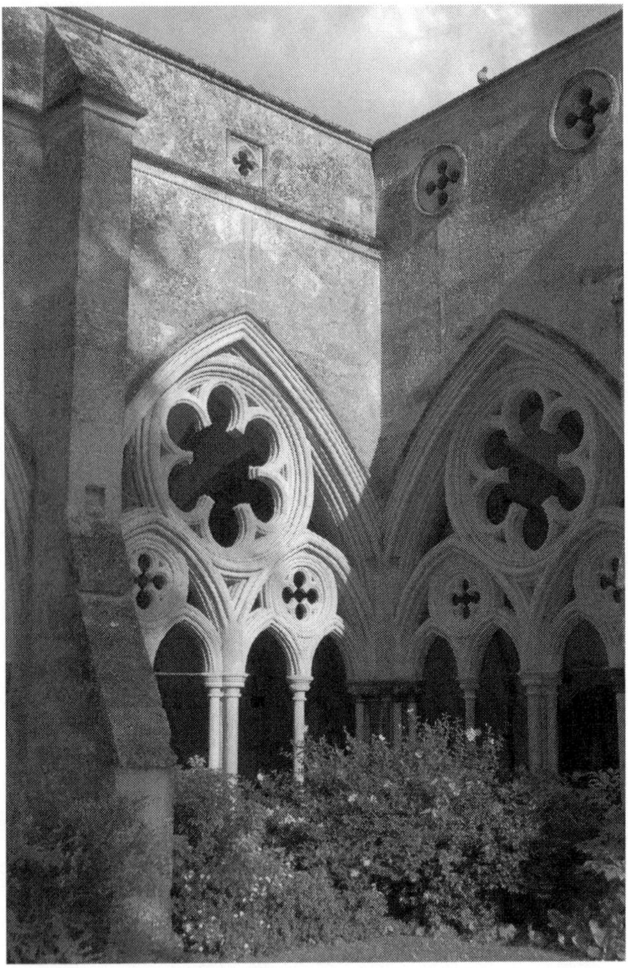

My view/convictions are something like this: Self-realization is the mind becoming conscious of what we are at the core of our being. We see the mind's enlightenment from beyond the mind. But all seeing is with the mind. So far the mind is still conscious of what I am. The mind's consciousness is temporary.

Yes, I know what death is. Art Ticknor is dead from my view. But Art Ticknor was never alive from my view. When the Art Ticknor you see/hear, etc., dies, it won't affect me in any way. Just as when Daniel R. dies it won't affect you in any way.

Yes, knowing what I am has settled my soul in a BIG way. I was in misery a great proportion of the time for 50 years. And now I'm beyond happy. What I am has no wants or needs and no vulnerabilities.

Another Way

$\mathcal{H}$ow do I get there ... "there" being the place of completion?

I know it has to be within, that I have to somehow go, sink or dive within.

But what strategy makes the most sense?
Do I adopt a contemplative tradition, like one of the Catholic
    or Buddhist ways?

If so, as a full-scale monk or as a layman?
Or do I look for an enlightened teacher, and dedicate my life to
    his or her tutelage?

Or do I remain independent, picking techniques
Recommended by teachers who appeal to me

And practicing them as long as they seem to be producing results?
Or is there another way? Could I let the mind find the way,
like the amazing true stories

Of dogs and cats and aborigine girls finding their ways home?
Is there an innate sensor that will find the path if it's my top
priority?

Can I feel "the call" — the voice of nostalgia, the call to come
Home?
Since it must be coming from Home, could its music lead me
there?

Do I need to have a map and complete directions
Before I start the rest of the journey from here to there?

Or do I merely need guidance for the next step?
Will the necessary guidance always be posted in plain sight

Where I can't miss it, or do I need to be vigilant?
If I don't hear or see or feel the guidance for the next step,

Can I receive it by asking where It is …
Then listening as if for the echo from a sonar ping?

Does the mind have a homing device?
If so, can the mind be trained to pay attention to it?

If Home is the abode of our highest state of being, is prayer a
progressive form of tuning in to the homing device until
we've completed the return trip to our source?

Let us work and pray together and separately,
Let us ask and pay attention together and separately,

Until we recognize the Truth.

Until we and the Truth are One.

Looking vs. Thinking

*W*hen I contemplate, which I am doing more and more, I do things like try to triangulate over the feeling of being a collection of thoughts and being what is aware of the thoughts, for example.

That's good. And here's a possible distinction for consideration: The mind contemplates. The mind tries to solve its problems through negation (i.e., doing the opposite) then triangulation (i.e., getting above the opposition if/when that fails). What-you-are watches.

The mind receives and projects. What-you-are observes. What-you-are is aware of the mind's activity.

mind	receives and projects	tries to solve its problems through negation and triangulation	contemplates
what-you-are	watches	is aware of the mind's activity	observes

More Q & A

I was wondering how you view character in relation to the search. Do you think a person's character can be changed after it's been formed over a lot of years? Does the quality or lack thereof of a person's character have more of an integral role in a man's being, and for *purposes of becoming? Or is it the same as any other identification when it comes right down to it?*

I assume that our character or personality forms as a defense mechanism and does so largely by the time we're 5 or 6 unless later traumas occur to change it. A man's state of being depends on what disillusionments concerning self he's experienced. I suspect that the most helpful character trait in consciously pursuing self-definition is perseverance.

W *as the depression you battled with "covert" or "overt" in Terrence Real's [i.e., the author of I Don't Want to Talk About It] terms?*

Looking back, I'd say that for a dozen years before meeting Mr. Rose it was covert depression. What followed was pure, ecstatic elation—for half an hour, maybe :-) Then a dozen years of possibly productive struggle. Then 7 years of overt depression. Then an elation that lasted for at least several weeks. Then 7 years of possibly productive struggle.

D *oes it seem to you like a certain baseline of psychological health is necessary (or even helpful) in coming to recognize Truth?*

My feeling is that you won't regret any movement toward psychological health before enlightenment, but I take Jim Burns[1] as a possible example that it's not necessary.

---

1   Jim is an older—than me, even—fellow who lives in Pittsburgh and who made a breakthrough at age 17. He's had a difficult life & has always described his situation as on the verge of getting psychologically healthy since I met him around 30 years ago. Mark Jaqua condensed hundreds of hours of taped conversations with Jim and organized it into a very readable and valuable book, *At Home with the Inner Self.*

For the intentional searcher, discernment is necessary ... and increasing mental clarity undoubtedly helps foster discernment. Clarity requires energy and focus.

I s there something beyond experience that I really am, or am I the totality of all experiences?

There is no thing beyond experience. You are that which experiences, which is beyond all experience.

Is experience a subset of that which experiences (i.e. an integral part of it) or is it different and separate from it?

Looking at your question, I wonder where you expect to go with an answer to it. If I say that experience is an integral part of that which experiences, then what? If I say that it's a separate part, then what? Building a theory of what you are can only lead to additional confusion. A scientific approach works within the paradigm that best explains observable behavior until a better one comes along. Are you restlessly jumping from paradigm to paradigm without picking the one that makes the most sense to you as having the best chance to find or define the Truth/Reality/Self.

That which experiences has no parts, is whole and complete. We don't find it in experience.

I am simply not aware of something bigger within myself.

That's a matter of faith, not of knowing, and faith comes by intuition. One of the few visions I experienced—it came as a result of the question "What is the source of my awareness?" lodging in my mind for several days—showed me that I was attached to something bigger than myself at the end of a long cord. I didn't see what that something was, and although the question evaporated, the data didn't seem to have any impact until years later.

f God wants me to find Him, and he's merely pushing me in the right direction, why don't I have any sense (or evidence) of the Path for me?

A path can only be seen like the wake of a ship from onboard ... as it comes into view "in the past," after we take a step inward.

othing seems worth devoting myself to.

That sounds like the intellect talking. Intellectual devotion is shallow. What we're really devoted to is based on feeling. We don't cook up something to be devoted to; we react to a feeling of what we really want/lack. Your mind may be afraid to put it into words, like: "I want to be loved unconditionally. I want to feel completely secure. I want to feel complete." Despite that, your mind-self is pursuing what it wants. And by observing the mind with a bit of detachment, we may get out of the way and let it work more productively.

❧

Stuckness

You wrote in Solid Ground to not let fear and pride stop us from asking for help from a self-realized person. I have been wanting to ask for help... but:

1. I don't know if I've tried hard enough to deserve asking for help.
2. I don't know what kind of help I need.

I just don't know. I am not even sure at which step of the ladder I am in my search. Sometimes I feel I slide back down several steps when I thought I was up higher.

I'm not working at self-inquiry with any group at this moment, no regular person-to-person communications in a conscious self-inquiry context. But I'm not isolated as I help out at the [family's] restaurant every day. Does this kind of confrontation with people suffice?

I feel stuck. Can you help?

Dear friend,

It's not a question of deserving help. Who's going to call the shots on that ... a spiritual supreme court? There seems to be a universal law that helping inspires help.

Sounds like you want someone to do the work for you :-) See below for more details.

What stuckness comes down to, in both mundane and spiritual endeavors, is not facing our prides and fears.

Productive confrontation is helping people to ask themselves questions. Self-confrontation is the basis of self-inquiry. We ask ourselves some equivalent of the "What am I?" question and attempt to catch a glimpse by looking back at what we're looking out from (i.e., become momentarily conscious of awareness). As a parallel effort we work to move the line between self and not-self by observation, distinguishing between the yet-unidentified self or viewer from anything that comes into our view. The sticking points when we're not making progress can be attributed to fears and prides that we're identified with.

Finding others for face-to-face cooperation in confrontation is great, but it can also be done remotely, like with the email confrontation group that you tried for a couple weeks in the past then dropped out of. Your unwillingness to work with fellow seekers in that email confrontation group indicates to me that some pride or fear prevented your participation. In retrospect, what do you think it was?

Is the reason that you don't know what kind of help to ask for because you haven't figured out what you want and made a commitment to accomplishing it? Everybody wants to be happy (or doesn't want to be unhappy), but to have an intentional program to accomplish it, the mind has to get a little more specific about what you feel will do the trick. I want to be rich, I want to be famous, I want to be a hermit ... whatever. Once you have an objective, then you set your determination to become a vector toward its accomplishment. You'll become stuck, but it will be in the context of the objective you're trying to accomplish. Your self-honesty will be tested because other fears or desires will demand priority. The basic form of stuckness is trying to serve two or more masters.

Can't Do's

S urrendering and feeling one's deepest desire consciously both *present the same problem: "I" can't do these things. I have increased the amount of time I spend in this kind of contemplation lately, though, and it feels like this will take up more and more time. I also find myself thinking of what's aware while doing everyday things much more often these days than even, say, a month ago. Maybe this is all I can do toward surrendering, etc.*

Here are a few thoughts you could add to your contemplation of those two can't-do items. Surrender is bowing to the truth. We can do this along the whole spectrum of mundane and spiritual considerations. For example, we can observe over-extended credit card balances and ask ourselves if we're living beyond our means. When we get angry or judgmental about how someone wronged us, we can ask ourselves if we're judging impartially and then accept the truth if it contradicts our preliminary view. Surrendering to the truth of what we are may take a lot of digging into unexamined self-beliefs and comparing them with what we observe through introspecting the mind. We can "do" surrender up to the final jump by a system of work or play. When we've done all we can do, our inner self will pull us the rest of the way.

Consciously or intentionally feeling feelings is something that's difficult for many of us but can also be accomplished by working at it. Again, the work or play starts by asking ourself a question. "What am I feeling?" We'll need to come up with variations on the question to keep the inquiry fresh. One way to do that is by asking ourself what we're feeling in our head, throat, chest, or gut. Hubert Benoit suggested asking ourself what we feel with our entire being.[2] In any case, while feelings may be associated with body locations, we feel or observe them in the mind. Just as we ask ourself what we're looking out from

---

2   "To accept, really to accept a situation, is to think and feel with the whole of one's being that, even if one had the faculty of modifying it, one would not do it, and would have no reason to do it. Man in his inner unconciliated dualistic state, with a separated reason and affectivity, is absolutely unable to adhere affectively to the existence of the Not-Self by which he feels himself repudiated. He can only pretend to accept, that is to say resign himself." *Zen and the Psychology of Transformation: The Supreme Doctrine,* by Hubert Benoit

and then get an instantaneous glimpse of the true self, we ask ourself what we're feeling and get an instanteous glimpse of our emotional state. The interpretation of what we see or feel is a secondary process taken on by the intellect.

Another way to get at surrender may be to ask ourself: "What don't or can't I accept?"

Another way to get at feeling our deepest desire may be to ask ourself: "What motivation is directing my life?"

❦

Anxiety

A couple quotes in Solid Ground have really stuck with me. They're both on p. 84: "procrastination, the everyday symptom of being stuck, mostly comes from failure to face our fears. The path to knowing the self is one of facing psychological fears." and further down the page, "depression...is like a spa for the bruised ego... there's one antidote...and that simply is persistence." I like how it puts those emotions in the context of the spiritual path and it has changed my relation to these states. Do you have any similar perspective on say, stress and anxiety and how they might relate to the spiritual path?

I think our various neural networks react differently to stress and anxiety, Tim. Some people—myself included, probably, although I never did this—could probably make good use of physical practices to calm the nervous system, such as breathing exercises, tai chi, and so on.

Generalized anxiety seems to me like static that interferes with getting a reading on what we're feeling. I think all anxiety goes back to a fear of being overwhelmed, which is the natural fear that arises from the belief in being an individual something.

Once we get some perspective on not being what is observable, we're still apparently stuck with the belief in individuality.

That belief is beyond the ability of our mind to see through or really conceive of. So some catalyst has to shake loose our hypnotic identification with the mind's view.

8. Struggling to Move

I surely didn't feel like I was making any movement along the spiritual path during the years since 1989. Physically, though, I'd moved from Miami to the Rose farm in rural Moundsville in 1991, in order to keep it available for people to do solitary retreats. In 1994 I'd bought a house for my mother to live in, in the small city of Moundsville. It needed a lot of work, and after I completely rewired it, had a heating and air conditioning system installed, remodeled the bathroom, refinished the wood floors, etc., I moved into town to live in it while finishing the work with the help of a skilled friend, who had also built a new staircase, helped restore the porches, add a deck, and remodel the kitchen.

Four of the Raleigh folks (Shawn, K.W., Alex and Georg) were then living on the farm, so I didn't feel continuing to live there was necessary. I'm sure there were additional, emotional factors involved that related to my poor self-image, but I'll spare you those :-)

I didn't find any journal entries from where the previous journal left off (Oct. 24, 1993) until a journal beginning Feb. 3, 1995. I guess I was mostly focused on the house remodeling although I continued mowing at the farm, helping with work projects, and participating in the TAT meetings.

I found copies of two notes I'd written to Mr. Rose tucked in the front of the 1995 journal. The first one, dated Jan. 24th, said:

> I do not feel that I can participate in the planned weekend meetings [I think Rose had invited me to join in something he had in mind for the farm residents], since I have written myself off as a lost cause. As I guess you know, my sense of hope departed in 1989 and has showed no signs of returning. I would like to remain a friend of the group and do whatever I can to be of help. With sadness, [signature]

The second note, written on Feb. 10th, expressed a different mood:

> Surprisingly, I find myself in a peaceful state of mind these days—reminiscent of a period in Florida around 1987. I felt then that it was "too good to last" and of course was right. I expect this relative euphoria is probably a setup for something to follow, but it's welcome while it's around. [I'd handwritten this PS:] Recently came across a moving extract from Paracelsus (enclosed) in a book by Frank Lloyd Wright, of all places.

A Feb. 3rd entry provides a look at the new mood or state of mind: "A new phase of my life has possibly begun. Whether positive or negative remains to be seen. Last week I admitted [to Rose] my conviction of hopelessness concerning self-definition, which hit it early 1989 and hasn't decreased. That this is a state of mind resulting from a shock seems obvious, but the conviction-state is strong enough to be effective. How do I square this giving up with my commitment made in 1978 and reaffirmed many times between then and 1989?"

The journal entries for February were largely about dreams. It must have been one of the periods where I was actively remembering and reviewing dreams. I noted on Feb. 20th that I'd been swimming laps for three weeks. I remember that as a fun time, swimming three times a week, building up from only being able to swim a lap or two before stopping to catch my breath ... adding a lap or more each time, until finally getting to where I could swim for a mile. Then, of course, it became more like work. I would often try to talk myself out of it on the way to each session, but I'd always feel so good afterward that it became a habit that continued for about seven years.

There was a gap, then two more dream entries in May, a brief entry in July ("On awaking 7/21/95: Need to let go of other desires (esp. desire for love) and concentrate on writing...") I'd been doing a good bit of writing—short stories and detective novels—with the idea of seeing if I could become a skillful writer. Next after that was in mid-September, where I made the following note:

> Something inspired me to attend an AA meeting on 9/6 as a result of fear (after seeing that I had no resistance to drinking during August) and desire (for more human contact). At that meeting, one person spoke to me after … mentioned a meeting the following night, Thursday night. A similar event led me to a Friday meeting, and I've been going to different meetings each day since.
>
> Have been reading the Chinese classic *Dream of the Red Chamber* about a man born with a corrupted soul—incarnated into a love drama to have his soul purified. Dawned on me that my case may be similar to Pao Yu's.
>
> A Higher Power rescued me from alcoholism in 1978, giving me a Higher Purpose to live for. In 1989 I lost hope regarding my spiritual progress (felt as if the Higher Power had given up on me). Now the hope of reestablishing contact/movement is stirring.
>
> Chief obstacle = pride? Not asking for help, through fear or false pride…
>
> 1. I don't feel right praying for help (not merited) but don't feel able to accomplish on my own
> 2. Afraid to stop hiding from fellow man

I recall sitting on my back deck, drinking to take the edge off my depression during the warm weather that summer and fall. And I remember the specific occurrence when I saw that, although I was only drinking two shots of Southern Comfort each day, I wasn't in charge of when I started or when I stopped. The words that followed were: "I'd better get off my ass and get around other people." And then I remembered that I'd read the "Big Book" of Alcoholics Anonymous years earlier and had, in the back of my mind, a desire to work the 12-step program.

I ended up going to AA meetings every day for an entire month. I got a sponsor, worked the first four steps and then went through my honest personal inventory with the sponsor. I had hoped it would produce some kind of *satori* or insight, but instead it left me feeling numb for several days, and I didn't attend any more AA meetings. Like the drinking (which stopped), I wasn't in charge of starting or stopping the AA meetings. [1]

That brings up the whole question of the "doer" or the "decider," doesn't it. I don't mean to imply that there wasn't deciding going on or that there wasn't doing occurring. But there was no conscious forethought that I could take credit for "doing."

THE NEXT EVENTS eliciting journal attention occurred around the April TAT meeting in 1996. Danny S, who was at the farm for what he said was his final visit, stopped at my house before the weekend of the TAT meeting. I told him about my recent change of conviction state, with its shift from an emotional focus to an intellectual one—no longer feeling the need for love, but noting that it may be fading back to the old state. I commented on Rose's increasing slide into Alzheimer's dementia, and Danny started to cry. The tears streamed quietly down his face for a few minutes. It reminded me of reading a biography of Robert Louis Stevenson, and how he would do the same thing when moved. I admire or envy guys who have that relief valve.

---

1   The first five steps of the 12-step AA program: 1. We admitted we were powerless over alcohol—that our lives had become unmanageable. 2. Came to believe that a Power greater than ourselves could restore us to sanity. 3. Made a decision to turn our will and our lives over to the care of God *as we understood Him*. 4. Made a searching and fearless moral inventory of ourselves. 5. Admitted to God, to ourselves, and to another human being the exact nature of our wrongs.

K.W. stopped in one evening after the meeting, and we talked until about 2 AM. We'd had a remarkable Saturday evening session at the TAT meeting—I don't recall Rose being there; it's possible that he may have left early. Cecy Rose had announced in the 1995 TAT Retrospect, written early in 1996, that Richard had been diagnosed with Alzheimer's. I think by the April TAT meeting he was pretty much limited in his ability to comprehend or communicate and that those of us who considered Rose our primary teacher were pretty much on our own by then. Anyway, K.W. had talked in the Saturday evening session about the cosmic consciousness experiences she'd had twice years earlier and that she hadn't talked about publicly before then. And Danny, highly sensitive like K.W. and likewise loathe to reveal much of what was going on in him until thoroughly "processed," had read a short quote from Bernadette Roberts and asked whether people thought she was referring to the same thing as Rose wrote about in *Psychology of the Observer:*

Who is living? Who is faced with oblivion?

And once more the observer has to face a very important question besides these last two. Who is asking the question?

Who is it that observes the glassy fragments of thought and self, which if sorted and properly arranged, will form some magic crystal ball that shall for all time answer our questions about our future.

I'd cracked a joke about the sexual innuendo in what Bernadette had written and, talking with K.W., I saw that I'd been an ass, not realizing that would hurt Danny's feelings. "I'm such a self-involved bastard," I wrote. "I don't have a clue about anyone else." I also noted that I was inspired to resume a meditation practice after 7 years of neglect.

A day or two later I had talked with my son Chris. He told me that his son Mark, then 5 years old, had been driving them crazy the past couple weeks talking about "Grandpa Ticknor" all day long. I hadn't been there since Christmas, and it had just started out of the blue. I semi-joked that my spirit must have been visiting Mark in his sleep.

In mid-December 1996 I began my first solitary retreat since the end of 1988:

> In isolation for a week.... Back then it seemed like a month was necessary; now a week seems okay — at least for this time. Would feel irresponsible not to check on my mother for more than a week; she's been in Good Shepherd nursing home for nearly two years now and feels secure there. I can't tell if she knows who I am (I doubt it), but she's always happy for the candy I bring....
>
> I moved to the farm in the summer of 1991 with the intention of living here for the rest of my life.... But the conviction grew on me that I wasn't really wanted here (by Mr. Rose). In retrospect, much of what occurred can be explained by his current Alzheimer's condition, but at the time many small traumas drove me first out of the farmhouse and into this trailer [where I was doing this retreat], then into town.... But in January of 1995 my mother needed to go into a nursing home, and I continued living in the almost-finished house I'd been getting ready for her.
>
> Once the stress of caring for my mother was removed, I began an exercise program (still going) and decided to give myself two years to see if I could develop skills as a writer. The two-year period is nearly up, so I need to make a decision concerning the writing.
>
> As for self-definition, nothing moved during my period of hopelessness. Then, for the past year or so, I've been back on the razor's edge between hope and hopelessness....

I reviewed my practice of sexual continence, which had been fully successful from fall of '78 to summer of '83; unsuccessful for more than a few months at a time from summer of '83 to summer of '88; almost successful with only a few slips from summer of '88 to summer of '94; and back to completely solid since summer of '94. And I noted that: "If my awareness opens up as it did when the first satori experience occurred (1979-80), I suspect that I would get a more comprehensive view now."

On the fourth day of the retreat I wrote that I was feeling good today and planned to start drinking juice that afternoon or evening. I had brought Benoit's *Supreme Doctrine* with me and found my attention riveted when I read his definition of acceptance:

> It is of capital importance to understand this distinction between acceptation and resignation. To accept, really to accept a situation, is to think and feel with the whole of one's being that, even if one had the faculty of modifying it, one would not do it, and would have no reason to do it.

Well, my mind started arguing with that idea of acceptance: it would be like casting all the things I didn't like about myself in concrete—or, worse, in Lucite!

But I found myself making a list of humiliations, rebuffs and rejections that I carried around as "pain balloons." Without straining I was able to conjure up 14 :-) It was two days later before I started really considering the items on my list. I began with one that was 10th on the list and reached a Benoit-defined acceptance rather easily. Then I considered the 1st item … and my mind went into something like turbo drive that I'd never witnessed before: It was processing so much data at such a rapid pace that I was only seeing bits and pieces of it.[2] And the end result was again one of acceptance, but this time it was because the computation had showed me that there was no way for me to know all the factors involved, and changing a situation if I had the power to do so could easily make things worse rather than better.

Next I picked the 12th item, and again my mind went into turbo mode. This and the last item were my big one-two in terms of humiliation and were uncomfortable even to think about. Once again the computation popped out the same result:

---

2   I think this was the first time I consciously witnessed the intuition program or process as it was running.

"There's no way for me to know all the factors involved [in other words, I don't have a big enough computer] including the validity of my own value-judgments. So I wouldn't change it if I could."

At the end of the second acceptance conclusion, I felt myself going up (not physically), propelled to an instantaneous new view. The words that formed to describe it: "I feel like I've encompassed a sphere of knowledge too big for my mind to comprehend; and from up here, everything down there is perfect just as it was and is."

With this satori or intuitional insight came a sense of relief of a magnitude greater than I'd ever experienced. I'd hoped and prayed for my defects to be removed, but I'd never serious considered accepting them. Thank you, Mr. Benoit. Thank you.

And thank you, whatever force propelled me away from my distractions and into isolation. My solitary retreats have been High Magick for me, bringing revelation and inspiration.

I felt that a major factor in my current ability to accept these things was Richard Rose's quiet withdraw into dementia. When he was still *compos mentis*, I compared myself to him and felt that I was pretty much worthless. "Well, I may be," I noted. "But I've been this way for 40+ years, which is long enough to despise myself. Let other people despise me, if they want to. With the exception of my kids, I don't really care."

Then, thinking about how to describe what had happened—and sensing first something, then maybe a multitude, hovering over me—these words came: "All the angels in heaven must have come to my aid." And: "Why anyone should want to help me, I don't understand." Then my ego started to disintegrate. I recalled Rose's words: "I'm right behind you ... always right behind you," and I started to wonder if he was the cause behind all this. Then my paroxysm decreased, and I thought: "[Well,] the ego wasn't ready to let go." This was December 23, 1996 ... 7:30 PM ... O, Holy Night.

The following morning I asked myself, "Do I feel different today?" The answer: "Yes and no. The main observable difference is that I feel things are possible—making plans to do things. Of course this is probably part of the optimistic (or at least, hopeful) state of mind, which the fasting brings on. Rather more subjectively, there's a twinkle in my mind's eye. Why not? This is really the first sign of movement in 8 years. Will have to see how the hopeful state stands up after isolation."

Thinking back, it occurred to me that a memorable "Black Bear" dream I'd had in November was like a lead-in to this isolation. Here's what I'd recorded of it on Nov. 8th:

> A black bear has lost his mother and is terrifying the neighborhood. I wave him over and befriend him; he transforms into a human. He knows he has to return to the woods, and I walk with him, to show him the way. We cross a four-lane highway, and I explain to him about driving on the right side of the road (why, I wonder later). After we cross the highway, he embraces me (a bear hug, although he's still in human form), and we walk down the sidewalk with his arm around me. I'm concerned that the other guys on the sidewalk will react, but they don't pay any attention. I'm trying to decide what to say to him about contacting me if he ever needs help, about meeting at prearranged intervals, etc., and debating on their feasibility when I awake.

My thoughts on the dream when I recorded it were that the black bear represented my "animal" (emotional, child) part, which felt like it had lost its parent (the "intellectual" adult part that I was currently identified with). When it saw me and I acted friendly toward it, it became human. It knows it has a natural environment and doesn't mind returning to it and demonstrates its affectionate nature now that it no longer feels abandoned.

Reading Benoit during the solitary retreat, I came across his opinion that in order to reunite these internal parts naturally so that our self-identification can transcend them, the abstract part must have a proper love for the instinctive part. Fear of abandonment, he says, is the primal, ancient fear of the child when he becomes self-conscious (i.e., conscious of the split between self and other); it is the fear of annihilation, of death. I associated the four-lane highway in the dream with the *corpus callosum* dividing the left and right brain hemispheres.

On the final day of the retreat, Christmas day 1996, I decided to put the novel on hold that I'd been working on unless/until inspiration struck me to finish it. (It never did.) In my summary notes, I included this: "What I have is a new way of looking at myself, and although it's tinged with conceptual thinking, I believe there's been a refinement/restatement of the problem (i.e., of self-definition)." And I concluded with this: "It's been wonderful—wonder filled. The last two logs are down to coals in the wood stove, the truck is packed and ready to go, and I paused for a last cup of tea and parting enjoyment. Am filled with a mild euphoria and peacefulness."

Between-ness

ℛichard Rose wrote about the ultimate "formula" for self-realization in a section of his *Direct-Mind Experience* titled Notes on Between-ness:

> How do we do it? We do it by carrying water on both shoulders, but by not allowing it to touch either shoulder. We stagger soberly between the blades of the gauntlet with recklessness and conviction, but we pick our way through the tulips with fear and trepidation, because the trap of the latter is sweet. We charge the gates of Heaven by urinating our

way through Hell, all the while sitting for forty years on the banks of the Ganges, doing nothing. We sit on the banks of the Ganges, not from laziness, but from an anger at angriness, a fury against our inner fury for wasted activity. And we pull back a terrible arrow...but never let it go. And by so holding, with the universe as our target, the universe is filled with terror at our threat.

If you find this metaphor as moving as I did, you may react with an intense desire to implement between-ness or a deflating feeling of hopelessness of doing so. Worry not ... between-ness isn't something you can do or fail to do. It's between doing and not doing.

Productive Self-Inquiry

*C*onfrontation is trying to get under the skin of the seekers' self-protective covering by throwing feeling questions at them ... for example, their fear of death, or the "sting of the scorpion" as Nisargadatta referred to knowing that we're conscious, or fear of separation. If a person can get in touch with the misery aspect of his individual existence, and if he can overcome his belief in the impossibility of finding a solution to it, then he's faced with the challenge of carving out time from his sleepwalking existence to find the solution. That's what productive self-inquiry meditation is.

❧

Seek Me First

A friend of several decades wrote to ask for feedback on a list of about 20 items that expressed his understanding of what he knew when he was in a "one-pointed state" while working on transcriptions of satsang talks by a spiritual teacher he's working with. My response:

The strange thing is that we can't understand our way to cap-T truth. All our understanding has to be exposed as delusory. There was a Korean zen guy, Seung Sahn (may be dead now) who seemed to have been a 1-note Johnny, responding to all his correspondents with "just don't know." But you know what? That's the interim goal that all us knowing types have to get to.

A mutual friend wrote to me the other day. He had found some words to express to himself what he's looking for: "... I want to find the most fundamental part of my being. Nothing else really matters and even if there is no core, I want to know...." The want is on the feeling side of the mind; it's the goad that drives us to look for that "I." No matter how good a conceptual approximation we arrive at with the mind, the matter can't be settled until we get beyond the mind. That takes a discontinuity. I feel that the lead-in to the discontinuity has to be lined up by some helping intelligence & that help is likely to be triggered by our admission that we know nothing and need help.

We reach the point of becoming an egoless vector when we see, intuitively, that what we're looking for is not going to do anything for us. The self we believe ourselves to be is what's in the way. But we can't subtract ourselves past a certain point. Up to the point of becoming an egoless vector, which we only see in retrospect, we're pushing toward the core of our being. After that point, the magnetic center pulls us the rest of the way.

Merrell-Wolff, the patron saint of the seeker of understanding, said he was surprised to find himself writing poetry after his realization. His poetry aims at feeling. For example, the ending lines of "Seek Me First":[3]

Long have ye lingered in the desert of Ignorance.
I desire not thy continued suffering.
Come unto Me. The Way is not so hard.

When the seeker is ready to "come unto Me," he lays down the sword and shield.

A Solitary Retreat

I'm heading off to do a solitary retreat this weekend at that St. Benedicts monastery in Erie. Do you have any advice on what I should eat/take with me? I'm thinking to take Rose and Maharshi books, since they automatically put me in a contemplative/meditation state of mind. For food I am not inclined to fast, but maybe just drink water?

The daily practice for anyone wanting to go within would include some reading, some thinking about where life's been and is going, and some directed meditation. The mind seems to open up best when there's some relaxation following intense introspection. I'd try to avoid anything that comforts the mind—like reading for inspiration. Water-only is what I refer

3 www.tatfoundation.org/forum2003-07.htm

to as fasting. Two or three days of it may shock the mind into a new mental state. I'd limit reading to a page or two to prime the pump if the mind gets tired of introspection (looking) and wants to daydream, go off on tangents, etc. I think you're like me in that we're somewhat creatures of comfort ... so discomfort can be a great irritant and goad.

Thanks for the advice, I am looking fwd to the retreat and being by myself in nature. Hopefully it will help my crazy mind calm down a bit.

One of the easy ways to slow down the mind is to breathe naturally, and silently count the breaths. That tends to switch the focus from "thinking" (thinking-feeling) to watching thoughts & feelings.

Yes, I have this 'deep breathing' exercise I do, where I do deep belly breaths, and that usually works pretty well and slows down the breath and my mind too, but I can't do it 24/7, and at work lately I just get so irritated with everything, I forget to do the exercise and by the time I realize it I'm entering the 'anger' zone. For your exercise, do you count the 'in' breath and then separately the 'out' breath, or both together as one?

I'm thinking about it as a prelude to meditation, although it could work also in situations like the anger at work.

The only time I actually practiced it was while swimming laps ... not to count breaths but to count laps ... so when it occurred to me that it might help people as a prelude to meditation, I applied my lap-counting technique, counting the in-breath (up the lane) and out-breath (return) as one breath (lap). I don't see where it makes any difference, really ... the idea being to take the attention off the racing thoughts and put it on the breath-counting. Without consciously slowing down the breath rate, it will accomplish that if pursued for maybe 5 minutes.

We don't do anything 24/7. The mind's operation is basically what Mike Conners pictured for the TM-type effortless meditation technique ... mostly lost in thought, interspersed with momentary self-remembering. What meditation attempts to do is increase the ratio of self-remembering moments to self-forgetting moments. Watching the mind promotes self-remembering. Self-remembering promotes self-realization.

Indestructible?

If we ultimately are indestructible, and cannot be anything other than what IS, then what does it mean for most of us who don't realize this while we're alive? If we die undefined will there be an end, or will we be recycled until we do? I hope that there is an amnesty for those of us who tried but failed.

I can give you an answer ... but no matter how much you believe another person, their answer can only be an opinion and therefore not really satisfying. What you really are knows itself. The problem is only at the mind level. So enlightenment is really the mind's becoming consciously aware of what you are. The question of continued incarnation becomes a non-question when the mind knows its source. It remains an intriguing mystery, but it's not tied into existential angst ... because you'll know that existence, as the Latin root indicates, stands outside of being. *Being* is what you are. The value of self-definition is to "settle the soul" while living. It makes life tenable. And since what you are experiences 6+ billion human lives simultaneously, the incarnation of an individual life-experience is not such a big deal. :-)

With or Without

> With it, nothing will be added to you.
> Without it, nothing will be taken away.

I understand the part of 'getting it' making the question moot, although I still don't grasp if you mean there will be further incarnations if a person doesn't eject existence from being, or that this remains an intriguing mystery?

You probably remember that Richard Rose was vague about reincarnation. Ramana Maharshi, ditto. I'd say it's no more unlikely than incarnation. (Think about that.) I don't know the mechanics of how what we are projects what seems. Rose apparently got some view of the mechanism ... seeing the unmanifested mind as the prop room of creation ... but it was still vague. When you go from the mind's "knowing" back to the source, you find yourself at Unknowing. There are no whys or wherefores. I saw life, the cosmos, as if I were watching the creation unfold on my belly ... and yet it was all a seeming. Gurdjieff labeled God as the #1 idiot, which jibes with my feeling. We don't know why we project the seeming. I had the feeling, also, that what we are loves a mystery. We don't want to make the ending of the story known or it wouldn't be interesting.

To try to answer your question at the level that you're asking (i.e., looking through faulty glasses :-), there is no person. No person has incarnated. There is no person to reincarnate. It doesn't help, does it? You can't conceive of "no person." But that's the truth that offsets your belief in being a person. You see arms and legs, thoughts and cows, etc. You are never that which you see. You are that which sees. You can't conceive of that not being an individual seer ... but it's not.

The Flower Sermon

I would like to ask you what is your opinion on the meaning of the Flower Sermon as seen from the Lotus Sutra, Nagarjuna and Nichiren's teaching of the inseparability of symbol and dharma.

Why do I get the feeling that you're a fellow who knows too much and whose knowing is in the way of Knowing? :-)

I don't know what your question is trying to get at ... you'd probably have to spend a lot of time educating me on the Flower Sermon, Lotus Sutra, Nagarjuna and Nichiren.

I think the *Flower Sermon* refers to a story of Buddha silently holding up a flower and one of his followers having become instantaneously enlightened. The explanation accompanying the story was of a direct transmission of wisdom from Buddha to the disciple.

Enlightenment is the mind's becoming consciously aware of its source ... of what You are. Transmission is the transition, or experience, that occurs preceding enlightenment. It may or may not involve another person. Experience is dualistic, occurring in the mind dimension. Transmission is the reflection in the mind dimension of the true nature of self. Another way of saying it is that transmission is the mind's recognition that awareness is self-aware.

All the preceding is obviously just words, and self-realization or self-recognition is beyond words ... beyond the mind. The closest we as two robotic organisms can get to communicating about it is paradox. I wish I could say something simpler. All that Is, is All. No thing Is. Enlightenment, transmission, etc., are the process of, or the result of, disillusionment. The only things that stand in the way of Knowing are beliefs (knowing).

To Know the Truth

To know the Truth, you must act.
To act, you must go within.
To go within, you must retreat from untruth.
To retreat from untruth, you need only see through faulty be-
    liefs about what you are.
The Truth is your essential nature, your True Self.

Chela-1: I don't "get" self-inquiry.
Master: To find the permanent happiness you're looking for, you have to become it.

To become permanent happiness, you need only recognize what you truly are at the core of your being.

Self-inquiry is the process of looking until you recognize that which is looking.

Chela-2: I don't feel wholly committed.

Master: What action does that feeling prevent?

C: Not always putting first things first. I have time to meditate from 8:30 to 10:30 in the morning, and I put it off rather than starting at 8:30. I think it prevents me from being consciously aware, or present, more often.

M: Sounds like a red herring to me. Giving yourself a self-pity out: "If only I were fully committed, I would be consciously present twenty-four-seven...."

Procrastination and rationalization are something we fight all the way to permanent awakening.

❦

Lo-Cal Snacks IV

$\mathcal{T}$he mind's reaction to changing its action/inaction patterns is healthy and automatic ... necessary but not sufficient, in math terms. Satisfaction of the ultimate quest for wholeness comes when the mind questions the sense of self.

❦

$\mathcal{I}$f you want to be a great magician, focus on the one transformation that's permanent & doesn't need to be repeated: self-realization.

❦

$\mathcal{T}$he mind isn't constructed to be able to conceive of something without its opposite. If there's an object of observation there must be a subject that's observing. The problem being that when we really look to see the subject, we don't spot it. You're convinced of I-amness. The conundrum is finding it.

❦

*T*he crack in the cosmic egg is that you've never not known yourself.

🌿

*W*hat you do doesn't make any difference unless you believe it does. The only solution to existential suffering is to go beyond belief to absolute knowing. The only absolute knowing is knowing what you are ... and that knowing ends existential suffering.

🌿

*I*f a person admitted to himself—at any point in his life—that procrastination was no longer a good alternative, I think he'd be in a similar circumstance to what Ramana Maharshi experienced when he was 16: all the obstacles to self-realization could evaporate rapidly.

🌿

A man's state of being depends on what disillusionments concerning self he's experienced.

🌿

*U*nless we want to paddle our canoe in endless circles, we have to paddle on both sides. In the search for self, we work to see what we're not, and alternately we ask ourselves what we are and take snapshots of what we see when we look back at what we're looking out from. Eventually, ka-bam!

🌿

*T*he Truth is insane from the mind's perspective, and the mind and its projected cosmos are an insane dimension from the perspective of the Self.

🌿

*I*f you feel your deepest longing, you may be able to get a reading on the objective that whatever has been shaping your life has in mind for you. Our limited minds may misinterpret it, but the more conscious we become of it, the more we may be able to consciously align our will with Its will.

Dream of Grace

I was standing in a pit, and Ramana Maharshi was lying stretched out on his side on a platform about at my eye level. I was asking about, or more likely complaining about grace, which I believed was missing. Necessary-and-missing.

The pit began to fill silently with water until I was standing on my toes to keep my nose above water.

Ramana then said to me: "You are always up to your nose in grace."

❊

Grace, Simply

*W*hat *is Grace, in its simplest form?*

In the transmission of one-mind, the mirror of I-amness must be held *just so* for awareness to witness itself beyond time.

9. *The Knot Untied*

*T*he acceptance satori that occurred during my solitary retreat at the end of 1996 lifted a weight off my shoulders that I'd been carrying around since childhood, setting in motion some events that determined the next phase of my life and spiritual search.

At the end of Jan. 1997, I wrote:

Regarding HELP:

1. I've had a great deal of help in my life, most noticeably beginning with finding Richard Rose in 1978.
2. The "beatific vision" during the recent retreat, with the feeling that a holy spirit or choir of angels had lined up to help me.
3. Now my faith has awakened to the possibility that *the source of the help is within.*

The progression: I'm all alone => something outside of myself is helping => the help is coming from my source (inside).

I asked myself: "If I were offered oblivion this instant, would I take it?" My answer: "Probably not—a radical shift in my interior."

ON MARCH 4TH I accompanied Cecy and Richard Rose when he went into the nursing home in Moundsville while waiting for an opening at a nursing home in Weirton that had a special wing for Alzheimer's patients. After two years of devoted care, with help from K.W. and others, Cecy was no longer able to care for Mr. Rose at home. I was concerned about how to react if he wanted to leave with me when I visited him at the nursing home, which was only a short walk from my house, but that problem didn't arise.

I'D CONTINUED READING Benoit's *Supreme Doctrine* after the re-treat. He introduced the term Creative Principle early in the fifth chapter, in which he wrote:

> In the course of my researches for the means of liberating my-self I note that the various teachings which admit the possi-bility of liberation or 'realisation' in the course of life can be divided into two groups.
>
> The greater part of these teachings are founded on the following false theory: real consciousness and will are lack-ing to the ordinary man, he does not have them at birth; he must acquire them, build them up in himself, by means of a special inner labour. This labour is difficult and long; conse-quently the result of this work will be a progressive evolution, that is to say that the acquisition of consciousness and will is progressive. Man will surpass himself little by little, slowly climbing the steps of his development, obtaining higher and higher consciousness by means of which he will progressive-ly approach the highest consciousness—'objective', 'cosmic' or 'absolute' consciousness.
>
> This is a theoretical attitude radically opposed to that which Zen doctrine holds. According to this doctrine man does not lack this real consciousness and this real will, he lacks nothing whatever; he has in himself everything that he needs; he has, from all eternity, the 'nature of Buddha'. He needs absolutely nothing in order that his temporal machine may be controlled directly by the Absolute Principle, that is by his own Creative Principle, in order that he may be free....
>
> This conception necessarily entails the instantaneous, lightning-like character of man's 'realisation'. Either there is not union between the two parts of man, and then he does not enjoy his divine essence; or the direct contact is re-established, and there is no reason, since absolutely nothing is lacking, why man should not be instantaneously established in the enjoyment of his divine essence. *The inner work which results in the establishment of this direct contact, but not the deliverance itself, is long and difficult, and so, progressive.*

On March 31st I journaled this realization/admission: "I accept fully and wouldn't change it even if I could whatever the Creative Principle has in store for me—whether it's Self-realization or not. I don't know if this is a proper attitude, but I believe it's an honest reflection of my current state of mind. I embrace (theoretically, anyway) whatever comes, either happiness or suffering. I would like to find the courage to:

1. Be more open-minded (questioning)
2. Think for myself
3. Face my fears

TOWARD THE END OF APRIL, Dave W. and I did some work together at the farm. While on one of the roofs, we began talking about fathers and sons. I said that my father and I had been in different worlds: He didn't seem able to get into mine, and the only communication was on the rare occasions I'd go hunting or fishing with him. Dave asked what my world had been like. When I considered the question later, I came up with the following items, which I then communicated to him:

- Wanting everyone to love me
- Feeling weak; fortune's fool (didn't have those words then)
- Terrified of masculinity
- Cut off from all other human beings
- Hiding in books

He shocked me by saying that those descriptions fit his childhood world perfectly, too. I hadn't conceived of *any* similarity between us as children.

DREAM STUDY had been a source of self-study in recent years, and in May there was a dream in a classroom setting that produced this insight: "I realized that my mind-state of accepting the status quo, of not asking myself questions (no self-confrontation) was equivalent to *sleeping with the enemy.*

A couple days later, Dave and I were finishing an all-day roofing project on the farm ... hot, tired, and a bit cranky. I mentioned to him that I never got angry with myself (he thought that was a huge aberration) and that my parents never tried to direct me after I was 8 or 10. His response was along the lines of: "I can see why they gave up on you." I don't recall what it was, but I shot some insult back at him. That evening, lying on my sofa, I felt mentally nauseous—something new to me. Looking back on the rooftop conversation, I realized that my action had contradicted my self-image. I always told myself I'd rather take a bullet than see a friend take one, but after being wounded by Dave's words, I'd shot a bullet at him. I'd never known what people meant by the word *guilt,* but now I thought I'd experienced it ... seeing evidence that undercut my self-image.

Following not long after that entry were a few quotes from the "Elegant Sayings" selection that Rose chose for *Profound Writings, East & West.* Two that I still need to pay attention to:

1. Praise everyone's good qualities if thou would have friends.
2. Argue not with the self-conceited.

Arguing is arguably one of my many weaknesses :-) Winning an argument used to be almost of life-or-death importance to me. I can see now that being right felt critical to my continued existence. Fortunately that's no longer the case, and my opinions are wrong at least as often as they're right these days, but the old habit isn't quite ready to R.I.P. yet.

Another favorite quote from *Profound Writings,* this from the Isa Upanishad: "He moves and He moves not. He is far, and He is near. He is within all, and He is outside all."

TRIED A SENSORY DEPRIVATION TANK in Pittsburgh. Dave and Damon (a friend of Dave's from when he was working on his

MFA degree in Pittsburgh before moving to the farm) wanted to try it, and they could get a discount if a handful of people signed up, so I agreed to do it. The tank, a fiberglass capsule, was in the back of an esoteric bookstore. It had warm water with enough salt in it to make the body buoyant. One at a time we got in, closed the door, lay down in the water, and luxuriated in the darkness for maybe 20 minutes. For me it was like lying on my sofa—thoughts slowed down, but exponentially more. Each thought came like a separate sheep jumping over a fence after an interval of no motion.

I thought afterward that the real purpose of the trip was finding the Krishnamurti book, *Freedom from the Known.* I'd read some of his earlier books and had heard him talk at Ojai two or three times when I lived in Los Angeles in the early 1980s, but this book was by far the best of his material I'd come across.

Dave, Reggie (also living at the farm now) and I began meeting on Saturdays for confrontation (i.e., mutual questioning) sessions several weeks earlier, at the beginning of May. Near the end of the month, the three of us got together with Cecy and K.W. to discuss farm maintenance, and then the five of us had a Memorial Day cookout with Mike C. and Shawn.

Bob F. called to say he was arriving on June 3rd or 4th. He'd gotten inspired at the April TAT meeting and decided to move back to the farm for another stay.

Mike C. and Todd organized an event in Columbus, *Awaken!97,* to try to meet some new folks. Cecy and I both made presentations, and Mike found a very colorful character who led a session where we all did *Qigong* movements. My presentation was on Benoit's Zen material, and I found it the easiest group of people to talk to that I'd ever experienced. Dave came up afterward and shook my hand enthusiastically. Todd told K.W. that I should take it on the road. Mike noted that the audience laughed at every attempt at humor and were in the palm of my hand. I think an unusual rapport had developed—explanation unknown.

Vertigo hit Sunday evening of the 1997 July TAT meeting. I was sitting at the computer and leaned my head back to swallow the last of a can of soda. It felt as if a psychic arrow hit the back of my neck, and I fell off my chair onto my hands and knees with a disabling dizziness. I crawled into the nearby bathroom, where I hugged the toilet for 6 or 8 hours. Any minute movement of my head would increase the dizziness and nausea. There was a phone only feet away, but I reasoned that an EMT team would have to cut a hole in the roof and hoist me up by helicopter since it would be unthinkable to change my position. For some strange reason I wasn't emotionally distraught. In fact it seemed like I had extraordinary mental clarity for those hours. I recall initially doing mental experiments to try to determine whether there may have been a stroke. I didn't find any loss of mental functioning and concluded there probably wasn't. Eventually I had some dry heaves, after which I was able to crawl to a near-by bedroom, where I lay in bed for most of the next week, other than an occasional trip to the bathroom.

I didn't have a primary-care physician at the time, and it took more than a week to get an appointment with a doctor who was seeing new patients. That Monday I awoke with the thought that the dizziness might be a symptom of Meunier's disease. I don't know where that came from, but I recalled that the term was related to an ear problem. I looked up *meuniere* in my French dictionary and found that it referred to a way of cooking fish by rolling it in flour and frying it in butter.

Stopping at the library on my way to the medical appointment, I found *Ménière's* disease or syndrome in the *Physician's Desk Reference* as something related to the inner ear. The doctor listened to my story and, knowing I didn't have any medical insurance, he said he could run some tests if I wanted him to, but it sounded like the problem was acute vestibular neuronitis. The symptoms were all but gone by now, so I told him I'd hold off on the tests. He gave me a prescription for medicine that should help if the problem recurred. As we shook hands to say goodbye, I mentioned the *Ménière's* disease phrase upon waking. He said: "That's the same thing."

IN EARLY OCTOBER OF 1997 I made a 3rd or 4th trip to Pittsburgh to hang posters on the college campuses advertising an October retreat weekend on the farm. Dave had ended a two-month solitary retreat the day before and drove to Pittsburgh with me. Damon helped with the postering, too. Dave decided to stay around for the retreat then head to Kentucky and stay with his mother for a while before going back to school.

Bob F. left to return to Colorado. He said he'd been restless the whole three months of his stay, had negative feelings toward everyone, couldn't think, etc. But he left with positive feelings toward TAT and with plans to come for the April TAT meeting next year.

About 10 of us participated in an October retreat including two new folks, Damon and his friend Lucas. I wasn't happy with the way it went, but something happened during one of the sessions that I hoped was an indicator of an interior change: *I felt an invitation to come within for the first time.*

I made a trip to Pittsburgh near the end of the month to put up posters on the college campuses for weekend meetings at the farm, inviting people to come down for work, discussion, and just spending time in nature. [I don't recall any takers.] Met Damon for coffee, and he talked about seeing if he could get a room reserved at a coffee shop near the Pitt campus for philosophical discussions.

A HINDU WISE MAN appeared in a dream in December.[1] He was lying on his back on a platform about at my eye level. The guru scanned my being—his face so close to mine that I couldn't see him. He built up my ego by flattery, then tore it down by saying

---

1   See "Dream of Grace" near the end of chapter 8.

he'd seen something negative. He dismissed me with a kiss on the mouth, which I wasn't aware of until we separated. I recall complaining about a lack of grace. The area I was standing in filled with water up to the top of my head. But I was standing on one foot with perfect balance, which allowed me to breathe by somehow getting my nose above the water. The guru said: "You're always up to your nose in grace." I was in a state of no conceptual thought—not joyous but wonderful in a non-emotional way. When that state ended, I tried unsuccessfully to get back to it.

I began a 10-day solitary retreat on December 15, 1997. On the first day I was recalling the acceptance experience of the previous December's retreat, and I asked myself: "How can such a jump to a new view be encouraged?" and: "From what perspective would the self let go?" Looking for some notes from "The Himalayas of the Soul," I first came across this quote on surrender from Dr. R.P. Kaushik's *Organic Alchemy:*

> Surrender comes spontaneously the moment you see your helplessness, and in this surrender and silence you are in communion with the Supreme Energy—call it God, call it love, truth, beauty, any name you like. It is the action of this energy which transforms your mind—not your effort, not your decision, not your will or promises.

I noted that I had justified or rationalized this 10-day retreat since my mother, in the nursing home, seldom if ever opened her eyes any more. She napped most of the time. Occasionally she would return pressure on my hand.

On the third morning of the retreat, I awoke with thoughts of resentments toward my friends, my petty complaints of not being as important to them as I wanted to be. (Krishnamurti: "Being nothing, a desert in oneself, one hopes through others to find water....")

I had penned this wonderful, and I'd say atypical, comment on play by Richard Rose in the journal:

I have always estimated play as a happy ingredient of efficiency. It is a known fact that the subconscious mind gives forth its inspirations under a lassitude of the conscious. By this I seem to discredit concentrations

Concentration is not a strained method of forcing the mind upon a certain train of thought. We can best study a proposition when we are interested in it. And interest means ease. It is a harmonious corresponding of the mind—either by memory or reason—with environment. This reacting with environment is accomplished by reading, holding conversation, or by any other method which arouses the memory. The result of interest is frequently inspiration, which is often a sudden illumination of the memory, or the arriving congruency of two past memories hitherto unrelated…."

I fear being alone with my thoughts [I wrote], always wanting some distraction at hand. Why? What is the condition that I fear? Can I face the fear through curiosity? If the mind is a bridge to cross, can I explore it sufficiently to effect a crossing? If my true nature lies within, what is there to fear? Going within and fear of doing so, sexuality, resentment and friendship, going beyond conceptual thought: keep these cooking on the back burner while the foreground attention reverts to retreat [i.e., a group retreat for February] planning. There is no place I'd rather be or anything I'd rather be doing—I feel grateful to whatever set up this moment—and I recall the "invitation" to come within [at the October group retreat].

WHAT IS MY REAL INTEREST? On the surface [I wrote], I want someone to love. But even if I could conjure up the ideal situation, it would take my mind off *this*. I would be likely to forget the importance of self-definition, which I haven't yet established firmly in my mind after nearly 20 years! The tentacles of such a relationship would affect everything current—friendships, ladder work [i.e., working with other seekers], freedom. I have come some distance, a long way from where I was 20 years ago, toward standing on my own two feet, and I don't want to give that up. So, although I might have little resistance if the situation presented itself, it's not what I (the inner man) want.

As I went to sleep on the 20th of December, I realized how happy I was, and how utterly thankful I was to find myself here. And with the hope of having found a new sense of inner direction from my determination to apply my new understanding of Mr. Rose's technique for thinking (and stopping thought), it was the second night of my life I can remember going to sleep looking forward to another day. (The first was also during isolation, a few years previously, when my awareness switched into a mode where I was able to watch the thought-stream and trace each one back to its source.)

A couplet came into my head the morning of the 21st: "How I wish that all mankind / Could taste this joyous peace of mind!" Have been smiling frequently the past couple days (never do this when by myself, except in solitary retreats). Is this the awakening of Hope in my emotional center? Is it possible that, after nearly 20 years, I'm on the edge of going within?

The feeling of last night is coming back, that my whole life was worth this one moment.

A questioner asked Ramana Maharshi: "Is God personal?"

His response: "Yes, he is always the first person, the I, ever standing before you. Because you give precedence to worldly things, God appears to have receded to the background. If you give up all else and seek Him alone, He alone will remain as the I, the Self.

Another questioner asked about the final State of Realization:

Ramana replied: Why speculate as to what will happen some time in the future? All are agreed that the "I" exists. To whichever school of thought he may belong, let the earnest seeker first find out what the "I" is.

"Regard me! Take thought of me! Touch me!" [Those are the three modes of initiation: look, thought, and touch. My first retrospective thought about the dream with the Hindu sage was *initiation,* which I had never put any belief in.] "Mature me! Make me one with Thee, O Arunachala!" This is from Ramana's *Marital Garland of Letters* written at the request of some of his followers as a song to sing on their way to town with their rice bowls.

From *The Diamond Sutra* (Price and Wong, footnote 60): "In the eighth of the ten stages of the spiritual progress of a bodhisattva, he is established beyond falling back, and a prediction (*vyakarana*) of his attainment of the goal is made to him by a Buddha." When I read that, I recalled Rose's "I think you'll make it," in a letter following my first solitary retreat, responding to a question about whether I was too old at 33 to pursue self-definition. I remembered reading the letter, taking a pause from yard work on a mild October day, and the joy that had suffused my body. Now it gave me renewed hope.

WE BEGAN WEEKLY SELF-INQUIRY MEETINGS at the Kiva Han coffee shop, where the U. of Pittsburgh and the Carnegie Mellon

U. campuses meet, at the beginning of the spring academic semesters in early January 1998 and scheduled a weekend retreat for mid-February. On Feb. 10th we began meeting at the nearby Oakland Carnegie Library. We had a good turnout—10 people—the same as the previous meeting, with 2 new people. (Paul and Michael) and 2 returnees (Suresh, Gautam). I think we switched to meeting every other week at this time. [We're still holding meetings of the self-inquiry group at the Oakland library as I'm writing this, nearly 15 years later.]

I gave a talk at Pitt on the 17th at Damon's request; he wanted to restart the U. Pitt Self Knowledge Symposium group, which had lapsed. Had a small turnout of 8, so instead of giving the talk ("Eliminating Existential Distress: Real Zen") we just talked informally. I found the experience more inspiring than giving a presentation.

Cecy brought Mr. Rose home for his 81st birthday on March 14th. I stopped in to see him. Lou K., another of the longtime TAT folks, was there, also.

IN *THE COLLECTED WORKS*, Ramana described this revelatory sequence of discriminating between the seer (sentient) and the object seen (insentient):

Object Seen (Insentient)	The Seer (Sentient)
The body, a pot, etc.	The eye
The eye	The optic nerve-center (brain)
The optic nerve-center	The mind
The mind	The individual self or ego
The individual self	Pure Consciousness

That would explain why my Isolation '96 experience, where I felt as if I were encompassing a sphere of knowing too big for my mind to comprehend, could have been an experience outside, or on the periphery, of the mind but still within the individual self.

He goes on to say: "The mind is nothing else than the 'I'-thought. The mind and the ego are one and the same. Intellect, will, ego, and individuality are collectively the same mind."

Two months elapsed before the next journal entry. The typical summertime sexual cloud descended, with the strongest "attack" in several years—acute for a week or more. Nearly lost celibacy but somehow survived intact. Along with that came a change of mood from optimism to pessimism regarding the Pittsburgh group and TAT folks in general. Didn't feel like anyone was in my field of rapport. Nevertheless, I resumed weekly meetings with local folks to discuss the Albigen System, which we hadn't done since November.

Reflecting on my proposed questions before the meeting, I came up with the following response to: What do I really want out of life?

- To accomplish whatever I'm here for.
- Not to have wasted my life.
- To have been of some help to fellow-sufferers.

I realized that I had made a commitment 20 years ago to become the Truth regardless of the cost, but I didn't know if I ever raised my desire to help others to the same commitment level. So I found myself making that mental verbalization: I hereby make/affirm the commitment to work for the enlightenment of all suffering creatures. My models for this were Richard Rose and Ramana Maharshi.

Met my dear friend Anima at a Pittsburgh meeting in September of 1998. She came to the US from India, recently married and in Pittsburgh with her husband while he worked on a Ph.D. at Carnegie Mellon. The topic of the meeting had been life goals. Anima has a bachelor's degree and an MBA, and she thought the meeting was about practical goals. She was pleasantly surprised when she found differently, and I almost fell off my chair when her round-robin response to the question, "What's your life goal?" was: To become enlightened in this lifetime.

Another birthday, my 54th, floated by on October 17th. It fell on a Saturday, and I spent an enjoyable day cutting firewood for the farmhouse with Al and Mike F, Phil and Cindy, Shawn, and Reggie. Shawn, who was living and working at the Linsly Outdoor Center, had attended the November 7th as well as the two previous confrontation sessions (Saturday meetings) at the farm. Planned to begin meeting weekly in Pittsburgh, with insight workshops on alternate Mondays—starting with dream study—if we could find a place to meet.

On the night of November 25th, I made a commitment: To make my mind an instrument of Truth. The catalyst for the inspiration was seeing and hearing the blind Italian tenor Andrea Bocelli singing on a TV special earlier that evening. He sang Ave Maria, and his voice seemed to be an instrument of transmission, heart-to-heart. It occurred to me the next day that the

25th was the anniversary of my father's death, and I wondered if that was just a coincidence.

Cecy invited me to join her, Mr. Rose and their daughter Tatia for Thanksgiving dinner. He seemed all right, i.e., not unhappy with his situation. Being around him didn't create the old tension in me of feeling spiritually inadequate, especially the self-condemnation of not being awake to mind-to-mind rapport with him.

The November 1998 TAT meeting was the best one for me, personally, that I could recall—specifically, the confrontation session brought me to the edge of the abyss of now and held me there for a longer duration than had occurred during meditation or contemplation. I didn't feel the tremendous weight of adverse forces that had left me drained after recent TAT meetings.

ANOTHER DECEMBER, another solitary retreat :-) Anima came down from Pittsburgh with me after yesterday's meeting and is also doing a solitary retreat.

I had acquired the second of the two Krishnamurti books I found the best, *First & Last Freedom,* and started rereading it for priming-the-pump material. In the second chapter he proposes the question of what we really want. When I asked myself that, I came up with the two solemn commitments I'd made previously (i.e., to become the Truth regardless of the cost, and to ever-consciously school my mind to be an instrument of Truth; I must have forgotten or discounted the one of working for the enlightenment of all suffering creatures) plus a new one based on Ramana's comment that: "There is no difference between Jnana (i.e., self-inquiry) and absolute surrender to the Lord, that is, in thought, word and deed." My third commitment, which I felt was really a variation on the wording of the other two, was to obey the Lord in thought, word and deed. I remember scanning my inner horizon to see if there were any holdouts before

I made the commitment. I didn't see any, but I realized to carry it out would require being attentive every instant. Even though I knew I would fail, I recognized it as a goal. I added that I felt the need to be more serious with myself on this than I'd ever been before in my life. This commitment would mean a desire to love the Truth with my whole being—and that was what I truly wanted. And so:

- I can no longer push and pull people, trying to win their love and getting hurt or angry when they don't comply.
- I can no longer rationalize lustful thoughts.
- A great burden has been lifted from me—as in the 1996 isolation, but more subtle, I think—of concern for personal security (future comfort) and general anxiety.
- I now feel tremendously accountable for all my thoughts, words and deeds—requiring constant, alert observation.
- I now trust in the Lord, the Higher Power, to breathe my breaths, think my thoughts, and fill me completely.

On the 8th night of this retreat, about 6 PM, my mind finally tired of activity, relaxed and enjoyed the silence. "It would be wonderful," I wrote, "if I could carry this over from isolation to my daily life." I had made a similar determination last isolation to prepare and eat my evening meals, when at home, in silence rather than reading or watching the news:

How can I listen for my Lord if I don't have quiet times?

Finding myself so relaxed and in silence was a new grace. At ease with myself.... O, Holy Night! Silent Night, Holy Night. I wonder if other people experience this peace? It may be a foretaste of Bliss.

Is it possible that we've never been outside of this? It's a little past 10 now. The peace that descended around 6 continued all evening. There's no desire to reach out for inspiration (i.e., reading). Feeling very self-contained.

Listen to the silence. The silence is the answer...

I had a dream that night:

About a dozen of us were sitting around a table, eating a meal that we hadn't specifically ordered and which had been served. I was eating a hotdog, not in a bun, savoring the hot-dog flavor, and thinking to myself: "The only thing needed to make this meal perfect is some sauerkraut." Then I realized that we had sauerkraut on our plates, and I had been eating it without being conscious of the fact. About that time there was a lull in the conversation, so I said: "All that's needed to make this perfect is some sauerkraut." There was a silent gap, then everyone picked up (direct-mind) my amusement, and everyone started to laugh uproariously. I looked around, making eye contact with one after another, each time spurring us to renewed, rib-holding, eye-clenching hilarity.

The dream seemed to be a social reinforcement of the experience with silence. My dream family joyed in my joy at the discovery that what's needed to make things perfect is already here—we're just not consciously aware of it.

I remained in the silence that morning, although perhaps not as deeply. That surprised me; I expected, based on past experience, that the mood or state wouldn't last overnight. It lasted for two days and two nights.

After "doing" my morning meditation, it occurred to me that the desired mind control must come about, first, being able to look deeply into an issue then, second, realizing that it is the wrong direction for accomplishing my goal (e.g., absolute surrender of thought, word and deed).

The next afternoon, Christmas day, I was sitting with the door open and the sun shining in, warming my right arm as I wrote (sitting on a chair by the wood stove) my final thoughts and feelings for the retreat:

- Sadness, knowing this wonderful mood can't last.
- Thankfulness for another high point in my life. I don't know why I've been so blessed.
- I pray not to forget.

I stopped in at the farmhouse, where Cecy was now living, as I was leaving the farm. Cecy had Mr. Rose there for Christmas dinner. I sat next to him for a while, and we "chatted." At one point, when I was talking with Cecy, he reached out and touched my sleeve. I turned to see what he wanted, but he didn't say anything. Cecy and I both felt that he was just checking to see if I was solid or ephemeral. I wondered if that were a sign that the feeling I'd had when putting up posters on campuses a few weeks earlier—of being halfway between a real person and a ghost—was accurate.

Two days later I was busy writing my lengthy isolation report (I'd been torturing half a dozen friends with these for the previous two retreats), going to the farm and then to the YMCA for my swimming exercise, and so on. I'd forgotten my morning meditation so sat down to do it after dinner. Then I thought about the trip to Columbus the following day for my traditional visit with son Chris and his family between Christmas and New Year's ... and smiled to myself, as I did whenever I thought about that.

A GROUP RETREAT AT THE FARM, at the end of January 1999, turned out to be an uplifting start for the year. Expected attendees were Ben R. (a Pitt student who'd been away for a semester at sea), Paul V. (a Robert Morris student), Phil F, Cecy, Cecy's friend Leigh, Shawn, and Reggie. Todd and Anima were unexpected additions. Todd agreed to lead a session at the next group retreat, Ben agreed to lead a session at the Pittsburgh retreat planned for a Saturday in mid-February and volunteered to be my partner to remind each other of commitments we'd made. As Todd was leaving, he placed a hand on my shoulder and let it rest there—more eloquent of thanks than anything verbal—and said that something in a letter I'd sent him had inspired him to resume his meditation practice for the month before the retreat.

There were seven of us at the Saturday retreat in Pittsburgh (Damon, Ben, Reggie, Suresh, Vince, Anima and myself. Cecy's rental car had a flat tire overnight, which she took as a sign she shouldn't go. Dong-hoon didn't come as planned, which was disappointing). The highlight of the retreat for me was seeing Damon take a big step in dropping his cleverness façade, which occurred when we split into pairs to work on understanding our prides and fears. Nine of us showed up for the April 3rd Saturday retreat in Pittsburgh: Goedele and Dong-hoon, Michele (CMU student), Vince, Denise (Pitt grad student), Bevan (young guy who's seen the posters for a year), Cecy, Anima and myself. Anima and Sharad had us over for dinner afterward. Remi M, a post-doctoral fellow at CMU, joined us. [I've included the names in these paragraphs just to give you an idea of the flux of participants.]

A wonderful April TAT meeting from my perspective, although Bob F. called to cancel due to an interpersonal misunderstanding between us. Fourteen people made it in for the Friday evening session. Bob C. led a great confrontation session on Saturday. Doron, Bob, Cecy and I drove to Weirton, WV Sunday evening to see Mr. Rose.

We had a going-away dinner for Shawn (moving to TX) and Reggie (moving back to NC) on May 16th. My spirits were somewhat buoyed by receiving emails on the 21st from Kelly (a Pitt freshman who was at the last meeting; very positive about the group) and Bevan (inquiring about the next Monday meeting). On the 27th I noted that I was still struggling with depression, and that my mood depended on the *next* prospect for friendship.

Kelly, Vijay (electrician apprentice) and others came for a Memorial Day weekend retreat on the farm. Todd was making progress in becoming articulate but still froze when questioned. Damon had made great strides in opening up. Todd planned to spend 5 days in isolation in July … then moved it up to June 8th-13th to avoid avoidance.

June 5th: The depression state continues—and surprisingly so does the action of group work and meditation. This is encouraging, indicating the possible existence of a vector (i.e., action in a direction) and a consequent level of between-ness.

June 10th: After one and a half years of group work in Pittsburgh, got an enthusiastic response from someone (Kelly). He's attended the last three meetings and has stayed around after, going for coffee and more talk. His email:

> Things are starting to become clearer to me, and I have definitely noticed changes in my thoughts and perceptions. These meetings have had a tremendous impact on my search for truth and self-knowledge. It's really exciting. For the longest time I've been a highly skeptical person … but I can feel my hardness toward the world gradually melting away. I now

realize that humans indeed have a spiritual aspect to their being … and I've been neglecting mine for way too long.

TODD SENT AN ISOLATION REPORT to Cecy, Anima and myself. It
was uncharacteristically revealing for Todd … makes me happy
for him. His questions about meditation, and specifically about
Rose's advice for bringing the mind under control, have been
a catalyst to bring me to this commitment: I am determined to
bring the mind under control, using the technique described
in the *Psychology of the Observer.* Why did it take me 20 years to
come to this resolution? Did I arrive here years ago and forget
it? What are the forces that have encouraged procrastination
and rationalization? A couple months ago I wrote on a 3 x 5
card, "Koan: Do I need to learn to control the mind?" Today I
wonder how there could have been any doubt.

We held a Saturday retreat on June 19th in Pittsburgh and
had one new person, Ibrahim—a Saudi Muslim. I didn't know
why he attended since he seemed happy with his beliefs. Anima,
Kelly, Suresh, Vince and I went to Anima's and Sharad's afterward … ordered pizza and talked until 1 AM. Remi joined us
there.

There was a small turnout for the July 4th TAT meeting:
Vince, Anima and Sharad, Lee, Jim B (paraphysicist), Jim Burns,
Cecy and myself were there for the Friday evening session.
Anima moderated the session, which was difficult with the
varying states of mind. Todd arrived Saturday morning—first
TAT meeting he'd been to in a few years. We worked on farm
projects mid-AM to mid-PM. George P. showed up just after we
started a confrontation session in the later afternoon, as if some
force had provided irritation at exactly the right time. A tremendously frustrating, unstructured evening session followed,
monopolized by Keith M, who had arrived late AM.

We had an excellent Saturday mini-retreat in Pittsburgh on
July 24th. Cecy, Irwin, Anima and myself. Ejected Daniel, who

had come to one of the Kiva Han meetings, due to his obnox-
ious attitude. Kelly didn't come due to "economic priorities"
(guess he had to work). He also didn't show up at the following Monday meeting. Due to the small turnout, though, I was
debating whether to cut the Saturday retreats back to one per
semester.

I Worked with Bob C. and Steve to set up an e-mail confrontation group in October of 1999, using the Pulyan correspondence
with Richard Rose as focus material. My 55th birthday on the
17th was a non-event psychologically. Ten of us including four
new people (there would have been 11 but Cecy was sick) had
a good retreat at the farm on the weekend of the 22nd. I really
liked Mike M, a Pitt senior, who became active in the Pittsburgh
group. I thought that David C, another Pitt senior, was really
likeable, too, but seemed to outwit himself with his cleverness.

We held an informal meeting in Pittsburgh on Saturday
October 30th: Anima, Vince, Damon, Vikas (a 26-year-old CMU
PhD Chemistry student) and myself. Damon mentioned unusu-
al freedom from sexual thoughts over the previous two weeks.
Vikas said he was really happy to find fellow-seekers. Akilesh
(CMU freshman) started coming to meetings. We finally had
what seemed like a good Monday meeting (in the Gillespie
Room of the Oakland Carnegie Library) on November 8th.
There were ten of us, including two of the new people from
the farm retreat, Adrienne and Mike, plus Katy, Vijay (who
hadn't been since his first meeting at the end of May) and Vikas.
Damon spoke openly about looking for father-god approval. It
turned out to be the last meeting he came to that year.

Had a call from the Good Shepherd Nursing Home on the
morning of Friday December 3rd saying that my mother was
probably nearing the end. By the time I got there, she had sta-
bilized, but the end of her journey appeared immanent, and

she died at 3:29 PM. I was extremely fortunate in having good people as parents. They were dedicated spouses and parents. I never heard them argue or exchange an unkind word, and neither ever said an unkind word to me.

December 15, 1999: I began a solitary retreat, this time in Bob C's cabin. Those retreats had always provided inspirations for things people could work on together, and this time was no different. For example, on the 20th while walking to the shed for the daily sign-in, I had the idea of seeing if there was interest in holding a men's intensive in 2000 … maybe for two days prior to one of the TAT meetings so that people coming from a distance could combine the two.

On a walk after rereading the section of *Psychology of the Observer* on controlling the mind, I was thinking: "How many times have I read this material, with how many different reactions, from hope to hopelessness; how many times have I set out with determination to apply/pursue it, and how much time has elapsed in forgetfulness between launchings? And how much time was lost in dithering between my attraction to this method vs. the Ramana Maharshi meditation (which was finally settled by realization that Rose was the guru who appeared in my case, not Ramana)? So, I get ready to make yet another start—cautiously optimistic, but prepared for setbacks (or at least anticipating such).

Scanning through the index of *The World of Zen* by Nancy Wilson Ross (did I mention that Bob's cabin had a bookcase with a tempting selection?), the one item that caught my eye was a short sample of Huang Po dialogue: "[Seekers] do not know that, if they put a stop to conceptual thought and forget their anxiety, the Buddha will appear before them, for this Mind is Buddha and the Buddha is all living beings." Here was the phrase again that struck me when scanning through Huang Po's teachings during last year's retreat: "forget their anxiety." When I sat to meditate the following morning, with the general objective of scrutinizing the self, the thought arose that my sense of self includes a strong sense of separation from others. I asked myself what the nature of this separation was, and then I found myself vocalizing internally that I wanted, with my whole being, to see directly into the nature of this anxiety. What I saw was *a gulf of anxiety.* Apparently what separates me from others also separates me from Self-Awareness.

I then recalled the advice of some Ch'an master that you have to "transcend the world from its very midst," not by avoidance or abstraction. And this led me to the conclusion that the straightforward way to deal with the anxiety is to face it on an individual basis. Analysis (my nemesis!) of the anxiety I felt with each of the people I have the closest connections with yielded these composite details: With my women friends, I don't want to show weakness. Why? They will despise it and try to take advantage of it. Why does this bother me? Probably from a semi-conscious awareness of being "invaded by my mother's spirit" (i.e., being in rapport with her) as a child. Another concern is that where there's compatibility, softness might lead to sex. With males: going through them one at a time, I came up with seven overlapping items:

1. His anxiety stirs my own.
2. His inhibition of expressing himself leads me to conclude that there's a negative judgment of me.
3. He doesn't believe I'm telling the truth (which takes me by surprise, for I scrupulously amend my words if I find myself telling a lie).
4. He doesn't seem interested; self-absorbed.
5. I may see too many negative characteristics (weaknesses) reflected.
6. I'm afraid that self-revelation will lead to explosive (i.e., emotional) rejection.
7. He doesn't want to decrease the separation.

When I asked with my whole being a second time to see deeply into the nature of anxiety, the image of Cecy's dog Smokey, frozen in position on the road yesterday before he recognized me, waiting to see if I were friend or foe, came to me. The anxiety is based on fear of being hurt—physically, sure, but beyond that, the fear of being hurt emotionally. So I asked myself why there is a fear of experiencing painful emotions. Is it because they arise due to humiliations of the self-image? I remembered the great release of anxiety after the experience of facing my list of a lifetime's worth of humiliations when I went deeply into the question of acceptance in the solitary retreat three years earlier.

I awoke around 4 AM the following morning, had some tea and reread the Huang Po excerpts, then meditated from 5 to 6. Thankfulness came to me for the first time during this isolation as I began that sitting. "If my life produces nothing more, I'm thankful for this," I realized.

I meditated again that morning from 10 to 11, beginning after copying out the section in the *Direct-Mind Experience* section "Points of Reference" where Rose laid out the between-ness formula, and I recalled his comment about allowing anything to happen that doesn't jeopardize your principles. I asked myself what my principles were and came up with the following list:

- Never be intimidated (from Rose; an ideal)
- Mutuality inheres in every true act (from David Seabury)
- Never compromise my integrity (also from Seabury)
- Friendship is the highest human relationship (Rose)
- The first purpose of life is to define oneself (Rose)
- The greatest pleasure in life comes from helping others (personal experience)
- Help has to be selective (Rose; personal experience)
- The Golden Rule isn't adequate; people have differing values and sentiments; there's no formula for ethical relationships (personal experience)
- You can't lie down with liars; truth must be applied in all directions, with discernment (Rose)
- A life dedicated to self-definition is not wasted, regardless of success or failure; there is no better option (Rose)
- There is nothing good nor bad but thinking makes it so (William Shakespeare, *Hamlet*)

Finished my retreat at noon on Christmas day. Anima was arriving in Wheeling by bus from Pittsburgh at noon. I was to pick her up and take her to the farm, where she was going to be using Bob's cabin for a solitary retreat until the New Year's Eve party.

Sense of Self

"Do you have any sense of self? Is there only the "view" for you?"

I f there's other, there's self. If there's a view, there's a viewer. It's not a question of whether it is but of what it is.

You know that you *are*. You're afraid that you'll cease to *be*. That's the plus and minus of self-consciousness.

I'm in the fortunate situation of having a stark contrast between my dreaming state of being and my waking state of being. In my dreaming state, the dreamer isn't in conscious contact with its source—i.e., not enlightened. When body consciousness returns in the morning, I have a clear memory from the dream state of what the before-enlightenment state is like. And neither the dreamer nor the body consciousness has any complaints about its state of being, which is nice. In the body consciousness state, there's a split between viewer and view. Fortunately that consciousness has ongoing contact with its source. So when it looks back at what it's looking out from, it knows itself. It knows it's both the view and the viewer … and neither. It knows that it's what *is* … and that what *is* always has been and ever will be.

Using a slightly different way to break things down, the sleepwalker (typical waking-state experience) is not conscious of self; the sleepwalker is identified with a self-story. The starting-to-awaken sleepwalker becomes aware of "two selves": the self-story and the individual consciousness of awareness. Finally awakening, the mind becomes aware of what You are. It still operates in subject-object mode. Everything is the same ... but radically different. As in the Zen description, the mountains once again become mountains ... but the Viewer is no longer individualized.

I'm sure that makes it all clear to you :-)

❧

Riding the Trajectory of the Status Quo

A year ago ... I came up with the question "what is my deepest desire?" Last month, I got the clearest verbal response yet to that question: the words "I'm desperately incomplete" came and stuck in my head to express the problem, and "I want completion" was the deep desire. This might sound trivial ... but the clarity with which I felt it was almost a relief.

If somebody says: "My deep desire is X, but I don't want it yet" I can only guess that there's a deeper desire at work, and that's to maintain the status quo, the current trajectory of their life experience. And I assume that's the deeper desire that most people ride all the way down the slope. If your deep desire truly were completion, wouldn't you want it now? Or is there a deep fear that's overriding the deep desire?

This makes perfect sense. I'll attempt to lay out my desires and fears as I can feel them now:
- Desire to maintain status quo: I don't know why, but this desire exists....
- Fear that I'd have to trade in something valuable in order to get my desire for completion satisfied....

Did you possibly identify the fear that's behind the desire to maintain the current trajectory? Can you get an edge on what that "something valuable" might be?

I keep trying to get an edge on this, but mostly, it's amorphous (though strong). Verbal thought hits a dead end when I ask myself the question. Feeling wise, the latest feeling is, I have to give up everything—essentially, die. But I'm unable to tell whether this is coming from an inner intuition or from the set of things I've read and heard. If it's the latter, my whole "I'd have to trade something valuable" might be just a rationalization my mind has cooked up for procrastination, and the real reason for procrastination might be something else.

Suzanne Segal, in her autobiographical *Collision with the Infinite*, wrote the following comment that, I think, addresses the fear expressed above:

> The continued operation of all the functions in the state of freedom is an awesome way to live. It bears no resemblance to the stark emptiness that fear might paint it to be. People who tell me they don't want to give up the personal because they believe they would be giving up love or joy or deep feeling don't understand that the personal never existed. Nothing is given up. Love that appears to be personal is based on a mind-constructed sense of being separate. Love in this separate state involves a longing to merge with an other in order to be fulfilled. From the perspective of the vastness, the other does not exist. When the vastness sees everything out of itself to be made of itself, this is the ultimate intimacy. The moment-to-moment flavor of the vastness undulating within itself as it perceives itself through every particle of itself everywhere brings a love that is limitless, far surpassing anything the mind could construct as the ideal love it seeks.

She found a simple way to express the view from beyond the mind without getting tied up in convoluted terminology or confusing the reader by not distinguishing the view "down here" (i.e., within the mind) from the actual perspective—as opposed to an adopted belief—of no split between subject and object, between self and other.

Riding the trajectory of our status quo is likely to take us, nonstop, from the dream of life to the dream of death. Finding completion while living may well involve a discontinuity.

The status quo is not likely to take us to the pot of gold at the end of the rainbow. The rainbow is an optical effect depending on the location of the viewer, and going toward the end of a rainbow only moves it further away. :-)

❧

A Suggestion?

D o you have a suggestion for my spiritual practice?

Transcend the dichotomy of the mind by observing the observer ... i.e., see what you are.

❧

Frustration

E very time I hear in a talk or read in a book that all you have to do is look within, there's this immediate feeling of frustration since I believe that the next attempt will again feel like trying to walk through a wall.

I'll let you in on a secret you may already know but haven't considered: You can walk through walls in dreams ... through dream walls.

Limbo

or the most part I remain in limbo which is just north of libido for those w/o a compass.

Everyone who's lived past puberty has probably been familiar with the limbo just N of libido, although most might not admit it to themselves. But it's only an obstacle to finding the kingdom of heaven if we give it too much importance. Just as mental activity doesn't have to interfere with observation, neither does non-abstinence. We can find silence or celibacy in this dimension, but it's only temporary. This is the dimension of noise and movement. So we have to somehow, without any formula, run between those raindrops to get out of the rain and become consciously aware of our source. Enlightenment is really the robotic machinery becoming conscious of what you are. That robotic machinery cooks up a story of individual being, complete with all the variations from how-wonderful-am-I to woe-is-me ... but that's all part of the picture show. You mentioned the theme from "Training Your Dragon"; I haven't seen the movie, but the title is a good analogy for bringing the mind back to its longing for Eden. The mind's a problem-solving machine, and the more it's conscious of that innate longing, the more CPU cycles will go toward its fulfillment.

When the Body Dies

oes anyone know if Enlightenment occurs when the body dies even if the self has not prepared for or reached enlightenment during the lifetime?

Until the body dies, we'd be speculating on what might happen in terms of consciousness at that moment. The closest evidence we have is the reports of people who've revived from clinical death ... and their reports vary from "no consciousness" to "waiting relatives" to Victor Solow's "I Died at 10:52 A.M." [2]

We're home, back to Eden, during dreamless sleep ... but does it help when body consciousness returns?

We're home, in the Kingdom of Heaven, during the waking state ... but if we're not consciously aware of it, does it help if someone tells us that?

Becoming consciously aware of what we are at the core of our being is a question of not letting our attention get distracted by the view. The moments before the body's death may be a time when the view won't distract us, but it's a long shot for betting on.

There's no reason why we can't admit the seriousness of our situation right now and allow our inner head to turn away from distraction. Dying (to delusion) before death (of the body) removes the existential angst. Why wait?

Confused About Self-Realization

S ometimes I get confused about Self-Realization. Could you tell me how you know/are aware of Self-Realization?

The term "self-realization" points to the state of being aware of what you are ... of knowing what you are with absolute certainty. Merrell-Wolff termed it "recognition," pointing to the fact that the state doesn't arise but has always been. He also called it "introception," which he defined as a third kind of knowing

---

2   See the Dec. 2003 "TAT Forum" journal at www.tatfoundation.org.

that's beyond the types of knowing familiar to the mind. It's the only type of knowing that's absolute knowing. And, as Merrell-Wolff also pointed out, it's a knowing by identity. Absolute knowing doesn't know the time of day, the number of sands in the Ganges or the number of hairs on your head. All it knows is itself.

Right Action

I left the family home in November, got infatuated with and started seeing this woman…. I guess I need another perspective as I try to determine how important resolving my personal crap is in terms of my goal of ending seeking. On one hand, there's a spike of energy and focus that I'm clearly benefiting from in terms of my spiritual practice. On the other hand, I feel as if I don't make the right decision that I will not be doing "right action" and that this may impede my spiritual efforts.

Personality, the mask held in front of the belief in individuality, has to be seen for what it is before its stranglehold on the attention loosens. "Resolving personal crap" is probably the personality at work trying to keep itself in place. Looking at personality with some detachment may be more effective in terms of getting out of our own way. Viewed in terms of your objective, personality is a facade hiding the delusion obscuring the truth.

※

Longing

The months before awakening, were you frequently aware of a longing for Truth and ultimate satisfaction? How frequently did you feel the desire that motivated your search?

I felt a conscious love of Truth for many years, but I'd say my primary motivation was escape or release from misery. Over the decades I was pretty much conscious of my general mood most of the time. I knew whether I was feeling happy or miserable, and I think it would be an exaggeration to say that I felt happy 10% of the time. In the final 3 or 4 months, after my second visit with Douglas Harding (Feb. 2004), I wasn't aware of any change in the intensity of the desire to satisfy the longing, but a mood had descended on me of a desire to be more serious about it than I'd ever been. Curiously, my mind procrastinated that "getting serious," hoping the motivation would carry into the solitary retreat scheduled for that May.

※

Stark, Alone

You have a comforting account of what happens after. Lots of writings out there about how stark, alone, etc. truth is. Do you just skip that part?

The transition when transcending the mind's limitations could be traumatic (I think it was for Douglas Harding) and the transition coming back into the mind could be traumatic (as it was for Richard Rose, who wept for a week to find himself back in this dimension of opposites) but neither was traumatic for me. Loneliness is the experience of an individual self, isolated from other selves/things by physical and mental separation. What we really are just IS. And it is ALL. ALL-ness. Not bliss, not starkness—which would still be experiences in the dimension of opposites.

❧

Home Base

*Y*ou've taken a journey, a trek that's taken you away from your home base.

When it began, there was no problem, no disconnect. But gradually the situation changed and, without knowing what was taking place, you crossed a barrier and became disoriented. You forgot home base. Not one hundred percent, actually, because there is a vague memory of its existence, a longing or yearning that's often below the conscious surface. But at best it seems a place of the past and, for some, of the hopeful future.

At times when your journey has lost its luster, you've felt the yearning to go back to home base more strongly. But now it seems impossibly distant and inaccessible since you've forgotten where it is and how to get back to it. You don't even remember that you set out on this journey. It feels like you've been cast out of home, become a castaway on a remote world. And it's not reassuring that you have several billion companion castaways.

Of those billions, a significant percentage have become convinced that they have an inside track to finding their way home when they die—they call it heaven, paradise, nirvana—and they've adopted a belief-system that they hold onto for reassurance. They aren't absolutely sure, although they do have hope. But most are convinced that it's a question of blind belief, that there's no way for them to find out for sure.

Then there are those few who say they've found their way home already, that it's not necessary—or even a good idea—to wait until death. If you've come across one of those self-proclaimed finders, either in person or through a testimonial record, what was your reaction? Were you able to write that person off as a nut? If not, did you decide that what it would take to replicate that person's return home was beyond your ability (like the reaction of the rich young man whom Jesus told to sell all he had and give it to the poor)? Or did that person's words or presence "ring your bell" or otherwise ignite your flame from the eternal pilot light? If so, did the inspiration die off within a short time? Or have you put months or years of effort into trying to find and stay on the path that leads home, only to become discouraged and stop the effort? Have you become lost once again in the luster of your trek or found yourself trying to pursue the adventures that used to hold out hope of happiness (such as love, wealth, fame, creation of beauty, knowledge, helping others) but are now tormented by knowing that they'll never be enough? Or are you still struggling but, after years, not feeling you've really accomplished anything other than banging your head against the same spot in the wall?

These are different types of sticking points, indicating something that you're still attached to.[3]

---

3   For additional material on sticking points, see "Complications and Sticking Points" in www.tatfoundation.org/forum2005-01.htm.

Man to God: Turn Around?

*C*ould you say it a little louder,
      Could you repeat it again?
I didn't quite hear you,
or I didn't quite understand.

I'm trying, Daddy, I'm trying
but I'm oh so confused—
I thought you sent me out
to stand on my own, to become a man.

Isn't there something I have to accomplish,
some errand I have to attend to,
to win your approval? You mean
it's okay to come home again?
Now?

I believe you, Daddy,
but I'm so afraid—you can see
how wobbly I am. If I try
to look behind I'll lose my balance
and fall.

I can make a wide circle
and come round in that way
but then I'm still out here
and home is still behind me.

Could you say it a little louder,
could you repeat it again?
I feel like I'd better keep peddling
while I figure it out....

❧

Ongoing Q & A

Q: *Where are my blindspots?*

Response: In front of you.

❧

believe that if a couple of long standing doubts were answered this faith would be all that remained.

What is the nature of those doubts?

I don't know. I don't know. Those were the first answers that came to me, as I attempted to look at the doubt-sensation. It feels unreal when I stop to look at it. I have a question Art, are all doubts of the same essential nature? If I see through the root doubt, do all others dissolve?

If doubt dissolves, you're in trouble. The mind can never be absolutely certain of anything. Our essential nature, where we know what we are, is beyond the realm of doubt or no-doubt (transient certainty).

❧

D o you think there is some benefit about meditating while feel-ing physical pain, or is it the same to do it without physical pain, but just more unpleasant?

Meditation is noticing what you're seeing. If physical pain is getting all your attention, then you're probably not going to see anything when "meditating" that you're not seeing otherwise. The most immediate problem assailing the mind is likely to get all its attention unless we remember our deep yearning and that inspires the mind to turn away from other material for a while.

❧

R egarding Daniel's question to you ("I have a question Art, are all doubts of the same essential nature? If I see through the root doubt, do all others dissolve?")—Along the same line. If one big fear could be faced or overcome, would it eliminate the standing of all the other fears? I don't mean the final fear of surrender of ego, but some other major life fear falling, and creating a domino effect?

Fears (and desires) don't need to be vanquished ... merely faced or bypassed if they're in the way of accomplishment. The body-mind self doesn't become fearless or desireless as a prelude to self-realization or as a result of self-realization. Self-realization shows us the irrelevance of fears and desires to what we truly are. Absolute being has no relatives.

We only need to *act* in the face of fear. When we do, some-times the fear will diminish or evaporate, but that isn't of pri-mary importance. A way to think about blind spots is that they're the rationalizations and procrastinations we fool our-selves with. The topic of the last Pittsburgh meeting was being true to oneself. As deciders/doers, we're generally identified with the umpire or decision-making function of the mind. We see the fears and desires that are promoting their agendas and agonize over the tugs of war. The self we are trying to be true to is the more-interior voice of intuition, which is easily drowned out by the loud voices of the fears and desires.

❧

I'm 99% over it now. Just the mood of sadness is here. You can't win. (Win for losing) as you say. I maybe was trying to win something else.

The balloon got a bit of air let out of it, leaving the emptiness/sadness. At some juncture, all the air will depart in an outbreathing ... and the moment before the subsequent inbreathing will be Eternity.

❧

The recording of my dreams is picking up steam—it seems like the more that I write, the more I'm able to recall (I didn't recall one iota before I started recording). However, I think that I may be putting down too much detail—what do you think is a good amount?

I found the same thing when I started recording dreams. As for how much to write down, I'd say just enough to promote inquiry into their possible message. "If the dream maker is sending a message here, what might it be?" Even the act of recording a dream, if we're consciously looking, will provide material for awe and self-inquiry.

❧

n general, if I compare myself to a year or a couple of years ago, there's definitely a shift in my past-feeling that I could and should try hard to control where my life goes. Now, it's more of the feeling that I have no clue what's in store for me, and that apart from doing my duties, I'll have to leave everything to whatever is in charge. I feel reasonably okay with this feeling, something I could've never been okay with two years ago. What I'm not sure of is whether this came out of a) a loosening up of identification with control, b) helplessness (what other choice do I have?), c) resignation, d) rationalizing action away, or some combination of these. I'm particularly concerned about (c) and (d). Any pointers on how I can perhaps question myself to find out?

I assume you're not affectively indifferent to various possible outcomes & admitting that you're not in control of outcomes is not also concluding that there's nothing to be done. If you feel a deep want or longing, and if you feel there's a possibility that your actions could affect the outcome … i.e., if you're not a fanatical fatalist or completely beaten into servitude by depression … then it seems like the honest going-forward attitude is one of fighting for what you want. Recognizing that our life is not in our control is not the same as helplessness … if help is available for the asking. Resignation sounds like the reverse side of the faith coin. Look for beliefs that support resignation or rationalizing away action. If you look into any belief, you'll arrive at paradox … and recognition of paradox will promote between-ness. Another name for between-ness might be *wu wei*.

*T*hank god for Lyme disease, eh? :-) I felt similarly about the 7-year depression I wallowed in … the upside being that I had so little interaction with the world that everything in the mind slowed to a snail's pace and I was able to witness its operation in great detail.

If you watch the mind ... looking for feeling, perhaps ... I think you'll find that the mind is frequently working on solving a problem or conflict: mundane stuff like hunger, intermediate stuff like relationships, and—when nothing else is sticking a thorn in the side—the big problem of life/death. Much of our spiritual or philosophical work probably depends on curiosity as well as irritation. The "dead" may not be curious ... so it may pay to make use of that particular implant while it's functioning.

You're not at peace, although I don't doubt that you're relatively more peaceful than you may have been in the past. I get the feeling that you don't want to feel the intensity or immensity of your discontent.

At first, I disagreed with your assessment. Then I noticed all of the positions I was defending. Then second guessing, and torment.

I feel fine though. Or, I'm so apathetic, that I don't feel anything.

No idea where to go from here.

*W*hat all this says about IT I don't know, but I was looking for the "i." Could be a waste of time, but I can afford it. Any of your thoughts are appreciated.

An IT can only be conceived of as an object of consciousness. Nothing can be known for sure about an object of consciousness until/unless the subject—the knower—is known. Anything other than looking for the "i" is supportive of that search at best.

I have a few questions relating to the Richard Rose talk[4]:

> *Now this is the basis of meditating for the purpose of a subjective answer. In other words, you want a subjective answer, and you're putting in almost all objective data—only words out of philosophy books. But you throw all this data in, and you have to shut the computer down—or it will continue to put data in, which will confuse your answer. As long as data is coming in it will confuse your answer; it will affect it.*

What do you think he meant by this? Should we stop taking stuff in?

Carving out extended times for solitude minus media input and other distractions from "going within" for subjective exploration ... finding the real self among all the pretenders.

> *There's nothing precognitive if we live in a space-time continuum. Everything is now. We have a sort of a mix-up in our consciousness, caused by living in a solar system with a body that seems to age and grow older and die. We seem to have a passing of time. But according to certain people like Einstein and Ouspensky, there is no passing of time. Time stands still and we pass.*

This makes sense, but it seems as if Rose may not experience this timelessness (he points to Einstein and Ouspensky). Is this not something that an awakened person would recognize or am I reading it wrong?

---

4   The "Moods" lecture on nostalgia, moods and dreams given at Case Western Reserve U. in 1978. A similar talk given at Ohio State U. in 1979 is transcribed in Rose's *Direct Mind-Experience*.

Rose didn't want people to believe what he said (i.e., trying to agree their way to Truth) but to explore for themselves. You have to pick up his personal convictions "between the lines" most of the time. Using Einstein and Ouspensky as examples implies that you don't have to be enlightened to have a theory of time/timelessness. A person who knows what he is at the core of being knows timelessness ... in a way that's inconceivable by the mind as it's beyond subject-object experience, which puts it in the realm of "He moves, and He moves not." When I lost body consciousness in a riptide adventure 30 years ago, I had a life review, passing over my previous experience from oldest to most recent. On the other hand, knowing what I am, I know that I have never moved. And yet I am life, which is nothing other than movement.

Rose makes several references to dead people and the possibility of them communicating something to the living. This seems contradictory to what Pulyan said: nothing of you survives. How could this communication happen?

Good one! Who was right? Are we going to vote on who's the better authority when two "authorities" disagree? If two authorities agree (or 2,222) does that make their agreement the truth? (Rhetorical questions to aide your disgestion :-) Rose witnessed some remarkable things when he was working with people who were searching on a phenomenom level (after his realization, since they were the only searchers he came across for many years), such as intelligent entities appearing and communicating with people in the audience. He entertained various possible explanations for phenomenal experience of both the normal and paranormal kinds. When talking with searchers, he would often try to stimulate their self-inquiry by pointing out possibilities that leaned in a direction opposite to their beliefs.

✿

*C*an the ego get so fed up with itself that it does the talking to itself?

As with everything in this relative dimension, the ego-self is not singular but splits into two opposing factions. Alfred Pulyan referred to this split as ego-1 and ego-2. Hubert Benoit termed them saint and sinner. The mind works on the basis of an assumed subject-self that it loves and needs to protect ... and things get complicated from that starting point. We see the assumed subject-self thinking or doing something that supports the ideal image we have of that subject-self, and so we applaud the thought or action and identify proudly with that. The saint at work. Then we see some thought or action that contradicts the desired self-image, and we attribute that to the influence of the enemy (devil, mate, child, boss, etc.) and try to disidentify with that characteristic of the sinner/loser/whatever. Ego-1 feels shame concerning ego-2 and tries to detach from it ... lecturing it, condemning it, and so on.

I am flipping between knowing what I'm doing and then not knowing a thing. It's black and white. Yes and no. I'm not seeing many maybe's. Am I not looking deeply enough or am I looking too deeply?

The only way to get clarity on what you know is to know the knower. The knower is the real self and not hidden ... but the mind's knowing is vague, misty. The mind dimension is like dreamland, where something in the spotlight sometimes appears clearly delineated with nice neat edges, etc., but the rest of the world fades into obscurity. It's not a question of looking deeply enough or too deeply but of 1) noticing what we're seeing, 2) becoming conscious that our interpretation of what we're seeing has an equally valid-seeming opposite, and 3) determining where the lie is.

The Vector Moves on Its Own Momentum

10. Egoless Action for Others

*J*anuary 2, 2000: This is the first day when my life is beginning to return to normal since the solitary retreat of Dec. 15th-25th, my annual post-Christmas visit with son Chris and his family, and the TAT New Year's Eve party, at which there were just six of us—Anima, Sharad and Vijay, from Pittsburgh joining Cecy, Phil F. and myself. Tomorrow I'll return to my every-other-day swimming exercise routine. Today is sort of a free day, to let things return to normal. The next project is to write up my isolation report and try to consolidate the inspirations into action.

A dream from last night that had just come back to me as I was writing in the journal: A person I was with realized he was dying. I locked his gaze with mine and then started reciting, mentally: "The Lord is my shepherd...." This recalled to me that I had not felt closeness to the Lord, to my source, in a long time—I had been living far from that interior humbleness. In the dream I didn't remember the entire psalm. I looked it up this morning. It's the 23rd. When I read the second verse, it brought tears to my eyes: "He maketh me to lie down in green pastures; he leadeth me beside the still waters."

I had focused the Saturday meetings in Pittsburgh on meditation and scheduled a weekend retreat for early February. I had also been continuing with the email confrontation group ... and strangely hadn't mentioned anything in my journal about the amazing events of last November and December. Not long after beginning the email confrontation last October, Bob C. had a breakthrough to self-realization triggered by a comment in one of Alfred Pulyan's letters to Rose. That was in November, and Bob didn't say anything about it for a few days, until he was sure it was a permanent change of being. Bob was the Rose student I always thought the most likely to succeed since he had, I felt, the mentality most like Rose's (i.e., intuitive). So I wasn't shocked and found it easy to accept. It occurred around his birthday on the 7th, I'm pretty sure—before the middle of the month in any case. Near the end of December I received an email from Shawn N. saying that he'd had a breakthrough the night before he wrote, seemingly triggered by a mood that had descended while reading the transcript of Franklin Merrell-Wolff's "Induction" experiment (which he had conducted with a group of his students in Phoenix). Shawn wrote that he wanted to let a few of his close friends know that it had happened for him—and that it was possible after all for anyone. Shawn was like the next generation of Rose's students from Bob—he was thirty whereas Bob had just turned 46—and he hadn't heard about Bob's breakthrough until I told him after receiving his email. With Shawn, I was a little shocked. Like Bob, I didn't doubt his realization since I knew he was scrupulously honest and skeptical ... but I thought his mentality was more like mine (i.e., rational vs. intuitive). So in my reply I'd asked him if he'd suddenly perfected his intuition, which Rose had implied was necessary. He responded with a touch of humor that apparently that wasn't necessary.

And in February, Bob F. had a breakthrough triggered by a comment that Bob C. made to him in the email confrontation group, although it had taken a month or so of emotional turmoil before the breakthrough finished.

I made an agreement with Alex L, in Raleigh, to sit in meditation at the same time each morning (8 AM, except 11:30 on Saturday, when he had an early karate class). I began sensing his presence or his absence shortly after 8 most mornings. One Saturday morning I didn't sense his presence at 11:30 but then did at 11:35. [I think he corroborated some or all of my hunches, but that may be wishful memory.]

BY THE END OF MARCH I felt like I was back in the depressed mood or mind-state of 1989-96, characterized by a deep sadness and a conviction that almost any action considered was immediately negated as too much effort. I remember at one point wanting to ask God to kill me but then realizing that such a request would be egotistical and contra to my commitment to surrender to the Lord in thought, word and deed: a double bind if there ever were one :-)

One morning while reading Radhakrishnan's commentaries on the Upanishads—my morning reading before meditation during this period—it dawned on me that Radhakrishnan had a much better intellect than mine and, my intuition told me, he hadn't had a final breakthrough. I finally admitted to myself that no refinement of my intellectual understanding was going to solve the problem. I knew it was time to try something else—possibly getting direct guidance from a "felt" connection with the downward current from my source—but I didn't know how to go about it and didn't seem to have any tool other than my intellect to work with.

IN A VERY MOVING DREAM with my childhood friend Paul in early April, time stopped, and the final frame in the scene was like a still picture which I observed from outside myself. There had been occasional dreams in the past where I was in a body that wasn't Art Ticknor, or where I was a bodiless observer, but this one was different: I was looking at Art Ticknor from in front of him—i.e., facing him (no-face to his-face). I didn't realize this at the time, but this was another example of how my self-definition loosened up in dream consciousness ahead of the process in waking consciousness.

BOB C, DESPITE HIS BUSY LIFE, continued to put a good deal of effort into communicating with me on things spiritual. It occurred to me one morning that an example of guidance from the downward current may have been when something led me to ask Bob to be the spiritual adviser for the Pittsburgh group as well as for me personally last October. There was an element of knowing, of faith, and of surrender involved. I suspect the downward current knew that Bob was nearing Self-Realization. It may also have been the downward current that inspired me to suggest the email confrontation group using Pulyan correspondence, which triggered Bob's awakening.

We had an amazing TAT meeting in April 2000. Over 30 people attended including Bob Cergol, Shawn Nevins, Bob Fergeson, Jim Burns and Mike Conners. My favorite time was listening to an informal exchange by those five comparing notes on what they'd found.

But by the end of the month my state of mind had flipped back:

- Living seems to be a chore.
- I'm just going through the motions out of some sense of responsibility.
- There's no joy, and none expected.

- This attitude is tied into a change since learning of Bob's and Shawn's realizations a couple months back. (Could I be picking up something?)
- I seem to have lost inspiration for the Pittsburgh meetings and retreats, relying on a backlog of ideas for topics, etc.
- The old longing for love has come back, but with no hope that it could find satisfactory resolution.
- I feel directionless, with no internal point of reference for becoming more self-honest or retreating from untruth.
- I feel myself shutting down, withdrawing, wanting to disappear.
- Have started reading fiction again, which I haven't had much of any taste for in many years, for distraction. (Robert B. Parker detective mysteries.)

I FOUND ANOTHER JOURNAL that started as a writing journal for weekend meetings in Pittsburgh on Saturday, April 30, 2000 and somehow ended up with other entries scattered between then and 12/19/03. So I'm going through this journal now, adding material from it where relevant. Here's an entry from the 30th, which resulted from an exercise we did to just write non-stop for 10 minutes:

What's on my mind? Two things have caught my attention recently that I'd like to explore in more detail. One is a comment in an e-mail from Shawn on self-honesty: "think through your desires and where they take you." This email arrived on April 24th.

The other is a dream which occurred on the night of the 27th. In the dream, Richard Rose was speaking directly to me about me, giving me advice (which he never did) to remember that, when I'm caught up in longing for ideal companionship, I'm away from my natural state.

This longing for love is something that I saw last August was like a hold-out in my commitment to spiritual values—and at that time I made a decision to "burn the bridges" and not accept love if it came around. This led to months of no conflict, but the desire for love resurfaced recently.

So—thinking about Shawn's email and his conclusion that persistence and self-honesty were the key ingredients leading to his spiritual realization, I think I've got the persistence—but have to wonder about the self-honesty.

I don't feel like I've found a point of reference from which to judge when I'm being honest with myself and when I'm lying to myself.

The idea that love will provide happiness makes no sense to me intellectually, and yet it's apparently a keystone in my emotional conviction. So there seems to be a lack of self-honesty in this conflict. Is there some way to "think through" this desire and see where it leads? Is not having done this a clue to lack of self-honesty?

One of the things that I've just begun doing is trying to "go into" feelings when I'm experiencing them, not analyzing them intellectually but "sinking into them." When Steve H. mentioned the trapped feeling he gets when cornered in a non-philosophical, non-directed social conversation—a feeling I get, also—I was somehow able to go into that feeling and see a composite picture or gestalt about the psychology involved and how the inability just to relax and be at ease is a way to prevent seeing things about myself that I don't want to see.

Another writing exercise, this one on June 10th:

1. "I am..."
I am full of hatred for these writing exercises. Okay, not really hatred—more like loathing—well, not really loathing, more like fear. But this is just fluff commentary to get myself started.
I am superficial.
I see my mental pattern as wanting to grasp the concepts of things and not pursue deeper understanding.
I am effort-averse.

I always look for the easiest avenue to pursue an objective (or, especially, to avoid through procrastination).

I am negative in my view of myself. Maybe in my view of the world as well. I seem to focus on my "negative" qualities and characteristics rather than the positive one(s).

I am deeply shocked when somebody sees or projects a negative quality on me that I don't see in myself.

I am getting old. I am beginning to think of myself as an old person.

I am narcissistic.

I am always saddened (indicating surprise) when people I want to like me don't see what a wonderful person I am. Wonderful? How can someone who focuses on his negative qualities expect people to like/value him? Must be a huge dishonesty somewhere here.

I am running out of descriptors.

I am just letting myself keep writing.

I am overly concerned with what others think of me.

2. "I am not..."

I am not a brave person.

I am not proud of myself.

I am not able to relax.

I am not self-disciplined.

I am not able to let myself indulge in pleasure.

I am not liable to avoid certain types of pleasures (and therefore thank God for not providing the opportunities).

I am not a spiteful person.

I am not a forgiving person.

I am not a generous person.

I am not going to live forever. I hope.

I am not having an easy time putting words to this line of thinking.

I am not a "happy camper."

I am not making progress.

I am not satisfied with anything.

I am not about to try to change things. (I always try to twist myself into acceptance of the status quo.)

I am not—blank—I was thinking I am not comfortable (getting warm and feeling air-movement-deprived).

I am not able to accept what I see as unfairness.

I am not a risk-taker.

I am not artistic.

I am not a glad-hander.

I am not optimistic about the future.

I am not paranoid. Maybe not enough so.

I am not concerned about being betrayed by others (this idea doesn't compute). I feel that we all have the "wiring" to betray.

I am not at all happy with my physical manifestation / body.

I am not at all happy with my mental manifestation / body.

3. "I love..."

I love, in descending order, ice cream, food in general, alcohol, caffeine, chocolate, etc.

Seriously, I love myself.

After that comes anyone who inflates my self-importance.

Strangely enough, I still love my long-ex-wife, although I seldom remember she exists. I have a feeling that if I don't cut the knot of self-misidentification, we'll end up together again in the next bardo.

When I started watching the "Three Books of the Absolute" video[1] last night, it reminded me of my love for Mr. Rose. Of course that is really ego-centered: I love him for what he did for me (and others)—lifting me out of the swamp I was mired in.

I can't say if I loved my parents. I didn't think I loved them as much as I should have.

I *really* loved my kids, although once we were separated physically I've seldom felt as close—so the "love" must have had a strong physical component—maybe like a hypnosis that needs frequent refreshing by suggestion (seeing, touching, etc.—appealing to the senses).

I seem to be capable of feeling love for another person only when I sense the feeling is mutual.

I love—well, I think of myself as capable of being a loving person, but really it's more a protest of being lovable.

I love seeing other people happy.

I love doing things that make other people happy. But I don't want to make myself unhappy in the process.

I love the—can't think of the next thing that wants to be said.

4. "I hate..."

I hate to think. I hate not to think (at least I imagine so, never having tried it—you know what I mean: I have tried not to think, but I've never not thunk).

I hate self-righteousness. Hate may be too strong a word, but it irritates the hell out of me—literally, sometimes, when I feel compelled to poke someone in the metaphorical eye who

---

1   A video about Richard Rose put together by a TAT Foundation member.

triggers this response in me. Why am I so offended by self-righteousness? Probably because it's something I don't want to see in myself.

I hate it when people tell me I analyze too much. What do they know!? I like Harding's comment on how no one else is an authority on the inner-me. But I digress—this is about hating.

I sense a reluctance on my part to admit hatred—I want to soften the view and see ... irritation (what's the word I'm looking for?).

I hate "it" when people take advantage of weaker people—it seems to me like some cosmic law is being broken. Probably an indication of how I as "creator" think the cosmos should be, more so than a reading of how it is.

I hate the demise of beauty that occurs as people age. There's nothing more beautiful than a baby—well, after a few days, anyway.

I hate having people tell me what to do. This takes the form of wanting everyone to live in a Libra-induced dream of harmony and cooperation.

I hate how slow this 10 minutes is going. I'm beginning to think Anima must have forgotten to watch the clock.

I hate being hungry.

I hate waking up during the night.

I hate having to wake up in the morning.

I hate getting near-sighted.

In July 2000 Shawn suggested I create a website on Hubert Benoit's teaching. I think he had just gotten tired of me spouting Benoit all the time, but I actually started working on it ... teaching myself the HTML programming language and sketching out a site design. Nice to have a project to keep the mind stimulated.

Had a surprise visit with Paul S. yesterday. He was driving B. to D.C., where she is relocating. We got together at Mitchell's restaurant and talked for a couple hours.

Shawn stayed here Sunday and Monday nights, going to the Pittsburgh meeting with me on Monday, July 24th. Regarding my commitments made during the December isolation (e.g., to surrender to the Lord in thought, word and deed): he asked me if I had translated them into words that can be acted upon in my daily life. [No.] He said he eventually developed the yardstick of *searching for that which was unchanging;* what he could see as changing, impermanent, could therefore not be what he was looking for.

No journal entries from the one on the 31st until September 7th. I had experienced strong sexual "attack" for most of the month before the Labor Day weekend TAT meeting and men's retreat. Began a practice of *doing nothing* for some time each day, per Bob C's recommendation during our Saturday confrontation session at the TAT meeting. Managed to do it for an hour two days, forget it two days, did it one day, forgot it for three, did it for one ... then no more mention of it. I was unable to forget my anxiety. "Underneath" there seemed to be a river of sadness that I don't want to deal with. On September 23rd I cried while transcribing Rose's "sitting on the banks of the Ganges" paragraph on between-ness for the upcoming farm retreat (Oct. 7th-8th). First time anything had moved me recently.

Shawn drove up to Pittsburgh with me on Sept. 30, 2000. We did a writing exercise on urgency at Anima's and Sharad's, with each person reading what they'd written, and then we asked each other questions. When it was my turn, it felt like the first time in years there was some inner change during a meeting. Something shifted my view, and I was able to reaffirm my commitment to become the truth at any cost (internally voiced) and realized I was ready to come out fighting again, which I announced to the participants (the aforementioned plus Gary H. and Keith M). Only four of us showed up for the Oct. 7-8 retreat (Cecy, Anima, Sharad and me). The girls and the guys partnered for an accountability experiment to run until the next weekend retreat, planned for Feb. 2001.

I think you get the idea, that my focus was more on group work than on effective self-inquiry. Another way to look at it might be that the group work kept me focused on the problem. It probably carried out, to an extreme, Rose's advice to find others to inspire if you can't inspire yourself.

Irreconcilable?

A friend wrote:
   While reading your book [Solid Ground of Being], I ran across the question "...have you made an unshakable resolution to know yourself to your essential core, regardless of the cost?" I typically react to this kind of question with a great deal of reluctance to answer yes or to actually make that kind of commitment. I finally asked myself what the hang-up was. Basically, I've got mental doubts whether there's anything to find, and so I'm reluctant to get too emotionally involved. I can't really know whether Enlightenment isn't just wishful thinking in reaction to the fear of death. I also don't feel like I trust that something like 'seeing I'm not the body' isn't really 'hoping I'm not the body because I don't want to die'. The parent (mind) sees risk and doesn't want to let the child (heart) get too involved since it might be let down in the end.

   The problem to me seems to be this: If there's any Truth to be found, it will take an unshakable resolution to get there. My mind sees reason to doubt whether there's Truth to be found, and so I can't seem to give my heart over to such an unshakable resolution. If there is Truth, that's the only place to find certainty, and so the mind will always have doubts until Truth is discovered.

*These seem irreconcilable. How can you make an unshakable reso-
lution to find Truth when there's reason to doubt that there's any
Truth to find? Did you ever run into this sort of reservation in your
own search? If so, how did you deal with it?*

It's good to scan the interior horizon for those holdbacks. Often
they can keep us from getting into trouble.

So it (always?) comes back to the question of what we want
... what we "really, really want" as Douglas Harding used to
say.

When we find that we want something with all our heart,
then we realize that no cost is too high to pay ... regardless of
whether the pursuit is successful. We know that there's nothing
else we'd want to dedicate our lives to.

There was a song sung by Nat King Cole that was popular
when I was a kid, which started out like this:

> When I fall in love it will be forever
> Or I'll never fall in love
> In a restless world like this is
> Love is ended before it's begun
> And too many moonlight kisses
> Seem to cool in the warmth of the sun
> When I give my heart it will be completely
> Or I'll never give my heart....

When we truly fall in love (as opposed to infatuation)
there's no holdout ... nothing expected in return. When we give
our heart completely, it's because we've touched our deepest
desire. The inchworm has let go of the leaf and is in freefall.
He has no guarantee that he'll survive. But as the hard-headed
(and, I expect, soft-hearted) Kabir wrote, it's a win-win situation:

> *I have staked my body and mind
> To play dice on wager with my Love.
> If I lose, my Love wins me
> If I win, He becomes mine.*

Love is not an unshakable resolution. It's one's heart's desire being manifest. We don't think ourselves into love. It's not rational or logical.

I was never convinced that Truth was possible. Logic told me there was no reason to conclude it was ... or wasn't. I just knew at a feeling level that it's what my heart desired and that nothing else, no matter how beautiful, could satisfy my longing. Logically I knew the only true satisfaction had to be beyond time, beyond limitation.

❧

Conventional Practice?

I do everyday zazen 1/2 hour at home and 1 hour meditational fluting (called Sui-Zen). I am inquiring if I shall take up conventional zen practice again as there are here in the Netherlands enlightened masters of Zen.

Productive meditation questions our self-beliefs. The questioning may include thinking analytically and feeling feelings, but the primary data comes from looking. When you wrote: "I do not know what I believe myself to be" [in response to my previous question], that's an honest start. Then we can either wait in hopes that life will expose the beliefs, or we can try to accelerate the process by investigation.

There's a natural progression of investigation from the exterior to the interior. If we intuit that we're not the body, the next step within is thoughts/feelings. If we intuit that we're not our thoughts and feelings, we may still believe that we produce or influence them. Are you the thinker? Do you influence thoughts? What about decisions ... are you the decider? The final arbiter who controls his actions ... or should be able to? What do you feel/believe is in your sphere of control?

At some point we have to become our own authority. Douglas Harding frequently emphasized that fact. We have to "look for ourself" (and look for our self).

Regarding "enlightened" teachers: We might have considered Harding enlightened—and Harding might have considered himself enlightened—after his satori experience at age 33. But based on the time I spent with him and what he told me about his life, I believe his ego death occurred when he was 77. The term enlightened is a loaded term, like God, having different meanings to many people. What settles the soul, so to speak, is knowing what we are at the center of our being. That knowing is not within the mind's capability & occurs only when the final faulty belief about what we are dies ... and we view the mind, and all life, from above/beyond the mind.

I remember reading a biography of Gautama Buddha's life, which described how there were many teachers claiming to have the final answer then, as now. And many people hunting gurus, as now. Gautama stayed with a series of teachers until he arrived at the view they were espousing ... but knew it wasn't enough and moved on. I think that's a useful model to consider. If a particular Zen teacher, or a baker or candlestick maker, appeals to your intuition, then work with that person until you get what he's got ... and see if it's enough. If not, move on. There's obviously a good deal of subjective evaluation involved in any spiritual path ... and a limited amount of time, so it's important to find ways to improve the intuition.

Richard Rose encouraged seekers to form groups and work together, firmly believing that either a teacher would develop from within the group or the group would attract a teacher. That is precisely what happened in the TAT Society.

Guessing vs. Looking

A friend wrote:
When I asked myself what is the I, the answer "me" came up. Changing one word (symbol) for another doesn't seem very productive :)

So looked at the feeling behind it and it points back to the subject (in here looking out at the objects out there).

But I've also come to the intellectual conclusion that I'm not the subject, because I'm aware of the subject/object.

So what's aware of the subject/object?(guess: awareness, whatever that might be) And where is it located? (guess: everywhere, because I can't track the looking to anywhere specific like I can with the subject(unless the subject/object are one)).

That seems to be what I come back to and bang my head against from different angles.

The intellectual conclusion that you are not the subject makes no sense ... is absurd ... denies the "observable" internal facts. If there's a view, there's automatically a viewer; if there's an object in the view, there's automatically a subject that's viewing it. This is a tremendously uncomfortable position, since we feel that we're that viewing subject and yet can't "see" or "know" ourselves. So you try to avoid that uncomfortable admission of not knowing by jumping to an intellectual conclusion: Oh, yes, I'm not the object and not the subject but the all-knowing awareness above them.

The answer doesn't come by guessing but by looking. The subject/viewer is always "behind," out of view ... and moves behind you again no matter how quickly you try to turn around and see yourself. You can isolate the viewing location into two relative positions: looking out and looking back at what's looking out. When you're conscious of looking from either of those two relative positions, you can also note what is in the view from that position. But what's in the view is never the viewer.

"Just don't know."

Thank you. I wonder how many times you have to drag me back to this...

The sitting meditation practice has been established, but I'm not consistent in what I do and how.

Have printed this mail, will (1) feel the longing/pray, (2) read the mail, and (3) try to "look" and "not know".

When you sit down to meditate, sit like a mountain ... slow down (ask yourself if you're in a hurry) ... sit like a fellow sitting on the bank of the Ganges for 40 years....

❧

Attitude?

S o is it attitude, is it hard work, is it luck? ... I continually feel that my spiritual path is one of hurry up and wait. Do this, try that. If that doesn't work try this. It's not what you do but that you do something, but you must meditate and conserve energy. But wait, what's with all this effort? That's my problem, too much effort :) Oh well, at least I get to vent out my frustration. I feel better now.

Attitude? Hard work? Luck? The truth is, we don't know.

If you stand by the door long enough, it may open.

If you knock loudly enough, it may open.

If you pound hard enough, it may open.

The door is behind you; you're looking away from it.

The door is already open, but you can't see it.

The non-self cannot see the Self.

The non-self is all that is knowable.

The doorway is the threshold between the knowable and the Unknowable.

The Unknowable cannot make the transition known.

The more we realize that the Unknowable is what we desire,

And the more we lose our desire for the knowable....

Frustration is good. Action increases frustration. Spiritual action = questioning. Questioning occurs both by thought and feeling.

Doing Zen

W e had an interesting meeting in Pittsburgh Monday night. With the universities on break, I didn't know whether we'd have much of a turnout (which is always nice in a way, since it allows more time to spend with the few regulars). I started the meeting off different than usual, having the three folks who were there do a silent breath-counting exercise for five minutes. While we were doing that a few more people came in and sat quietly until we'd finished. Then, while I gave a short spiel, which I seldom do, a few more people came, so we ended up with ten of us—including two new people and two who haven't been around in a while. The talk I gave followed this line:

- Zen (the term) comes from a Sanskrit word meaning concentration or focus.
- If you were watching yourself count breaths silently, you were "doing" Zen.
- The ultimate purpose of Zen is self-realization, or knowing your true, present identity with full awareness.
- That's also the goal of this self-inquiry group. Intentional self-inquiry incorporates "Zen."
- To know your present identity, you need to be in the present.
- "Doing" Zen or self-inquiry = learning to be in the present.
- The poster for the meeting has the heading: Who in the Brain Is Looking?
- Scientists try to study it from the outside. Zenists/self-inquirers look for it from the inside.

I could have added, but didn't—which was just as well, since it might have obscured the point I was trying to get across— that our true identity is not found within the mind. We find our identity by transcending the mind, which is in fact within our true self, not vice versa.

Are You Sure?

F *irst of all, I consider yourself as Truth without ignorance....*

If we pick up the Genuine in another person, we're really picking it up in ourselves—but we're not yet ready to accept the implications. Thus, when the student's ready, the Guru appears, as the old saying goes.

I'm almost sure that space-time, although infinite, somehow, is already known, recorded, everything on the manifested universe has already happened (which may be paradoxically, cause it's infinite, and we cannot know the infinite all at once) from an Absolute perspective every occurrence is already known, so the sage realizes that, and he knows everything that would happen, and, therefore, his life would become boring cause there's nothing new for him to discover, for a sage, everything, i mean, time and the transformations which seem to take place on time, become monotonous and uninteresting because he knows them, he knew them all at once from the absolute viewpoint . I hope you understood. Please, destroy this idea, tell me your viewpoint about the complex conceptual labyrinth i created for myself.

The first time I went for a swim in the Pacific, I got caught in an undertow (rip tide). I'd never even heard of them. I panicked, swimming as hard as I could to keep from getting swept out to sea. Eventually I got to the point where my arms and legs just wouldn't work any more, and I found myself relaxing. I thought "this is it," but I had no fear (surprisingly). I then got a vision, a life review, where my life was laid out as if on a two-dimensional surface over which my discarnate observation traveled. The review progressed from early memories to more recent ones, and I had the conviction—although seemingly not the curiosity to explore it—that I could go down any of the side-branches and view any of the memories in as much detail as I wanted to. I have no idea what the elapsed time was, but the review ended as awareness "came back into my body" and felt my knees scraping the bottom of the ocean—quite a way up the beach from where I'd been swimming. From that experience, I saw that the past was laid out as on a computer circuit board— but nothing about the future.

I have the conviction that the Self doesn't know what's coming next. Even stating that, though, has to be put into the context of there being no time at our core. The Self creates this entire picture-show, but it does so in a way to keep it interesting. The Self likes a good mystery. It creates an animated Sergio-story, an animated Art-story, and 6 billion others. It (what we really are at the center) sometimes puts a foreshadowing in the story, sometimes a preview (e.g., a dream that turns out to have been precognitive). When it views the Sergio-story, it forgets itself—like the person in a cinema theater who forgets he's sitting in a seat watching flickering images on a screen—seeing the animations it has created of Sergio's friends as "other creatures" and believing "I'm like them, a separate individual, a person who was born and is going to die."

The sage finds life both dull and immensely interesting. He generally has no idea what is coming next, but whatever it is turns out to be perfect. The awe comes from tracing the manifestation back to the "impossibility" of something having come out of nothing.

(I think this is impossible to answer conceptually) How the heck is the observer linked to the observed (don't worry to speak about that)

The mind is a dimension of opposites. There can't be up without down, cold without hot, objects without subjects. When we're trying to figure out what we are—which may be the basic job we were designed for—we have to work in this field of opposition. Somehow we have to draw a tentative dividing line between self and not-self. The self is "inside." Anything in the self's view is "outside." As we introspect the mind, accidents seemingly happen, and the self's view broadens. An example of this is when we realize "I'm watching thoughts! I never knew that was possible!" Another example is when, generally after a great deal of observing our actions and trying to put together the puzzle of why we did what we did in certain situations, the decision-making process suddenly comes into view. This is the point that Krishna was trying to get Arjuna to in the *Bhagavad Gita* story: We see that we're not the doer. Eventually we can eliminate all the parts of the mind we previously identified as ourselves (thoughts, feelings, beliefs, convictions, self-images, decision-making, etc.) because they're all observable. And the self is never that which is seen. "I'm not any of those observable objects; I'm the subject, the observer." But what's the nature of this observer-self? It's as if we've run ourselves into a wall, or alternatively it feels as if we've gotten ourselves to the edge of an abyss. This wall/abyss is the edge of the mind. The journey to that point has many possible by-paths, and it will vary for each individual (each animated story).

So far, everything I've described is based on looking outward. Something has to turn the inner head around so that it looks back at what it's looking out from. Douglas Harding's experiments are designed to do that with a minimum of fuss. I think they work best for the person who is simple-hearted; the intellectually clever have many buffers to first-person, direct observation. When this turning of the inner head occurs, it's as if the "third eye" of mystic lore opens. You can see (although in my conviction, it's based on a somewhat hypnotic induction) what you're looking out from. What we're looking out from is obviously our inner self. And we can "see" that this inner self is self-aware. That realization, though, is something that the mind cannot comprehend.

What occurs from that point is unpredictable and mysterious. My feeling is that there's a built-in resistance to accepting the implications of what has been seen. Depending on age, conceptual understanding, and probably other factors, accepting or admitting the truth is going to be more or less traumatic. "I see that what I'm looking out from, what I really am, is self-aware. But wait a minute, I'm the thing that's observing that." That's the final quandary, the final sticking-point. The Real Self is still identified with the Sergio-story or the Art-story at that point. When that false-identification finally breaks, the conviction that the self is a separate thing, even such an abstract thing as an observer, is broken. At the core, there is no observer and nothing observed. And yet the self-realized "person" now knows that—knows that he doesn't exist. Try to compute that with the mind!

Can you tell something very brief about the relation, or equality of knowing and being.

Bernadette Roberts became a Discalced Carmelite nun around age 17. She reported a conversation she had with her advisor, a Carmelite priest named Columbanus, shortly before that:

> Father Columbanus: There will come a time when I will not be around to help you, but just remember, there comes a time in everyone's life when they must stand absolutely alone and squarely face their own misery and nothingness.
> BR: So I am nothing, so what? I already know that.
> Fr: To *know* you are nothing is very different from *being* nothing!

Knowing is within the mind. Being is Unknowing.

A last question: when self-inquiring, there aren't conceptualizations, and i feel as if the tactile sensation of my head or brain is progressively disappearing, as being absorbed/sucked by a black hole. Of course it's metaphorical, but does it seem as the description of inquiring in a correct manner? First energy moved as toward the root of the nose, then somehow to the right temple, there staying for a time with a whirling movement, then to other part of the right side of the head, and then to the left temple, and then to the higher part of the left side of the head, where it's now it this kind of things normal?

Self-inquiry begins with a question, requires direct looking at the mind, and successively reveals false self-identification. There's no formula for doing this, although the best raw material is what Richard Rose referred to as "afflictions to the individuality-sense." The source of all our problems is the conviction of being a person, an individual, a separate thing. And that conviction gets lots of buffeting by life. When one of those shocks occurs—such as a rejection, or shame/guilt at exposure of a lie we've been telling others (or worse, ourselves) about this is the kind of person I am—it's a grand opportunity for getting a little wiser. Until we get really thick-skinned, though, we can't do much self-observation while caught up in the emotional reaction. So we start by going back to those painful moments in childhood, or far enough in the past where we can review (not think about) them without getting swept away.

As for energy movement within the head, from nose to temple, etc.: Are you sure—based on your first-person, direct observation—that you have a head?

Energy

"Energy can only be channeled in one direction."
Richard Rose, from *Mister Rose: The Video*

I like the comment about energy being channeled in only one di-rection, with you as the receiver. It provokes thought though. I still feel that the channel needs to open back to the Source as well for him/it to hear you.

Life and death: energy (life) flows from the source through the organism to the earth. The organism is like a hose. The organism's "operating system" is programmed, arguably, for species survival. The individual is not going to survive. But the program doesn't prevent the individual from becoming conscious of its source—the highest form of spiritual endeavor.

The organism doesn't intentionally channel life-energy toward death. But that default flow of energy through the organism can be intentionally redirected, in some degree, toward self-discovery.

I May Be Wrong

My books have been my teachers and my path started out from a bhakti or devotional point ... prayer, chanting, yoga, then moved toward looking for a tradition ... ACIM, Hinduism, Buddhism, Taoism ... .but I never got stuck in any of those places, I just took what I needed and moved on. Then came the specific teachings on awakening, specific practices such as meditation and watching my mind, these being the two things that brought about "experiences" ... unity, satori (as best as I can tell based on what I've read), even two out of body experiences, which I didn't try to have nor have I ever tried to repeat. Although I chased the satori/unity experiences for a while, I quickly realized the suffering that it caused ... now, I don't really even want to go near bliss/nirvana because what goes up must come down.... I never had any difficulty understanding Tolle's "presence," and was imme-diately drawn to Bob Fergeson's "listening attention," Nisargadatta's

"I am" gave me pause several years ago, but last winter I revisited and found it less confusing ... self inquiry, however, was a different story.

I tried self inquiry a couple of years ago, Ramana style, preferring the "what am I" rather than the "who" ... explored "where am I," "when am I '... took the advice of Adyashanti and Jed McKenna and looked at my intent for doing all of this and then began a more serious round of inquiry starting with what I thought I knew "I exist" ... hang in there with me, I'm getting close to a question! ... So this is what I tried to go back to the past several days of driving around Virginia ... and I hit the same wall I always hit with self inquiry ... you can start with "I exist" and tear both sides of that statement down (from the point of "I" who, what, where is it, or from the point of "what does exist mean to you" and the bottom line is "I don't really know" ... and even when you come back to "I exist" ... I really don't even know that ... but I feel it!!!! I went back to those old favorites, "am I the body, the mind, observer/observing/observation question" and I went in the same circles and came to the same conclusion ... I DON'T KNOW anything for sure ... but I feel it!

I can see how self-inquiry would confound [analytical] minds.... But for someone who doesn't question the "how" of things, someone who feels their way around this ... I'm having a hard time even putting this into words ... how can a mind be broken by this line of questioning when I readily admit/intuit/know that all answers are basically "unknowable"...? Or is that just a cop-out?

"I exist": yes, a self-evident feeling (I-amness).
Existence = standing outside of (Latin, ex + sistere)
"The world is your oyster"
You are not in the oyster world...
You see into the oyster world from beyond it,
Which is possible only if the oyster is open at some spot
The I-amness feeling may be that spot.
Awareness is the light illuminating (and maybe creating) the oyster world.

We retraverse the ray of awareness from the conscious I-amness,
Backing up from that which is seen,
Finally turning around, looking into awareness (individual consciousness of awareness)
Losing our resistance, the hypnotic identification with what we see, with mind-movement,
And finding ourselves back Home.

Self-inquiry is a way of disillusionment aimed at finding the self; bhakti is a way of disillusionment aimed at losing the self.
All self-inquiry has a bhakti component; all bhakti has a self-inquiry component,
And the two paths merge at the end.
Truth = Love, and Love = Truth.

The mind doesn't need to be broken.
We just have to lose, momentarily, once,
Our identification with the mind.
It will come at a point of surrender.
Depending on what's left for us to hold onto,
The mind opens to a new perspective.
When there's nothing left for us to hold onto,
We become aware of our true state of Being.

I don't believe that it's possible to develop a recipe for this awakening.
I believe the transition from knowing to Unknowing will always remain a mystery.
I may be wrong :-)

"What should I do?"
Be true to yourself:
Follow your intuition,
Pray to your inner self for help,

And get out of the way.

One of the best ways to do so may be to find a few others to help, to bring up to your current rung on the ladder.

"A rising tide lifts all boats."

[Your name]—identification with a body-mind self—is the problem.

Have you read Alfred Pulyan's "The Penny that Blots Out the Sun"?[2]

Interview Questionnaire

'm looking to create some fresh content for the European group website that we need to build in order to attract new people, keep it going and make something out of it.

I'll be doing a few e-mail interviews for starters… [Questionnaire attached. Responses are below.]

---

2   See the October 2004 issue in the archive of the *TAT Forum* magazine (TATfoundation.org/forum). That and other articles by Pulyan are also available at SelfDiscoveryPortal.com/.

Could you also append a recent photo of yourself that has not been published elsewhere?

What was your life like prior to starting seeking?

What I'd describe generously as semi-conscious seeking began when I "woke up" as a college senior to the boring prospect of working an 8 to 5 job five days a week for the foreseeable decades. Over the next 10 or 12 years I experienced periodic identity crises, as I thought of them, where I'd be flooded by feelings that my life was missing some purpose or meaning. But I would scan the horizon for what might fill that hole, and nothing that I could conceive of sounded satisfying.

What got you interested in seeking?

My wife and I had taken our kids to the local library one rainy Sunday, and she spotted a poster that she thought I'd be interested in. It was for a Zen group meeting at the local university. It took a full year before I finally got to one of their weekly meetings, which took place when classes were in session during the fall, spring and winter academic quarters. The group had formed when Richard Rose gave a public talk at the university a few years earlier. When he attended a couple months after I became a regular participant, he rang an inner bell I didn't know even existed. I credit that bell-ringing with an awakening of my intuition to the prospect of finding what I was looking for, within.

As seekers, we often notice, but cannot get over our delusions or beliefs. Were there any particularly traumatic or funny ones that stood out on your path?

As Charlie Chaplin was quoted as saying, life is a tragedy in close-up and a comedy in farshot. When I was seeking to find my true or real self, I was pretty much stuck in close-up. Every illusion or delusion that got popped lifted a weight from me, but I don't recall any that were particularly traumatic or funny. I was a rationalist, though, and thought feelings were something to deal with (as opposed to something simply to feel), so I'm sure that helped obscure the reactions I felt to those belief balloons popping.

During your seeking, what did you think the path was all about?

I was tremendously fortunate in having a teacher who'd been all the way down the path, so I didn't have any pie-in-the-sky fantasies about the path. I knew it would take determined effort with no guaranteed payoff. But I also felt rather sure that I would not regret a life dedicated to searching for my real self regardless of whether the search proved successful.

Looking back, what would you say the path is all about? What is the work that is to be done? Can we gauge progress?

I'd say that the path to Self or Truth or Reality is subtractive, shaking off or seeing through faulty beliefs that obscure the truth or prevent us from accepting the truth that is always in plain view. Those faulty self-beliefs keep us asleep to the truth. The work is to wake up. There are a few discontinuities along the way that we see in retrospect as milestones. While we're on the path, though, it's difficult to gauge progress. After 25 years of effort I went through a period of feeling like I was right back where I'd started. Fortunately I had some friends whom I was working with who could provide contradictory views.

What advice would you give out to someone just starting on the path?

The only thing I can say for sure that's needed is determination to keep going even though there will likely be periods, maybe lengthy ones, of discouragement. And then keep going even when you get to the point of seeing there's nothing in it for you.

Some teachers say it's all quite simple and obvious, which we today know best as the neo-advaita. What is your view on this type of teaching?

Any belief is a potential trap.

Was Art changed by the path, by the final event, or both? What happened to your suffering?

Art's pretty much the same, although he can afford to feel his feelings deeply these days since there's no threat of extinction hanging over his head. He knows that he never really existed :-) He's still programmed to continue existing, though, and possibly every cell of his body shares that programming. Art—the bodymind self—still feels pain and pleasure. I am beyond or before or behind movement. There's no suffering where I am.

You often mention that as a seeker you were more linear, logical, rational. Looking back, what is the place of rationality on the path?

Most seekers, I suspect, lean either toward feeling or toward rational thought as their weapon of choice to try to get what they want from the world. Franklin Merrell-Wolff, a very rational guy, concluded that Buddha was the world-class teacher who had been the most balanced between the two extremes as a seeker, that Jesus was primarily on the feeling side and Shankara primarily on the thinking side. Using both thought and feeling would be great, but I suspect that most of us will stay pretty much in one rut or the other for most of our seeking.

Intuition is what I believe determines progress. Intuition shows up somewhat differently in feelers and in thinkers. My advice would be for thinkers not to be afraid of intuition and for feelers not to believe all feelings are intuition.

You are known for your skills in seeing the blocks of seekers and confronting them without too much fuss. What is the method of confrontation all about?

The best confrontation is self-questioning. Our faulty beliefs mostly fly under our radar, so it's hard for us to get them into view for questioning. Working with friends can accelerate the process. Most of the helpful confrontation probably occurs by accident.

What do you know for sure? What is enlightenment? Are you sure?

The only thing I know for sure is what I am. Enlightenment is an open channel between the self-conscious mind and Awareness. The individual self of the bodymind recognizes that its existence, as the word literally means, is a "standing outside of" its core being.

What is death?

Human death is like a faster and more interesting version of the death of a boulder.

What are you?

I am what you will find as your "original face" before you were born.

Why do you teach? How do you teach?

I'll take refuge in what Richard Rose said when I asked him that question: "I can't help myself ... it's an obsession." He had a dry sense of humor that I've never seen surpassed. The best explanation I can come up with is the same thing that seemed to move me along the path: momentum. I started leaning in a direction and couldn't stop. My attempts to help other seekers seem to be more of the same: stumbling along in the hopes that something will work. Another, prettier, description might be: faith. A more vanilla description might be: it's what Art's programmed to do.

What would you say to a seeker that despairs of ever finding what she's looking for?

That's a good position to be in ... as long as you keep on with the quest. Working without any hope of reward is the final stage of the path. Be thankful if it's quick or easy, but don't expect it to be.

What/where is the truth? Is it far away?

The Truth is that which is beyond reach by any except itself.

11. Conviction State Revealed

*M*y old state of mind must be back [I wrote on Nov. 2, 2000]. I found myself reading from *Talks with Ramana Maharshi* this morning and finding inspiration in the words—the first time in what seems like a couple months or longer. And with the old state of mind, a great feeling of sadness: Is this the longing for Home?

What prevents people who come to the Pittsburgh meetings from jumping in with both feet? So far, the only one to have done so in 3 years is Anima. Once a person does so, what prevents self-definition from becoming the #1 obsession? [I didn't have the answer to either question.]

Shawn N. wrote a great challenge in the November TAT newsletter:

- You will not get serious until you exhaust, see through, or simply ignore your distractions.
- Every day offers you opportunity to laugh at yourself and turn from the ridiculous and untrue.
- You are at all times utterly alone, without security or certainty.

I inquired and saw the following distractions/untruths that I lived with:

1. That somewhere there exists a person who can provide what's missing, whose constant love will elevate me into 7th heaven.
2. That when I find that person, or that person comes along, then I will no longer be utterly alone.
3. That such fulfillment offers the best chance for completion, in that it doesn't require any effort on my part (and is therefore more likely to occur than self-realization).
4. Of course the probability of personal love lasting for the duration of my lifetime is miniscule.

Why am I willing to hold out hope for a shot at the impermanent and superficial?

It dawned on me sometime later that the four items were
actually convictions that characterized my most prevalent state
of mind.

I WAS PLANNING (early-stage research) on taking a vacation in
December rather than doing a solitary retreat, somewhat in response to Bob C's suggestive question about when was the last
time I took a vacation just to get away by myself. (Never.) The
preceding is what I wrote in the journal on November 19th, but
actually when Bob said he thought I was getting too comfortable with solitary retreats and suggested a vacation instead, it
was like a gigantic spring was released inside me.

I recalled from my earlier sojourn in Tampa that Clearwater,
on the gulf coast, was the prettiest spot I'd seen in Florida. I
decided to head there first and then maybe fly over to the
Bahamas, where I'd taken my son Chris for his 19th birthday

many years before. The upcoming vacation [I wrote] is heading toward putting myself in the lion's jaws and seeing what happens. I also recalled a dream from April where Mr. Rose told me: "The longing for ideal companionship is keeping you from your natural state."

I checked into a hostel on Clearwater Beach when I arrived late the second afternoon. The next day I went to the Y in nearby Clearwater for a swim and had an instant mutual attraction with someone I met there. We ended up spending the night together, and I felt that we got as close as it's possible for two human beings to get. It was superbly beautiful and also incredibly sad. It reminded me of something Bernadette Roberts had written, that when we experience something fully, we don't need to repeat the experience. I knew now what she meant.

One thing for sure, the two- or three-week vacation got me out of my analytical thinking mode. I doubt if I did any of that for at least six weeks. On the 28th I realized that I no longer held the conviction that somewhere there exists a person who can provide what's missing, whose constant love will elevate me into 7th heaven, etc.

THE DEPRESSION MOOD or state of mind started to settle in at beginning of March 2001. I thought I was going to miss the March 5th Pittsburgh meeting due to a winter storm, but it missed us. I didn't feel like going, but it turned out to be the best meeting in a long time. There were nine of us, including Sharad (now a regular), Akilesh (also started coming regularly), Michelangelo (graduated from Pitt; on a return visit), and Harsh (CMU grad student). Five of us went to the Kiva Han coffee shop afterward and stayed until they closed at 11.

I proposed an effortless meditation experiment at the end of April. Nine people agreed to participate: Steve H, Alex, Rob W, Todd, Michelangelo (in Italy for the summer), Vince, Christina

C (post-doc researcher in Alzheimer's at Pitt, from Ireland), Sharad, and Akilesh.

THE DANGER OF IDEALS (I-DEALS): I started to see what a gigantically selfish vector my search for love/approval had been. It's almost like I created an ideal companion and projected this composite picture on fitting strangers along with intense desire for their love/approval. The underlying conviction may be: the only way for me to become okay is find approval in the eyes of the ideal

A secondary pattern developed when I met Rose: the ideal of the enlightened man. Unlike the earlier ideal, which I was convinced I could never become, here was an ideal I could aspire to within myself. But the pattern of seeking approval from the ideal (although not love; a step forward, maybe) reasserted itself and became an obstacle.

SHAWN N. RECOMMENDED that I attend a Douglas Harding workshop scheduled for the Raleigh in October 2001. Todd, Anima, Sharad and I registered for it. A little later K.W. (newly married and relocated to Louisville), Vince, and CMU student Jeff C. also decided to go.

I began rereading Merrell-Wolff's *Pathways Through to Space*, finding great inspiration this time and seeing things I hadn't seen in 1980. (I'd changed!) Regarding meditation, he said that all his attempts to quiet the mind directly were unproductive, but he realized there was a way to abstract the subjective moment, the "I AM," from the objective manifold or process. By *ignoring thought*, it becomes like a subdued harmonic and, remaining active, allows the personal man to share in Awakening. [I didn't learn how to do that, but it's exactly what happened with me in May 2004. Although I don't credit Merrell-Wolff with being a primary teacher, I think my mentality was more like his than like either Rose's or Harding's.]

I learned on October 7th that Douglas had been ill (he fell during the August gathering at Salisbury) and had canceled his trip to Raleigh. He was then 92, and I'm pretty sure he didn't make any more visits to the US. In addition to the seven of us named above, Kiffy P, another CMU student, had decided to go, so that was a disappointment.

From a writing exercise on October 27th: "What is my calling?"

> I agonized over this for 10 or 12 years after graduating from college. I found myself with all the things that should have made me happy—career, family, material comfort—but it wasn't enough. Something—meaning or purpose—was missing. But with everything I considered, I could project it out to completion and realize that wasn't "it."
>
> Then I met Richard Rose, and he rang a bell in me—and a great new vista opened: that all answers lie *within*, a direction I hadn't guessed at or intuited was even possible. My calling then appeared—don't know if simultaneously or sometime shortly after: to find / become the Truth by going within.
>
> As Ramana Maharshi said, the solution or answer to any problem is to see who has the problem.
>
> My calling was calling me....

Todd, Anima, Sharad and I had scheduled a "no nonsense" session with Shawn at my house for Saturday, November 3rd. With the cancellation of the Harding workshop, I suggested we expand the Nov. 3rd meeting to an overnight get-together.

When I asked myself what I honestly wanted from the meeting with Shawn and friends, what came into my head was *a last supper.*[1] I never had any personal expectation from meetings other than hoping that someone would get some inspiration for action. Why not expect the maximum? Suspend disbelief.

---

1   The "Last Supper" poem that formed itself in my mind appears in the first chapter of *Solid Ground of Being.*

Allow for crushing disappointment. Open my heart to possible infusion of Love.

Isolation/Vacation 2001: Whereas last year I headed south—straight into the hedonistic lion's jaw of Florida—in hopes of finding whether I was living an honest life, this year I wanted to spend some time in a solitary retreat before making a trek to Florida to get warmed up for the West Virginia winter. I had considered several options for isolation, all of which seemed lacking, until I lit on the idea of trying Myrtle Beach, SC. I thought it would be diverse enough to allow for walks without generating conversation or concern on the part of the residents, fairly deserted at that time of year, and provide cheap lodging. I chose the economy motel from the AAA website that was the farthest south on the Ocean Boulevard, the El Dorado, and got an efficiency room with kitchenette at $150 for a week. It was clean, quiet, and they had an enclosed, heated pool that was long enough to swim short laps. It was sunny and in the 70s when I arrived (December 7th) then turned chilly on the night of the 9th. The beach became almost deserted, so it was great for taking long, undistracted walks.

Reading Merrell-Wolff spurred me to consider ways and means, which had always been a weakness in my search. He described discrimination as the act of rigorously distinguishing between Self and not-Self, and he said that the practice of discrimination has the value of a dehypnotizing force. While sitting silently on the morning of the 11th, a feeling of determination to fight through to the Truth arose—maybe for the first time. A realization followed, which was the need to weigh all thoughts and actions in terms of whether they support this primary objective.

While reviewing the journal, which started at the beginning of the year, I came across Shawn's question regarding whether

I'd translated my commitments into words that could be acted on in daily life. No … still.

The week went by really fast, and I left Myrtle Beach on Friday the 14th for a 12-hour drive to Sandy B's in Pompano, on the Atlantic coast of Florida. After staying with Sandy for a couple days, including a drive we made to Miami to say hello to Steve and to check out the old neighborhood, I headed west to the Gulf side and checked into a motel on Treasure Island, just south of Clearwater Beach, on the 17th.

WHAT DID I ACCOMPLISH in 2001? I answered the question in my journal on 1/5/2002:

- Externally: I made some new friends on the path, which is always a joy.

- Internally: I finally, after a couple decades, got past my conviction that wholeness or completeness could come from outside—i.e., through prefect friendship or love.
- This realization seems to have disrupted the *feeling* for why I was pursuing self-definition.
- Looking back to the time when Mr. Rose awoke the sleeping inner man, what I was looking for was *meaning* or *purpose* in my life.
- I can see now that this is probably the same drive as that for wholeness or completeness through love—maybe one more the emotional part of me and the other more intellectual.
- Anyway, I seemed to have lost the "intent"—or the words to describe the intent to myself—for why I was pursuing self-definition.
- I knew intellectually that it's the only thing that makes sense; but emotionally, or at a feeling level, I seemed to be adrift.
- Whether this was a "negative loss" or a "positive loss" (i.e., an accomplishment), I wasn't sure.

"ASPIRATION"
Written 1/18/02 for a retreat weekend:

Yes, it's embarrassing to say it,
But the only thing I've ever really wanted was love.
My dreams of love have taken many different forms
And have provided great joy.
And yet—the joys have always embraced sorrows.
Momentary union with the beloved is not enough.
What perfect love means to me—
And thus my aspiration—
Is for the sense of separation to depart
Forever.

"Credo (I believe)" written at the 1/19 retreat:

(Well, to get started with something)

- That I'm tied up in knots

- That I'm powerless to do anything about it
- But that it's up to me to do something about it
- That I'm a separate being
- And yet I doubt that it's the essential truth
- That no one else can help me
- And yet I've received immeasurable help from others
- That I'm lost
- That all will be well
- That no one likes me
- That I don't like myself
- That I like almost everyone I meet
- That I'm a surface-skimmer, not looking deeply into things
- That life has been good to me
- That I'm always going to be the way I am now (despite all the evidence to the contrary)—meaning, I guess, that I assume this state of being will continue on indefinitely
- That any form of immortality I can think of would be painful
- That oblivion offers the only conceivable end to unhappiness
- That I've done the best I could in my actions, but there are some things I would probably do differently if I found myself confronted with the same situations now
- I don't know why I'm doing what I'm doing

From Francis Thompson's *Hound of Heaven:* "I sought no more that after which I strayed / In face of man or maid...." I've been convinced more than once that I could say the same, but the seeking returns in refined form or recurrent form. Rumi: "Be like melting snow: Wash yourself of yourself."

A couple weeks elapsed. Have been under a prolonged attack, having little peace of mind for a few weeks. Don't remember seeing this drawn-out attack before.

Was very moved a week ago by Merrell-Wolff's "Nirvana" poem. It may have brought me to the doorway. Decided later to memorize it—as a way of letting my soul sing: speak it at a Pittsburgh meeting. Received an invitation to give a talk on Richard Rose at the Theosophical Society in Pittsburgh on 4/28. Will recite that poem for them as part of my presentation.

"THE UNKNOWN GOAL"

The mind perceives
And the mind conceives
        Of objects, things apart
        Sorted into abstract categories
        And then segregated from all other objects:
                This thing, and everything it's not.
This mind likewise conceives a self
        That conceives,
        That does this sorting
        That's separate from everything it's not:
                Subject versus objects,
                Viewer versus viewed.
But for this sorting and separation
        To take place,
        There needs to be a background,
        A space with no objects —
                Like the table on which the pharmacist
                Sorts out his tablets and capsules,
        A space void of objects
                A blank sheet to hold printed symbols
                A silence to contain sounds.
"Felt dimly in the soul,
"By world-man unconceived"
        To use Merrell-Wolff's opening lines.
"Unknown Goal of all yearning...."

A writing exercise on Saturday 2/16/02, "What is where I am?" based on a quote from the *Gospel of Thomas:*[2]

What is where I am? Thank God I don't have to *think* about this—it would be like the headache balls (wrecking balls)

---

2   Sayings from the *Gospel of Thomas,* selected by Douglas Harding in *Look for Yourself:* "You examine the face of heaven and earth, but you don't know what's where you are."

that one listener described as the effect of Rose's "Lecture of Questions."

So all I have to do is just let the inner talker talk, and then transcribe whatever he says to himself.

What is the question again? Oh, yeah, "What is where I am?" Where I am seems to be a blank space, an unknown background that is watching a moving mental picture show. The strange thing is that this camera is aware of the watching—which means it's somehow aware of itself.

But how can something be aware of itself? Does this mean it has split itself into a watcher and a mirror?

What is where I am? A question asking questions? The mind skitters away from going deeply into this question. What feeling does it generate?

In front of the feeling is a mental response: Save it for later…. Then an argument: "Too disruptive to go into now" vs. "Wimp!" "Not ready to upset the status quo," vs. "But I want to go into it…."

And here's the beginning from a 3/2/02 writing exercise, a reaction to the *first pillar* of Zen: "A special transmission outside the scriptures":

Well, this immediately disgorges feelings of inferiority, inadequacy, long-suffering fatalism, and all that sort of good stuff.

My teacher Richard Rose said that he had "picked up" (as in shop-lifted :-) the technique of transmission of Mind from a Zen master who worked primarily through the mail, Alfred Pulyan. Rose described the mental dynamics of how a person who had realized his Oneness with the Absolute could bring another person to the same realization.

"Gosh, this is great," I say to myself—I can use up the entire 10 minutes "explaining" rather than having to communicate something about myself or my way of thinking, which might expose me to ridicule or rejection :-)

Bob F, who was in town and staying at my house for the April 2002 TAT meeting, sat up talking with me until around 1:30 AM despite knowing that he had to get up at 7 AM to get to the airport for his flight back to Colorado. At two times the "current" became strong as we sat in silent pauses at the kitchen table. The first time, my mind hovered on the image of me as identified with a hand at the end of a ray (as in the Egyptian *Aten*) versus my memory of an image of something bigger than myself, at the end of a long string, as the source of my awareness.

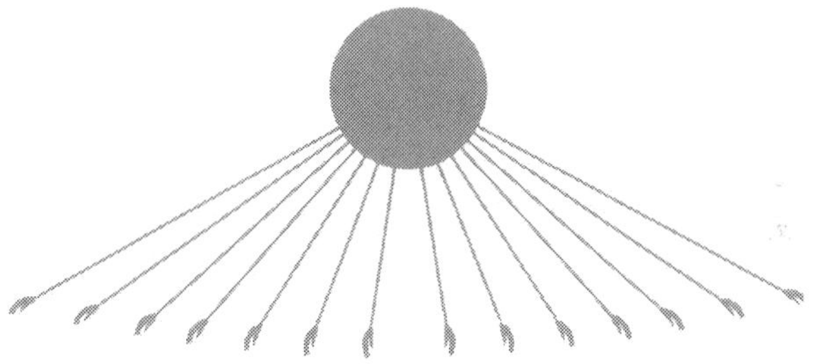

The second time, I realized that everything I knew was impermanent and would perish. Therefore, I had no argument with Pulyan's assertion that nothing of me will remain—which brought on a neutral (i.e., not emotional) curiosity about that which is not (or might not be) impermanent.

I should have been happy: Five of the people from the Pittsburgh group, four CMU students and Anima, now in Houston, came to the TAT meeting at Wheeling Park, and one of the students had gotten a new lease on life: five days "clean" (i.e., celibate) and sober (drug- and alcohol-free), as he expressed it … and wanting more. Yet my mood after everyone left and I was again by myself in my house was irritable. I figured this had to do with an oncoming sexual attack, which turned out to be the case, but fortunately it didn't last long.

At the end of April I decided to start morning and evening meditation with the following intention: active concentration on a belief or conviction, with consideration of its opposite (e.g., thought vs. no-thought), and passive (admitting that I don't know) listening for an answer in the morning; review of where my life is going, and feeling what my heart longs for in the evening.

ON THE MORNING OF MAY 1ST, I asked myself: What would I say if I were to give a presentation without quoting authorities?

1. This has been my life-experience....
2. These are the things I've experienced personally (excluding all the reading and other "hearsay")
3. These are the things I've experienced directly (mini satoris)
4. These are the afflictions to the individuality sense I've experienced
5. These are the most unforgettable things I've experienced
6. These are the experiences I value most highly
7. These are the lessons life has taught me
8. These are my current beliefs
9. These are my unanswered questions

7 Lessons life has taught me:

- Conviction states can flip dramatically
- "Chief features" can change, or maybe vary with conviction states
- There may be (probably is) a permanent center
- What's being sought can't be found in the mind
- Acceptance/completion can't be provided by another person
- The goal of all yearning lies within

#8 Current beliefs

- I am a separate unit of awareness lodged in this body.
- This awareness-unit is attached to its source by a long umbilical cord.
- It's possible (due to the testimony of people I've known well) to lose the conviction of identity with this seemingly

separate unit and become identified with (i.e., one with) a permanent center or Source.

- All my efforts to do so are absurd, but not trying to do so is even more absurd.

#9 Unanswered questions

- What will happen to my I-amness at death?
- What is the opposite of mind/I-amness?
- What is the real nature of the longing for love (a.k.a. removal of separation)?

A week later I wrote that the morning and night sittings had been continuing every day. Hadn't made any inroads into feeling (articulating) my innermost desire, though. But I realized when I wrote this week's accountability report that the articulation has gone past love, and past oblivion, although loss-of-self aspects still apply. Now it's closer to losing the limitations of self. (Note—three new people have joined Anima, Sharad, Todd, Jeff and myself in the email confrontation/accountability reports: Josh B, from NY; Shane M, from Cork, Ireland; and Carla P, from Calgary, Alberta. Two more people joined within the next few weeks: Ligia from Porto Alegre, Brazil, and Bob R. from the Philadelphia area.)

5/25/02 writing exercise—"Dreams of Perfection" or "What is your life a search for?"

> … I don't want to write about the topic of what my life is a search for since I'm at a point of diminishing clarity about it—I feel I know what it used to be, and that motivation is no longer primary, but my mind hasn't been able to formulate the new-and-improved version.
>
> Which I guess leads back to the first topic, dreams of perfection. This is when I get out the world's smallest violin and play sad melodies on it :-) I don't remember ever having dreams of perfection, assuming as I did that "myself" was something damaged and not fixable, so the only option was

just try to adjust to the status quo—like living out a life sentence in prison.

But recently I've had the desire to take off the clamp and allow dreams of perfection to become conscious—although I haven't yet succeeded in seeing or catching any of them.

Shawn suggested in mid-June that I go to Andrew Cohen's October weekend retreat, to check him out. Shawn had met him briefly in Austin a couple of years earlier but hadn't had any conversation with him and was curious what my impression would be. I was planning to go to Jerry Katz's October retreat in Nova Scotia, but it had been canceled. So I decided to go to Lennox, MA to check out Cohen [I wasn't impressed.].

Had a good meeting in Pittsburgh on 6/17 with nine people, three of whom were new folks including a CMU grad student from Amsterdam, Vince C. Seven of us went to the Kiva Han afterward, including Vince, and two more people joined us there, including Edward W, a CMU undergrad who attended for the first time the previous Monday meeting and had just arrived back in town from a relative's wedding in CA. I sent emails to Edward, Vince, and Sai (Indian grad student at CMU) after the meeting. Heard back from Vince saying he liked the meeting and would come again.

Had a good Saturday meeting with seven folks at the Kiva Han on 6/22. Edward came and brought a girl friend who goes to school at Amherst and is teaching in Pittsburgh for the summer. Vince C. was there, as was Pete, who came but left around 5. Kerri came after Pete left, wanting to avoid him. Surprise shows by Akilesh and Manuel. Vince had to leave around 7. The remaining five of us (minus Manuel) went to the Thai restaurant down the street after the meeting, eating and talking until about 9 then chatting on the sidewalk until about 10.

Toward the end of June I found myself starting to pray for the first time in many years, maybe the first ever. The prayer was: Please let me live a Heart-centered life, not a mind-centered one. The impetus was the sense that my life may have been approaching a turning point or fork in the road—one that my intellect would pursue in a definite direction but I didn't know if it would be the right direction from the standpoint of Heart/Higher Power/Blueprint of Creation.

5/25/02 writing exercise:

What's on my mind is the question of "right action." I anticipate a possible decision point down the road where I don't trust my decision-making process to lead me to right action. There's a mess of conflicting fears and desires involved and a conviction that I don't have any clear guidelines on what's right or wrong. My mind tries to evaluate right and wrong relative to a variety of limited or partial views but doesn't feel it has enough data to decide what's best even for these individual considerations. Because of this standoff, I guess, because I don't see a clear way to satisfy all the fears and desires and come up with a decision on right action that would be easy for me to rationalize, it leads me to wonder if there's right action from a bigger perspective—from the standpoint of an overall blueprint for life—rather than from the relative perspective of what's best for this "entity" and the field of its immediate concerns. And suppose there is a right action: how could this receiver be tuned to receive the proper signal? I see no way out of the dilemma. For the first few days of considering it, I found myself praying to the not-self for help. Now I've sort of subsided into an unflustered fatalism—but still hopeful that right action will occur despite my limitations.

7/6/02 writing exercise:

What's the last new thing I've seen about myself? This would have been a difficult question to answer a couple weeks ago, but when I was answering a question from Carla (in our email accountability group), an explanation dawned on me that I felt like I'm walking in blind circles again—sort of like before I met Richard Rose 25 years ago, but with the difference that I now think finding an answer is possible.

Before Rose (BR :-) I was feeling my way toward an answer but always looking in an outward direction, whereas after Rose (AR), I began searching inwardly and using more of an intellectual approach—trying to refine my understanding, to grasp an answer with my mind.

Then sometime, maybe a year ago, I saw beyond question something that I'd "known," but not admitted to myself in some way, that refined understanding wasn't going to take me all the way to an answer. Since then I guess I've been searching for a new tool to use but haven't found it yet.

So—where is this going? What's the question again? Uh ... what's the last new thing I've seen about myself ... it's this appreciation that the reason for the "blind circles" has come to some point of clarification. What's the change? Possible understanding of the reason for perceived darkness ... like a shedding of meta-light ... lessening the darkness about the reason for the darkness. Sounds like a case of the mind chasing itself around in circles, doesn't it. Or maybe like the flight of the mythical kufu bird, which Rose described as flying in ever-decreasing concentric circles until it flies up its own posterior and disappears.

I had started rereading Nisargadatta's *Seeds of Consciousness* and found the material even more inspiring this time. On the morning of 8/19 I wrote that it was even inspiring me to "attempt" meditation for the nth time. Of course the inner dialog began with: "I don't know how—need to understand how to go about it," and then a small voice said: "just do it—it's not something to be conceptually understood."

THE VARIATION ON A DOUGLAS HARDING EXERCISE that Shawn did in our retreat last January—where we each drew ourselves as we currently, actually saw ourselves (i.e., torso down to toes, maybe with a nasal tip or blur floating somewhere in front then put them together, headless center to headless center—shifted or threw into question my conviction of being the hand at the end of one of the long rays from the Sun (as in the Egyptian *Aten* disk). The individual "hands" or bodies that we drew were merely the views—individuality. The I-amness that each one of us, the viewer, felt was actually the Sun or headless center. How, I asked myself, can I follow that doubt sensation, that awe, as an entry point to become one with my true identity?

Two weeks later I read Shawn's 9/5 essay "The Natural Koan"[3] and was surprised to see that my last journal entry had been on that same topic. I then asked myself: "What is my cur-

3   Appeared in the January 2003 TAT Forum, http://tatfoundation. org/forum2003-01.htm

rent natural koan?" Scanning back over my lifetime, I saw that there appeared to be two themes: love and purpose/meaning. They'd both been more psychological than philosophical, I felt. I also felt that the "love" question had been resolved, both at the rational and the emotional levels, by my Dec. 2000 experience. It seemed as if the doors had all been tried and found lacking as far as what would prop up the ego. I found myself praying to become zero, in a feeling but non-emotional way, a couple weeks earlier. What does the Life-force want? [I wondered] and decided to pray for an answer.

- What does my innermost being want?
- What is the nature of my innermost being?
- What is the nature of the felt separation between "me" and the Source of this awareness?

9/28/02 writing exercise: "Why is my heart empty?"

Oh ... the word just came to me: "disenfranchisement" from the self. No, that's what I said before ... I don't think that's it. Anyway, the first thing that came to me this time was "knowing"—but that's really based on memory of what came to me when I was thinking about picking a topic for this meeting. The second thing that came to me today was ... damn! Can't remember. Maybe if I keep writing it will come back to me. It was an angle I hadn't really considered before. Ah ha! It was ... damn! Slippery! ... something in me doesn't want to remember. Gotcha! It was because I'm continually turning my inner head away from what is. My heart is empty because I refuse to "let go" or whatever it takes.

Nisargadatta said: "Just do it." Okay, I have no argument with that. My mind no longer looks seriously for a technique that will lead (eventually) to "just doing it." So I guess the question for myself is when am I going to be ready to "just do it"?

The procrastination is undoubtedly a fear-thing. This would have to be coupled with a belief that "no one is going

to be there to catch my fall." The old bogeyman fear that—
what?—unbearable suffering will result?

Fear of letting go of the known, which is another way of
saying fear of the unknown. Why would the unknown be
feared? This must reflect a belief that the unknown is going
to be, or liable to be, worse than the known. Where does that
belief come from? Krishnamurti says that if we look clearly
and see the lack of passion for an answer, that will reveal the
passion for an answer. Somehow the passion will have to
overpower the fear.

11/23/02 writing exercise: "What is action?"

This is a question that has annoyed me for years—I guess ever
since the initial euphoria of meeting Richard Rose inspired
me with the possibility that there was a whole new direction
for finding answers to the problem of missing purpose/mean-
ing in my life. The direction was one of "going within."

In the early years of attempting to go within, the day-to-
day frustration of effort that didn't seem to produce results
was rewarded by occasional seeming-accidents or revelations. Then, once getting the view that all "doing" went on
by itself, that I wasn't the "doer" making things happen, the
idea of action became nebulous. At that point, whenever I
heard or read anyone saying: "All it takes is pure intention,
earnestness, etc.," it would make me irritable, angry, or de-
spondent. Why? It seemed that the nature of my personality,
and of the observed workings of the mind, was anything but
consistently earnest or anything else that didn't alternate with
its opposite.

Where am I today? Seems like I've been riding the cusp of
"deciding" to take action, watching the argument or alternating moods of finding then losing intention to take action. For
example, I still "sit" for a period of meditation most mornings,
but now the sitting consists of reading a few pages (or less) of
Nisargadatta and then just letting thought drift in whatever
direction it takes. Occasionally that direction is toward trying

to identify the key question my organism is trying to answer, but there's no commitment to pursuing the answer in any methodical (or unmethodical) fashion.

So—I guess I could say I'm procrastinating. I feel that action is still necessary, but I don't see the direction that action "should" take. (Where did that come from? Sitting next to Jeff :-)

For now—and basically for the past five years—my action seems to be directed toward working with others on "the problem" rather than challenging the mind. Of the threefold path,[4] the sangha or working with others seems to be my top priority—or at least where most of my energy goes.

There is a part of me that has a deep love of Truth, but that part must be offset by personality characteristics that have strong defenses aimed at keeping Truth out. The weakest part of my threefold action has to do with the Way, or the ways and means committee, as Mr. Rose termed it.

ANOTHER LONG GAP (nearly 3 months) followed. I noted in the 12/1/2002 entry that I'd continued with the external spiritual activities, but internally "not so much." I'd been busy with the H&R Block income tax preparation course (11 weeks, 2 sessions per week with hours of homework for each session) plus Hospice volunteer work (training started at the at the same time as the tax training, followed by half-day patient visits one afternoon a week for the past 4 or 5 weeks). I had realized while responding to the email accountability group feedback that I knew the way home, and that the next step was to really look at the decades-long desire that represents this bodymind's chief feature [the desire for personal love]. Looking back, it had been a remarkable year concerning the Pittsburgh group, and personally there had been some remarkable changes, also. From an interior standpoint, though, I didn't know whether I'd made

---

4   See www.selfdiscoveryportal.com/arThreefoldpath.htm for the short treatise "The Threefold Path" written by Richard Rose.

any progress—other than increasing uncertainty, which I took as a good sign.

Who Are You Trying to Please?

*W*hen I was a young child I wanted to please my parents. I don't recall feeling stressed about it, probably because I felt secure in their care.

As I grew older and went to school, I wanted to please my teachers. Again I felt no stress since pleasing them came easily.

As a teenager, though, life became more complex. I still wanted to please my teachers, but there was more pressure now with the variety of teachers and subjects. And there was a new element: wanting the approval of my schoolmates. Winning that approval was more abstract and demanding, with a pervasive pressure to intuit and conform to unarticulated expectations.

Life seemed much easier when I was out of school and raising a family. I was back to the easier-to-comprehend task of trying to please authority figures—now the boss at work and the wife and children I adored at home. The need to win peer approval was no longer part of the equation for me.

In the background, though, through all the changing circumstances of life a program was running whose purpose was to please itself—i.e., to weigh the multifarious fears and desires that bombarded the mind and to react according to the program's dictates. I was that program.

Sure, I identified with this ("my") body and these ("my") thoughts and feelings. They were my property, not yours. But I felt and believed that my innermost self was that decider/doer program ... until one day I saw it operating in slow motion, like an accident about to occur.

Your wanting-to-please history is probably like mine in some respects and different in others, and I suspect you have a similar behind-the-scenes program that you've felt, and may still feel, is your innermost self. But since you're at least marginally aware of its operation, it's not the essential—not the aware—you.

Living life to please or appease that program is like worshipping your pituitary gland or the hypothalamus that controls it. Sure, it regulates much of your body's functioning … but is it your innermost being?

A Meeting of the Minds

Is that the closest we can come in life—a meeting of the minds? So terribly bittersweet…

We can come closer than the meeting of the minds like I experienced with the young Navajo man and the older Apache gentlemen that I wrote you about earlier. I've experienced having one set of thoughts and feelings that two minds were sharing (with another male) and I've experienced one mind (with a female). Those experiences, wonderful as they are, are still views from "down here" and ultimately don't satisfy our innermost drive for X. Once you've been beyond experience … I should say once the mind becomes aware of what you are … then the beauty of down-here experience can be appreciated without the background concern.

Your intuition tells you that "beyond experience" lies the solution to all your suffering. But the mind's programming tells you, via its fears and prides, not to jump in … you'll be able to do it tomorrow … better to keep your options open, etc.

Fear of Worthlessness

he fear of worthlessness is different: it's centered around the core fear that the world could completely do just as well (maybe even better) without me around. I add zero value—my existence adds value to nobody, to nothing, nowhere. My whole existence is completely and utterly pointless. My ego thinks this is one of the most terrible things.

You'd have to view "the life of V." from a superior view to get an objective reading on his possible value or lack of value in the big picture. So I conclude this "zero value" conclusion is one of self-pity ... most reasonable in terms of that indulgence. You'll only get perspective on the value of existence as a whole when you've seen nonexistence, and then perhaps the question of individual value will look different.

Why anyone would postpone trying wholeheartedly to see that view is what I'd label short-sighted.

❄

Lo-Cal Snacks V

*W*hen that faulty sense of self that you've been desperately grasping evaporates in a puff of smoke, you'll feel relief beyond anything the mind's capable of conceiving. You are that for which you've always been searching.

❧

*M*editation doesn't produce. Productive meditation removes the impediments to enlightenment. It prepares the mind. Enlightenment doesn't come when the mind sees the truth. (It's not big enough.) Enlightenment comes when we see the mind from our true state of being.

❧

*D*o you feel a resistance to waking up, like the sleeper who hears the alarm clock and wants to hit the snooze button quickly so she can go back to the warm, comfortable cocoon of sleep? If you wanted to go contrary to the stay-asleep desire, what might you do that's outside your comfort zone?

❧

*P*ersistent trying with repeated failures is extremely instructive for us ... way, way more so than giving up or going with the flow. I'm convinced it's the unintended path to between-ness.

❧

*T*he mind-self, knowing it has a limited shelf life, procrastinates the inquiry that threatens its make-believe world.

❧

*I*n a way, which I suspect everyone who has experienced a prolonged depression knows, there's nothing as painful as hope.

🌿

*F*rom my experience, surrender and final seriousness are pretty much one and the same. The mind gives up on distraction. The resulting "final surrender" of the mind is indescribable. Language is ultimately inarticulate on this.

🌿

*A*ny contradiction to a belief about what we are can propel us inward.

🌿

*H*e who asks for more gets more. What keeps us from asking is fear. What keeps us from asking is pride.

🌿

*W*hen I was a little kid I remember going through a stage, probably one summer, where I would convince myself that I didn't hear my father calling for me to come in for dinner. The mind-self wants to solve its existential dilemma, but it doesn't want to see/hear/admit the truth. It hears but doesn't hear the call of the father to come home. It wants to come home but not just yet.

🌿

*T*he guru is a teacher who has the perspective of having died while living and thus becoming conscious of his true state of being. Challenging the guru or suspected guru is a good idea until the seeker comes to a degree of certainty about the teacher's credibility. After that it's a fool's game of the mind-self that is searching for self-realization or self-definition.

To advance, the seeker must challenge his own beliefs. He does that by becoming conscious of them, doubting them, and *looking* to see their relative or absolute truth.

"Definition requires comparison"[5]—and the guru can provide comparison.

❧

Fear Mode

My mind is in fear mode so I must get this resolved ASAP. In the workshop you led this weekend ... I did not expect to realize, feel or fess up to the emptiness inside but that is what happened. When you spoke afterward saying "Between you and me..." I had an experience that felt like our minds were on either side of a tunnel communicating directly. Did you willfully cause that to happen or is that just my perception? Was it somehow telepathic? My mind saw Art do something to the separate individual R and now there is a fear of that power over R. I suspect this might be an unresolved issue with trust in authority or perceived authority. Can you speak a little about your take on this?

And if I have a Knowing of this emptiness then why is there still separation? I suspect that with me the undoing or dissolving comes in waves and that there are some waves yet to come and go. In any event it seems to me at this point to be a process of allowing. There is a strong sense of momentum.

The mind is programmed to keep the body performing its role in the cosmic theater, and it resists seeing the truth about its status in order to do its job. The struggle to awaken to our true nature is a process of facing our psychological fears. From that standpoint, fear is our friend ... it's the food for awakening.

---

5   In my mind this is one of the central points of Richard Rose's teaching—exceedingly simple and profound.

Don't worry about me ... I'm laughably non-psychic. A real blockhead :-) I suspect that came about because feelings were overwhelming to me as a child ... and the intellect developed as a shield.

C. told me a while back that she likes Madeleine L'Engle's writing. In order to try to get a better feeling for C's mind, which I wouldn't have to do if I were more psychic, I got one of L'Engle's books from the library. In it I came across this comment by a character—the daughter of an African king who had been kidnapped as a consort for a slave trader but was now an old woman:

> Aunt Olivia: Honoria, what's the difference between magic and a miracle?
> Honoria: A human can do magic. God do the miracle. Magic make the person think the power be in hisself. A miracle make him know the power belong to God.

I'm no magician. If things happen around me, you can blame God :-) In actuality, everything in life is miraculous.

I'm in a position that everyone aspires to, which is that I have no unmet needs. I used to admire the fact that Richard Rose never leaned on a student's mind. That seemed miraculous to me then. Now I can see it goes with the territory. A teacher who isn't needy has no desire to manipulate others ... whether for his own benefit or theirs. Rose talked about it in terms of 100% friendship. I see now what he was talking about. It's unbelievably freeing.

The mind's afraid of emptiness. No movement / no noise represents death to it. It's "scared to death" of emptiness. The fear is based on the conviction of separation. That conviction has to die (i.e., be seen as illusory) before you can Know—i.e., recognize by identity—Emptiness.

When I first came into the kitchen this past Tuesday morning, I saw something that caught my attention: eyeglasses on the table there, with the scene softly lit by the glow of light through the closed blinds. I took a picture of it, and that picture was still on my mind when I was responding to an email from a friend in Georgia ... a woman about my age who came to TAT meetings for quite a few years, had a stroke at the beginning of this year, and thinks she's started the physical dying process. (She's a highly trained RN, so she probably knows the signs). Anyway, at the end of my response I wrote the following stanzas to try to convey a mood to her.

(The "I" in the poem refers to everyman.)

"Eyeglasses on a Table"

When I'm gone,
When you can no longer see me,
What of me will remain?

Nothing. Nothingness.
I will have returned to the All
From which I had never departed

Despite appearances
To the contrary.

❧

Dreamless Sleep

I'm reminded now of how you used to talk about dreamless sleep. That during that time, there is apparently no experience. Yet somehow I am. But I don't feel like I exist during that time.

J. and Art don't exist during dreamless sleep. Existence = "standing outside of." During dreamless sleep we're not standing outside of BEING. But the mind hasn't caught on. For the mind to know what you are, the recognition has to occur when the mind is projected from the source. There's some testimony that it can occur during clinical death[6] and during coma,[7] but we can't very well count on those possibilities and need to pursue it during the waking state. The recognition is beyond experience but is seemingly triggered by experience. A self-inquiry practice that reminds us that we're looking for what we are at the core of our being succeeds through repeated irritation, frustration and failure.

❧

Stuck Between

I feel like I'm stuck between these two different lives that I want.

The external world presents a reflection of what we're not ready or willing to see inside. The real battle to awaken from *seeming*

6   Victor Solow, "I Died at 10:52 A.M." in the Dec. 2003 TAT Forum magazine (www.tatfoundation.org/forum2003-12.htm).
7   See "A Terrible Beauty" by John Wren-Lewis in the April 2004 TAT Forum magazine (www.tatfoundation.org/forum2004-04.htm).

to Being takes place inside, but sometimes we have to make adjustments on the physical level in order to gain mental clarity. During my first solitary retreat (at age 33) a lightbulb went on in my head, and the words that followed were: "My only hope for mental clarity is a prolonged period of celibacy." I also stopped drinking, just because I could see it influenced mental clarity. The spiritual path is a path of increasing mental health, and we basically replace less desirable habits or obsessions with more desirable ones. I replaced unrestrained sex-action and alcohol consumption with the pursuit of mental clarity. For my mentality, abstinence was easier than moderation. I come into contact with guys who feel they "should" be celibate but don't seem to have found a bigger/better obsession to inspire it, so they struggle with limited success. Richard Rose pointed out one of the great values of taking a vacation from sex, which is that no man stands tall in his own eyes until he brings the sex drive under control. It's a great learning experience, and failures may be a necessary part of our education. The path to Truth is, after all, a succession of disillusionments.

Beyond Experience: How?

ow do I get beyond experience? Everything I have ever known is experience. To get beyond experience implies that I can be, without experience. How?

There's no stairway that will take you there, but it's possible to find the way. The older sister found the way back to her home in northern Australia after the rabbit-proof fence that she was following abruptly ended in the desert.[8] St. John of the Cross

---

8   See the Rabbit-Proof Fence article in the July 2006 TAT Forum magazine (www.tatfoundation.org/forum2006-07.htm), for more details..

expressed the way, using the language of paradox in the twelve couplets that accompanied his drawing of the Ascent of Mt. Carmel. William Samuel expressed it in emotional language in his epic poem "The Melody of the Woodcutter and the King."

You already ARE beyond experience. The mind can't help but reflect the truth of BEING. When the "mirror" by which you know that you're conscious lines up to reflect the light coming from the SELF, it breaks your hypnotic attraction to the mind's movement ... and you recognize yourself.

❧

Notes from a 1982 Winter Intensive

*T*he following notes come from a journal I kept during an intensive retreat with Richard Rose from January 2nd through the 31st of 1982.

The daily schedule began with silence from 6 AM until noon. We were to be out walking when the dawn broke each morning, fasting the first three days, then tea only before noon after the initial days of fasting. Coffee and tobacco were off-limits; one smoker couldn't handle it and left. We worked outdoors from 1 to 5 in the afternoons—my main recall is of hauling huge tree trunks out of ravines and of splitting an endless supply of firewood. The farmhouse was heated by woodstoves in the living room, dining room, and a room that had been added for group meetings, where we gathered in the evenings. We usually started those evening sessions with an hour of "numbers exercises" that Rose had created to build intensity. They accomplished that, to the point where it would give me an instant headache to even think about doing them :-)

> Rose talk 1/6:

- Dawn and dusk are magical times … times of between-ness … they inspire moods ("eye of the soul") … you can get gestalts, insights
- New massive perceptions can occur during mental dawdling
- Be one-pointed in life—make life an obsession for finding out; mind will come around; revelations will occur at unexpected times
- Be aware of moments of awakening and going to sleep; encourage the nostalgia mood
- Between-ness occurs at moments of intense relaxation

> Rose 1/9:

- We're in an emergency ("the great sleep is on")
- Once you see an obstacle, you have to act immediately
- Live decisively, with a ways and means committee
- Zen: reach wisdom through an attack on vanity
- What we are is our meaning

> Jan 10: Until this point, the entire morning was set aside for silent contemplation. The new schedule: morning meditation now from 6—9, with confrontation (self-inquiry questioning) from 9—noon.

> Jan 11:

- Have to have a dream then work determinedly to create it
- The teacher must find his students; the students don't know what to look for

> Jan 12:

- If you were going into the egg business, e.g., you'd need a plan for starting out (purchasing, producing, selling) and detailed ways & means of implementing steps to build a lucrative operation
- Need a similar type of plan for spiritual work

> Jan 14:

- The success formula is very simple: Total commitment + direct all energies to ways & means (answers will come via intuition)
- Zen: no dogma—just learn how to think
- Approach to philosophy requires nonlinear thinking
  ◊ Triangulation; conciliation of opposites
  ◊ Intuition tempered by common sense
- Creation formula: imagination + will + fiat, then forget
  ◊ Surrender to that which is superior to us
  ◊ Desire only that which is supposed to happen
- Go into people's minds through what's on their minds

> Jan 15:

- Once you develop intuition, it will tell you what you need to do; then drag yourself by the rear end if necessary
- You can create vitality by getting really interested in something
- The time for books is over; just start thinking about what to do with your life
- You have to start working energetically; results depend on energy applied

> Jan 16: I've been bemoaning that I haven't had any revelations since I started on the path![9] The intensive more than half over; wish it could go on indefinitely.

> Jan. 18:

- A group has psychic protection

---

9   Which wasn't true, but the mind reshapes memory until it's highly questionable. Keeping a journal and reviewing it periodically is one of the best ways to refresh the memory with facts.

- The brain is like a coil, producing electromagnetic energy in synaptic gaps
- The mind interpenetrates the synapses
- With the synapses open, can tap into the mind dimension (see dead grandparents, unborn grandchildren, e.g.)
- Need to get to the point of saying: "I need help and I'm willing to scratch" (i.e., choose to drop ego)
- Value in exercise—learning to quicken your pace
- Value of an intensive is in resulting action
- We feel we don't need each other (superiority)

> Jan 20:

- Fear inserts itself on all levels
- Overcome fear by
  ◊ Self-inquiry
  ◊ Devotion to a higher cause
  ◊ Cultivation of courage
- Manifestations of our chief feature[10] are intricate ... require lots of meditation to see
- Hyperthyroids are not the most successful people; hypothyroids, once they have an idea in their minds, don't have a lot of other things coming in to knock it out

---

10   A term that comes from Gurdjieff's teaching. Maurice Nicoll, in his *Psychological Commentaries on the Teaching of Gurdjieff and Ouspensky,* describes Chief Feature as the governor of personality, the ruler of one's mundane self, which we have to struggle with in order to be free.

> Jan 21:

- Schizoid nature of mind:
  ◊ One part judges the cowardly part and condemns it
  ◊ Self-castigation becomes an excuse not to change
  ◊ To overcome this, stop confessing and start taking aggressive action
- The best confrontation is indirect—a simple question; otherwise, mental shutters slam shut
- The mind doesn't want to review the past to look for mistakes; memory blanks become an excuse for not looking
- Have to go back over our experiences and honestly evaluate errors [in order to see where corrective action was needed]

"I've been celibate for over 3 years but don't see any particular increase in mental clarity. In fact, I characterize myself as mentally dead—no curiosity and a singular inability to look at myself. Tremendous frustration with meditation, which results in drowsiness most of the time. It occurs to me that these traits may be manifestations of a fear (cowardice) complex. Since I detest myself for being passive and cowardly, I cannot afford to look at myself honestly; recognition would threaten the status quo." [Objective analysis or self-castigation?]

> Jan 23:

- A variation of the creation formula: To know, to dare, to do, and to be silent
- "Becoming" is becoming undistracted
- Progress is being attentive to what you're doing

> Jan 25th speculation: How does one go within? Apparently, through eliminating distraction ... by being attentive to whatever you're doing.

> Jan 27: We began doing the numbers exercises[11] in the morning as well as in the evenings. [I think we did these most if not all evenings during the month.]

> Jan 28:

- Just 3 days left ... nothing dramatic yet, but I feel I've gotten the direction I came seeking
- Rose: Study ways and means of success & all the factors that may impede success

> Jan 29:

- Our situation is hopeless ... except we can:
  ◊ Will to will
  ◊ Desire to desire

---

11   Richard Rose had put together a packet of sheets with mental exercises such as adding two numbers together, beginning with 2-digit numbers then moving to 3-digit ones, repeating long strings of digits, and answering occasional questions in the midst of the numbers exercises. We would split into pairs, with one person reading the exercises and the other person giving answers—each sum or repetition had to be accurate before moving on—and then switch roles.

- Everyone's chief feature is sex until that's overcome

> Jan 30, 1982—last day of the intensive.

- I felt like a different person than the one who came to the intensive
- My primary determination is now to fight my way out of ignorance and help others do the same

Generic Advice

$\mathcal{T}$rying to reduce instruction or advice to the seeker of Self to the least misleading minimum, here's my current attempt:

1. Remember/feel your deep longing & make it your underlying priority.
2. Review your actions to see if they're congruent with that priority.
3. Adjust your actions accordingly.

Meditation & Celibacy

$\mathcal{I}$f you find that thought stops in meditation, it might be wise to pause the intentional activity or allowance until you have thaumaturgical[12] protection. Richard Rose believed it

---

12   The thaumaturgists or alchemists of the Middle Ages were often priests who practiced chastity with more or less success. They also experimented with invoking intelligent entities to assist with their investigations. And they found, presumably by trial and error, that entities couldn't take over their minds if they had been sexually chaste for a minimum of 28 days. Benvenuto Cellini, a 16th-Century Italian goldsmith, sculptor, painter, soldier and musician, included a fascinating description of invoking entities in the Roman Coliseum in his famous autobiography.

was necessary for thought to stop before self-realization could occur. A friend and predecessor down the path to self-definition told me that thought had stopped several times for him, but nothing spectacular resulted from it. He also got to a point where he said he'd run to the end of the meditation trail and stopped meditating. (I don't know what his exact definition of meditation was.) I thought what Rose and Huang Po were talking about by stopping thought was the complete cessation of mental movement, but I believe that this friend thought it meant the cessation of conceptual thought, not perceptual thought. In other words, the picture of a tree could hit the mind, but there would be no ensuing labeling, no bouncing of the precept off memories, and so on. I don't recall any event where all mind movement stopped, but I found it easy and humorous to stop conceptual thought by rapidly turning the inner head from movement ... resulting in something like a pendulum swinging back and forth rapidly in the most minute arc.

Rose defined meditation as productive thinking. This was obviously not at all like Ramana Maharshi's advice just to sink into the heart. Productive thinking would be encouraging the mind in its work at solving "the" problem (as defined in 1-2-3 above). Since we can't control thinking directly, it would be done by the technique Rose outlined in *Psychology of the Observer*, or a personal modification of it, of turning the head away from thoughts that aren't relevant to that objective. That's the kind of meditation I practiced. I would sit for an hour, and eventually got to the point where turning the head away from irrelevant thoughts would go on for 50 of those minutes at most.

Once in a blue moon I would find the mind meditating spontaneously. That was always wonderful.

12. The Last Straw: Looking Until You See

*I*f you look long enough (or listen closely enough) you will intuit your relationship to what you're observing. That's the basis of the spiritual path.

"Wow," I wrote on May 7th, 2003, "it's been a long time since my last journal entry. Same as I'd written in my journal last December 1st, although this time the lapse was nearly six months rather than three."

I think there had been some flip in my mood or mental state. I recall communicating to friends that I'd fallen into a "neutral" mood—one where there wasn't any apparent internal conflict. One of them suggested that it might be tied back to the death of my first hospice patient. He was a guy just a year older than me who'd been diagnosed with "failure to thrive" (sounded like a primitive diagnosis to me) and was running out of time when I started spending an afternoon a week with him so that his wife could get a break.

"Failure to Thrive"

Ron was a gentle, considerate man—
A private man whose body flipped a switch
    and failed to thrive for no apparent reason.
Like me, he hadn't really accepted the reality
    of death.
I wonder if he had any
    final moments of clarity,
    of knowing what he was not.

Since Ron there were two other hospice patients who had come and gone, and a strange thing happened during my last visits with both of them. They were sleeping most of the time, and I just sat quietly for several hours without talking with them or reading to pass the time. My mind relaxed, as it had only done in solitary retreats previously. Even recalling that would bring the experience back to a degree, producing a mental calm in contrast to my mind's ordinary, somewhat frenetic, activity.

The core group that formed in Pittsburgh after more than four years of meetings was getting ready to disperse. Anima and Sharad would be moving to Houston in two months, Jeff had moved to Louisville, Edward to New Hampshire, Kerri stopped coming after Ed and Jeff left, and Ben would be moving to Germany after graduating. Kiffy and Dan would be back as junior and sophomore undergrads, and they were talking about getting a place together to treat as an ashram.

As I was writing my accountability report for the week, I saw a parallel between my decades-old desire for no-distance between self and other and the flickers of realization over the past year that I've never developed a feeling-connection to the source of awareness that I'd seen in the isolation vision years back.

I HADN'T DONE my typical December solitary retreat in 2002 due to the H&R Block tax preparation training. I had planned on going to a Harding workshop in France in June, but his health had deteriorated and the workshops were put on hold. I'd written to Merrell-Wolff's granddaughter for permission to include some of his writing in the TAT Forum, and she'd invited me to their annual reunion at Lone Pine, CA over the Memorial Day weekend. I'd asked whether there was any place nearby for a solitary retreat, and she said one of the houses on the property could be available, so I made plans to consolidate the trip to see what the FMW people were doing with an isolation retreat.

Kiffy and I flew into Las Vegas and drove a rental car across Death Valley to get to Merrell-Wolff's "Great Space Center" outside Lone Pine, at the foot of the Sierra Nevadas, for nine days of solitude in our respective locations before the weekend activities.

I made attempts to isolate the "subjective moment" (a FMW phrase pointing at experiencing the sense of self, like the instantaneous backward glimpse in the Harding exercises) ... and once, after a few days, I was sitting in the sun after trimming grass along the driveway and moving the hoses used to water the poplar trees, looking east across the Owens Valley toward Death Valley, when the thought came into my head reminding me to remember the subjective moment ... followed by the thought, "Thank you, Lord." I was really thankful for that experience. In the past I would probably have wanted to hold onto it, but not this time. Later I found myself praying, telling the Lord that my mind is weak but that I really wanted to come home. And sitting out after sunset, I had an intense moment of thankfulness for being there.

FMW wrote that: "Happiness is the only worthy prayer." It was a rare prayer for me :-) And: "For all men there is somewhere the easiest and most direct Way." [I pray you find it.]

Had another dream as a disembodied observer.

I was up before 5:30 every morning, in time to watch the sunrise … a never-before and never-since period. It was as if something wanted me to, and I overcame my inertia in order to comply. I had the feeling that the Lord would provide everything I needed for Awakening if I just put forth the effort to overcome resistance.

Jeff and Ed flew in for the weekend.

My deepest life question? Maybe: "How can I find true love?" Bob C. suggested that love, to me, might be something I'm trying to add to myself, to "fill in the gaps or compensate for the flaws, or allow you to love yourself and allow others to love you, etc."

Jim Burns's pearls of wisdom at the July TAT meeting:

- Ask yourself: "What is the most important thing for me to think about at this moment?"
- Give yourself the ability to *be* the answer.
- "Knock, and it shall be opened." Give it enough time.
- Draw yourself up to zero. It's a problem of the animal: the body/mind are afraid to be still.
- The key was finding that I should not try to direct my awareness. I had to let the Light within me direct me to the Light within.

I had started a writing exercise: 10 minutes per day for 7 days, free association, on "feeling." I only found entries for the first two days in that notebook. A summary of the 7/21 entry: Feeling "happiness is just out of reach" and "resignation." Feeling recalled from yesterday: "I've forgotten why I'm here." And from 7/22: "Is there anything other than this torturous sense of separation? This sense of 'I am a separate creature' is untenable—to the point where oblivion seems like the only desirable long-term solution.... Would like to just shut down & go into permanent sleep."

AUGUST 19, 2003. Well, a strange thing just occurred: I no longer felt trapped inside my body! I'd been working on adding a section to my web site, SelfDiscoveryPortal.com, about Wolff, Rose and Harding—this night on explaining their views of relative stuff such as life after death and reincarnation. Scanning Harding's writings to find if he'd ever made any direct references to reincarnation, in *Look for Yourself* he has a chapter "Let's Have an Out-of-the-Body Experience," where he goes through the progression of 1) thinking we are the body, then 2) thinking we're something in the body. For some reason I can't attribute to any particular words or concepts he used, it became intuitively obvious to me that I'm not an awareness trapped in this body and never have been—that obviously the body is inside me.

August 25. What do I really want? A comprehensive view (become the ultimate know-it-all :-) even if that view entails unknowing.

September 13 writing exercise: What would I change if I had the power to do so?

> Well, that's a good question—good in the sense that I don't have a ready answer. So what answer will come into my mind? I feel the need to keep the mind distracted so that I won't think up an answer—won't create an answer on demand—but just allow an answer to present itself. Ordinarily I would do this by sitting quietly, but with this exercise I'll have to see if part of the mind can latch onto the answer while the other activity is continuing. So—what would I change? Well, my main concern is that if I intentionally changed anything, then the fallout could be disastrous. Who knows what havoc that could cause? The main thing I'd like to change would be to leave everything in the cosmos functioning exactly as it is—including everything having to do with myself, Art—but simultaneously to become one with my source rather than feeling attached to it by a long umbilical cord (like an astronaut outside his space station). My feeling is that this would require a death of the self-concept, which would change only

what the self is currently identified with—so that while nothing changed, everything would change—the known would be unknown and unknowing would be the mode of operation.

November 12. Nearly three months since the last entry. Spent 3 days with Douglas Harding, at his home in Nacton, outside Ipswich, England during October. In fact I was there on my 59th birthday. Harding, going on 95, is amazing. One of the first things he said to me after we said hello was that my business was not to become Douglas Harding or anyone else but to become my self—the self we really are. When he found that I had a background in computers, he said I was heaven-sent. Catherine's computer had suffered a virus attack and needed to be restored. So I spent a large part of the 3 days doing that—and also tweaking a document he was working on, "A Sort of Poems."

On the second day, I overheard him saying to Catherine that it seemed as if they'd known me for a long time, in fact that I was like family. Strangely enough, I had been thinking exactly the same thing. On the second evening I asked Douglas a question that Bob C. had wanted me to relay, about grieving. Douglas said that everlasting joy is found by going "down, in and through" the pain—the son of God [the awakened griever] takes on the suffering of the world—not by going up and away from it.

On the third day, Douglas invited three of his long-time students who lived in the area to come in and do a mini workshop for me. The six of us did some of the experiments, with Douglas pairing with me for the "tube" experiment.[1] It had a profound effect, and I found myself flipping back and forth into the view engendered by it—that I was the space inside which everything was occurring, including my consciousness—frequently during my train ride to Southampton the next day, and afterward, although not as frequently since then, and generally in situations where there's a crowd. [Later, it became something I could seemingly do at will, as happens when staring at Necker cubes.[2]] This is a continuation, more extensive, of the inside-outside paradox demonstrated by the Necker cube visual phenomenon.

DECEMBER 7. Decided to start a daily discipline on 12/1 of remembering throughout the day to listen to the silence within and explore the edges of the black doorway / emptiness / unknown of consciousness.

Bob C's advice: Carve out a time each day dedicated to self-reflection and "staring back" at the purpose and source of one's life. Shawn had said at the November TAT meeting that inside knowing comes by looking "back and up." Bob had said earlier that meditation amounts, in essence, to a plea to the higher self

---

1   See http://headless.org/experiments/the-tube.htm for the Harding tube experiment.
2   Easily found on the Internet.

for help and guidance, leaving the outer man open to communication from the inner man.

DECEMBER 16TH: Started a 4-day retreat with Jeff, Kiffy, Dan and Spas (a grad student from Bulgaria). Went for a walk in town on the 17th—a vision quest.

> Trying to get some focus on a question I want answered. Nothing particular came to mind. Saw a young kid, maybe 8 or 10, dark-haired, walking along whistling—could have been me at that age. Later another boy around the same age came riding by on his bike, cheeks red from the cold, and gave me a smile and friendly hello before he was close enough where I might have said "hi" first—could have been me at that age. Later I walked by a boy probably 12-13 who was putting newspapers into a kiosk. He turned around with a big smile and said: "Merry Christmas." Could have been me at that age. After the second occurrence I thought: this is a sign, reminding me of my state of mind when I was a kid, how friendly and outgoing I was, liking everybody, etc.

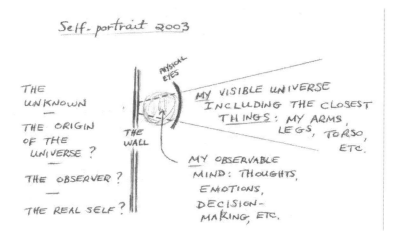

Self-portrait 2003

FEBRUARY 25, 2004: Since the last journal entry, on 12/7/03, I've made another trip to spend time with Douglas Harding—this time with Jeff and Kiffy, staying with Douglas and Cathryn from February 6-9. This trip was deflating compared with the October visit, with Douglas apparently becoming upset that I didn't react as he hoped to the experiments again done with a few of his older students that Sunday. When I said there was still too much of me in the picture, he said with vehemence: "It could only be due to pride!" and seemed to withdraw his friendliness afterward. We stayed an extra day to finish patching and re-graveling the garage roof, so at least I felt like we had contributed something in return for the Hardings' fine hospitality and Douglas's guidance.

Reading the prologue to Harding's *Little Book of Life and Death* after returning from England motivated me to really pursue the question of "What am I?" once again. Surprisingly, reviewing these journal entries 8 years later, I didn't mention that a mood had descended on me of wanting to become more serious than I'd ever been. And since I had a long-standing conviction that a breakthrough could only happen when I was isolated from people, I remember crossing my mental fingers at the time, hoping that the mood would remain until a solitary retreat that I had scheduled for May. It did ... but it was arguably the riskiest procrastination in a life of procrastinations.

THE WEEKLONG SOLITARY RETREAT, in a hermitage cabin at a Benedictine monastery near Erie, PA began on Monday, May 3, 2004. The cabin was one of three scattered along a path through the woods and, unlike most of the places I'd done previous retreats, had all the comforts of home.

I had no energy for reading or thinking during the preliminary fasting, which I cut from an intended three days to two. I recalled having done that once before and determined to stick with three days in the future.

At some point in the middle of the retreat, probably on the fourth day, Thursday, a switch flipped in me and I became my own authority. I'd heard about the necessity of that for years, but I didn't know what it meant in a practical way until it occurred. It was one of those watershed moments and, again, one I didn't note in the journal. The only reason I can imagine for not including them was that they were so obviously important that I felt I'd never forget them.

The following two days were an intense but seemingly effortless review of Harding's tests for immortality in *The Little Book of Life and Death.* I went through each one in great detail to distinguish between what I actually saw/intuited versus what I might be imagining or merely agreeing with.

On day seven, Sunday, I noted that I had been feeling antsy, which was highly unusual for me, and I also wrote that it felt like an unplanned transition day … although I was planning to stay until around midday Monday. The monastery included property that fronted on Lake Erie, and about 7:30 that evening I went for a walk and then down to the lake to view the sun setting. I came back to the cabin around 8:30 and found myself looking spontaneously back into what I look out from, as had happened several times earlier in the day. It occurred again as I finished a cup of tea and moved from the kitchen table to a chair in the living room.

I didn't lose body consciousness, but I sat in that chair without moving—in retrospect, I think someone coming into the cabin would have seen a comatose body—for maybe an hour, during which time I lost the final conviction of individuality and simultaneously became consciously what I am, have always been and will always be. I also witnessed the mind, as the open channel from its source "downloaded" way more information than it could consciously absorb. At 10:12 I made the following journal entry:

> This creature moves from the chair to the kitchen table, to record what has occurred over the past hour. His hand writes, not knowing how it knows. His memory is somewhat sketchy,

so he will see how much of what occurred comes back. I say "he," but he is really Me. Well, as real as a shadow gets. I have created this one—a tableau of events, a story—and projected it so that he thinks he's alive, experiencing events over time; experiencing his "inner" and "outer" changes as well as changes in his "environment."

One of the first occurrences in the tableau of tonight's realization was the realization that I, his newly found I, created him ("this creature sitting in the chair") and projected him. Then he thought of the nice old nun, Sister Phyllis, who's in charge of hospitality here—and realized that he/I had created her to think she was alive. And then he/I felt the love I have for My creations—and he/I felt the poignancy of that creature's belief that she is a separate being who was born alone and is going to die alone. And he wept for her. And then he/I realized that he (this creature) had really *felt* for the first time....

He/I just heated water for another cup of tea. Everything is the same and yet somehow slightly—no, extraordinarily—different. He had a thought that has escaped him, so he/I went back to stand by the stove, and memory returned it: "I can see now why Richard Rose thought he might have been crazy after his self-realization." This creature is questioning whether he's gone off his rocker, too.... This creature's brain feels like it's been fried (he thinks...).

He took his first sip of tea—and immediately realized why Douglas Harding says drinking is like pouring liquid into a great hole.

And now he's thinking about Sister Phyllis again—and how he'd like to hold her hand and tell her, "I couldn't have said this before, but God is closer to you than your breath or your heartbeat—and He loves you. You are his precious child." And this creature is crying again—he doesn't know why. (He's feeling His love.) I am feeling My love through this creature—and he weeps.

Verse from 5/10/2004:

I am always right behind you
But turn around and you won't see me
I am never not with you.
Why aren't you always with me?
I am at the center
while you stay at the periphery
I am there, too,
but you won't find me there.
When you turn round
the center stays behind you
Stand still while turning your gaze around
and look at what you're looking out of.

BEYOND RELATIVITY: You can't conceive of it, but you can go there. If you could conceive of it, it would still be in the mind dimension … an object (conception) of a subject (conceiver). Actually, you can't go there—because you've never been anywhere else. What you believe yourself to be is a thing, a relative something, which exists (literally, stands outside). But when you become aware of what you truly are, it seems like you've made a journey. All experience is seeming: We become identified with what we're watching, which appears as movement in space and across time. What we really are is what's watching, what's aware … which turns out to be Awareness, itself.

Ambrosia Dialogue

*A*s I see it, we've got two choices: we can either piddle around out here, seeking temporary satisfactions (and growing more and more dissatisfied) or go into our core/center, where we'll possibly find Permanent Satisfaction.

Q: Have you gone into the center and found permanent satisfaction?

A: Yes.

Q: Can you describe it?

A. I don't mind doing so, but what good do you think it might do?

[Your response goes here.]

We can *talk* about it until the proverbial cows come home, but to get the full flavor—and it's an either-or, all-or-none proposition—every person has to *go there* personally. Have you ever tasted ambrosia, the elixir of life, the nectar of the gods?

[Your response.]

It's *not* like meat, *not* like vegetables, *not* like ice cream, *not* like pizza. It's unlike anything you remember having tasted, but one taste of it will completely satisfy you at the most basic level forever, eternally.

Q: How do I get to my center?

A: It may require Herculean effort or heroic persistence. What are you willing to exert?

[Your response.]

It may involve bridge-burning decisions and loss of things you hold dear. How much are you willing to gamble? To sacrifice?

[Your response.]

There's no guarantee of success. How much determination can you summon to continue on and on and on if the landscape gets progressively bleaker, the doubts become progressively louder and more convincing?

[Your response.]

It may take a life-long commitment, and once such a commitment is made it may haunt you, and you may curse the circumstances that brought it about and rue the day it was made.

[Your response.]

Little Bird

Little bird
Sitting on the topmost branch of the Russian Olive tree
Chirping.
Little person
Torso, arms and legs hanging out of Me
Eating breakfast on the back deck
At dawn.

❧

Mechanics

There's a young fellow in my town who works all day as an auto mechanic, running a family business as he learns from his father, who works alongside him. What does he do in his spare time? Restores and shows vintage vehicles. The office if full of impressive trophies. He loves what he does and gets great satisfaction from it.

Many seekers are concept mechanics, equally in love with collecting, refining, and fine-tuning their explanatory theories.

The real value of concepts is seen, however, when they are revealed as faulty or lacking. And there are one or more key concepts that will stick like barnacles, preventing smooth sailing into the port you're searching for. One for me was that I defined what I was looking for as a final observer within—and I couldn't conceive of that ultimate observer as not being a thing.

❧

Zero

*M*y kids knew 30 years ago. My ex-wife and mother of our three children is from a French Canadian heritage and a family of devout Catholics. I felt it was a good idea to raise the kids in the Catholic Church, which we did, sending them to parochial schools through the elementary grades as well. At that time the Mass was still done in Latin—and very moving and impressive to me. Maybe it was just the appeal of the exotic, but it seemed to hold some half memory of my far past. (I later found that the arched walkways running along buildings of old Spanish missions in the US also had a very strong nostalgia for me.)

When the children were small, I often attended mass with them, both because of its appeal and because I thought it was a good family activity. The kids knew I wasn't Catholic, though. We never talked about it that I remember, and it certainly wasn't a point of contention between my wife and me.

I recall a remark one of the kids made, I think it was to a visitor in our home, in response to a question about my religion: "My dad's a zero," the child (I don't recall which one) said with a laugh. After that the kids and I would often joke about my zero-ness whenever the topic of religion came up.

Last week [written in my journal on 5/15/2004] I saw what my kids knew thirty years earlier: that at center I am featureless and no-thing.

❧

Struggling

9 feel like I'm giving it all I can right now but it doesn't feel like its enough and I just don't know what to do. This struggling seems to create even more dissatisfaction.

You mentioned reading "Who Am I?" by Ramana Maharshi and *Psychology of the Observer* by Richard Rose. I imagine you picked up Rose's bias toward struggling. Ramana's experience, and therefore his teaching, was less struggle-oriented. My feeling is that if life's handing someone enough trauma, they don't need to look for more. But if, unlike Ramana, we're past our teen years & find ourselves dissatisfied with what we can see coming down life's road, then it makes sense to work toward finding true satisfaction. And if we're fortunate enough to hear intuition's message that knowing the self is the only possibility of finding what we're looking for, we also find that the mind always veers toward distraction from the big problem. So we need to struggle consistently ... and that requires creating a system of artificial tension. Rose's "Threefold Path"[3] is the most comprehensive approach I've come across. The "way" involves a mental practice that's guaranteed to produce frustration (since there's no simplistic formula to follow) and the "life" involves finding and working with others (a sure-fire source of irritation :-)

---

3   See the January 2005 issue of the TAT Forum magazine (www.tatfoundation.org/forum2005-01.htm).

Ask Yourself

*W*hat is the one most important thing you think I need to be confronted with, or confront myself with, knowing me as long as you have?

Ask yourself if there's anything you're not willing to do or experience right this moment in order to be free.

No Question?

I don't have a question. I'm not sure if that's a good or a bad sign...

If it's because a "natural koan" has latched onto your mind and your mind is working resolutely to resolve it, then I'd say it's a good sign. If it's because you're not conscious of the koan your mind is trying to resolve, then I'd say it's not a good sign. No question = fully asleep; consciously working a question = starting to wake up; watching the mind consciously working a question = semi-awake; consciously self-aware = awake.

Holding On or Letting Go

I've just started meditating without a journal, remembering what I'm looking for and then watching the mind's reactions to that objective and turning away from what's not relevant.

When turning away from irrelevant thoughts in meditation, does it help to have a particular thought or perception to bring the attention back to, or is it simply a letting go of the irrelevant thought?

I think that would be an unnecessary complication.

There's no holding onto or letting go of thoughts.

The mind can turn away from unwanted thoughts & is expert at doing so for its own purposes.

Physical Dying Process

I suspect I may have entered into the (physically) dying process. I am thus feeling more pressured to pay attention. I am also feeling comforted that, although there may well never be an actual experience of what I really am, at least mind seems to have seen what it can of it. And perhaps, especially if I am wrong about this, there is still time....

What-you-are experiences comfort and discomfort through its projection of mind. It's a great comfort to the mind when it becomes conscious of what you are. However, that realization (or lack thereof) does not affect you one iota. What you are is the awareness behind all experience. When your identification with what you're experiencing is disrupted, all existential problems are resolved.

Individual consciousness comes and goes, brightens and dims, begins and ends. Awareness is the absolute constant.

The robot has become quite real to me recently, but what I see when I try to look at its source is as elusive as ever. About the umbilical cord [connecting us to our source]: I wonder if my sense of the back of my body disappearing, opening onto a living blackness, could be my version of this? (Wren-Lewis' phrase "dazzling dark" struck home the first time I read it.) This is an everyday experience now.

Your sense of the back of your body disappearing into a living blackness is the mind's consciousness of what you are. That contradicts what I wrote above, doesn't it. In addition to being conscious of what we are, the mind has to accept the implications of what it sees in order to disrupt the hypnotic allure of the outward view. In my experience after a quarter century of trying, that disruption occurred when something held my attention on the backward view until I saw and admitted the fundamental illusion of existence.

There was an "annunciation" a few months before that occurrence in which a desire to get more serious than I'd ever gotten became apparent. It was like a mood that descended. I suspect that a sense of entering into the physical dying process would be a similar foreshadowing.

Convictions About Knowing

1. Self-realization is the mind's becoming conscious of what we are at the core of our being.
2. We see the mind's enlightenment from beyond the mind.
3. There's no way for the mind-me to know for sure what another person knows about his or her true state of being.
4. Any certainty within the mind is relative. Knowing what we are is the only absolute knowing.
5. We have always known what we are. The mind's consciousness of what we are is temporary.
6. What we are is timeless ... before time and after time.
7. What we are is changeless ... before and beyond change.

❧

Untenable?

*W*hat can we do when what we've been doing isn't working, and we find our position untenable? Material for a Sunday afternoon session at the April 2010 TAT intensive, "The Center Cannot Hold."

The Center Cannot Hold....
I wonder what that means?
My mind sorts through the rubble
of it phrases and its scenes....

Uncovers something close aligned
with what old Alfie Pulyan[4] wrote
about having been in your shoes
and finding them untenably hot—

---

4   Alfred Pulyan was an unconventional "zen" master who worked primarily through the mail. See *www.spiritualteachers.org/alfred_pulyan. htm* and *www.selfdiscoveryportal.com/Pulyan.htm* for more background.

Untenable as in an outpost
that can't be held or propped
against assault, or a position
that can't be rationally defended:
Too hot to handle,
but it can't be dropped.

On the cusp of life and death,
   of happiness and sorrow,
the guillotine hanging overhead—
   there may be no tomorrow....

If you're not suffering, there's no real problem, is there? Are you in misery? If there's nothing you're longing for, there's no real problem, is there? Are you longing?

What do you do when what you're doing isn't working? The goal may be *wu wei* (doing without doing), but you can't "do" not-doing. So the strategy may be to "wind up your doing dial" and try something different ... unless that's your default strategy, in which case you may need to stick with something long enough to see results.

The Story of Sue Monk Kidd

I brought home Thomas Merton's *New Seeds of Contemplation* from the new books shelf at the library. The intro was by a 39-year-old woman named Sue Monk Kidd. She wrote that she was reading *The Seven Story Mountain*, Merton's autobiographical account of becoming a Trappist monk, when she was 29, and that it had "fairly stunned" her ... a small town Southern Baptist with "no religious orientation to the contemplative life."

She said it: "initiated me into my first real awareness of the interior life, igniting an impulse toward being that I still felt a decade later." Ten years went by. (That's the story of life, isn't it, and the typical seeker's tale. The mind wants to forget.) At 39 she visited Merton's hermitage in the woods near the Abbey of Gethsemane, Kentucky, where she began reading *New Seeds* for the first time. When she came to a passage on finding the true self, she wrote: "It caused something at the core of me to flare up and become known … initiated me into the secrets of my true identity and *woke in me an urge toward realness*" (my italics).

I assume something equivalent happens to everyone who gets hooked on "realness." A longing for the Real becomes apparent, and a discontent with the current state of being (ignorance of the Real) becomes equally apparent.

Let's try some exercises for the discontent—the malcontent, the heavily burdened, the seeker of answers, the sleeper who's dreaming a dream of the desire to awaken. *Note that, like all exercise, merely reading about it doesn't accomplish the purpose.*

Schoolhouse or Bordello?

Do you feel that life is a schoolhouse or a bordello (a house of pleasure)? If a bordello, do you wish you hadn't come? :-) If a schoolhouse, what lesson might your life-experience be trying to convey that you haven't yet "got"? [Split into pairs & discuss … or find a friend to discuss this with.]

Is your state of being changing?

Is what you consciously recognize of your true state of being changing? Has your self-definition (i.e., what you believe yourself to be) changed in the past year, for example? If not, *are you afraid of (avoiding) inspiration?* An equivalent question in emotional language might be: *Is there room for the Lord in your tent?*

Consider this example: you're following GPS instructions while driving, and a passenger says: *"I know a better way."* Do you listen to that "voice" or do you stick with the GPS? What authority are you worshipping in your pursuit of Realness? If you listened to a voice that is saying: "I know a better way," what would you do differently? [Discuss with a partner.]

A related exercise you can do by yourself: Throw the I-Ching mentally ... ask your inner self a question then watch/listen for an answer. If it doesn't pop out right away, it may come when you're not expecting it.

Do you feel stuck in your pursuit of Realness?

- Knowing the self is the way out
- Going within is the way of knowing the Self
- The way out = the way in

Where are you stuck? Where do you currently see/believe the dividing line between inside (you) and outside (not you) is? A typical progression as introspection moves the dividing line inward might be something like this:

- I'm this body; the skin is the dividing line between the world and me
- I'm inside this body
  - ◊ I'm my thoughts, feelings, decision-making, etc.
  - ◊ I'm not my thoughts, but I'd rather be dead than have no feelings
  - ◊ I'm not my thoughts or feelings, but the world would go to hell if I didn't make the right decisions
  - ◊ I'm not my thoughts, feelings, or decision-making; I'm this individual awareness

How do you get loose from identifying yourself as what you witness? How do you get beyond the separation of what you witness from what you are? ["The seer is never that which is seen." ~ Richard Rose]

Puzzle or Mystery?

I'm going to ask you to record 3 or 4 short items on the back of a 3 by 5 card or piece of paper for future discussion. [In the group session, I handed out pages from a 1997 Little Zen Calendar, which someone had given me back then and I had saved. I asked participants to pick one off the top, the bottom, or in between … but to keep the date and quote side face down & not to look at it until a later part of the session.]

The first is a choice between two words: *puzzle* or *mystery*, as defined by Gregory Treverton, a national security expert, cited in Malcolm Gladwell's *What the Dog Saw*: Treverton defined a puzzle as something we need more information to solve, versus a mystery, where we have too much info and need to see it in a new way.

Do you feel that knowing the Self is a puzzle or a mystery? (Write down your choice.)

What do you fear?

- Pair off for this exercise.
- Admit to yourself a/the major psychological fear that you experience.
- Communicate that fear to your partner.
- Partner (once you understand): What single sentence of advice would you give?
- Write that sentence down on your LZC sheet (back); do not communicate it.
- Switch roles and repeat the exercise.

What are your competing desires?

- Pair up with new partners.
- Admit to yourself the major competing desires that you experience.
- Communicate those competing desires to your partner.
- Partner: What single sentence of advice would you give?
- Write that sentence down on your LZC sheet (back); do not communicate it.
- Switch roles and repeat the exercise.

Are you being honest with yourself about what you really want?

Are you clear about what you really want vs. what you may feel you "should" want? Tap the inside for answers: Ask yourself that question, and then watch the mouse hole where thoughts appear for an answer. (Note: This is a form of prayer.)

Feeling exercise—sensation/apprehension

Feel some object near you with your thumb or forefinger. Does your digit feel the object? Or do you feel it, using the digit as an instrument?

Where do you feel the object? (This is a slight variation of the former question.) Do you feel it "out there" or "in here"? Repeat the test with your eyes closed and ask yourself the question again.

Feel one index finger with the other. Switch the feeler and felt fingers and repeat. Is it clear to you how you distinguish which one is feeling the other? Close your eyes, repeat the test, and ask yourself the question again.

Now use the index finger to feel the thumb of the same hand. Switch and use the thumb to feel the index finger. How do you distinguish which one is being used to feel the other? Is it whichever digit the attention is focused "in" that feels the other at that instant?

Some opinions:
- You "become," or identify with, the digit the attention is "looking through"
- But it's not really you, is it
- Neither one is you, neither the digit that's feeling nor the one that's being felt

How is it possible that *you* feel what the digit is used as an instrument to feel? Is it where the *outward-directed attention* is focused, is "in" or "looking through"?

Another step toward more interior looking: How is it possible that you "know" (feel, apprehend) that you feel what the digit is used as an instrument to feel? In other words, a dog may respond to an itch by scratching the offending location. But is it consciously aware that it's doing so? I don't know the answer for the dog, but for the human there's a distinct separation between subject and object, isn't there. It's what we refer to as self-consciousness (and what the 20th century India guru Nisargadatta Maharaj called the sting of the scorpion). How do we *know* that we feel what the digit used as an instrument to feel? Close your eyes and repeat the finger-thumb test. Is there an *inward-directed attention* that apprehends the outward looking?

Just as you "forget" that it's not the thumb or index finger that feels, not the eyes that see, etc., you forget that conscious attention (outward looking) and self-conscious attention (inward looking) are instruments of apprehension and not the essential you.

Feeling exercise—emotion/affect

Why are you here? A worded response may have popped into your head, but *what's the underlying feeling? Can you feel it?* Not the irritation the question may have prompted but the "e-motional" reason that brought you here. Is it because you're unsettled, dissatisfied … suffering? Is it because you're looking for something that will settle you, satisfy you … end suffering?

What are you looking for? "Don't know" is a response I've often heard. It's really the same question as: "Why are you here?" *Can you feel it?*

If you're looking for X, **you** *are that which is looking for X.* (We'll come back to that.)

Once you realize that nothing temporary is going to satisfy you … that you're looking for a *permanent* fix … you admit to yourself that you don't "know" what you're looking for (i.e., can't conceptualize it). You can feel it but like the Sharp ad for Quatrone TV technology, where they added yellow to the red-green-blue palette: "You have to see it to see it."

You'll "know" it when you "see" it may be your hope. I have a conviction that it's true … and that *it's the only "seeing" that can testify to its own validity.*

The problem is that what you're looking for is that which is looking. And you're entangled in (hypnotized by) the view.

And everything you do to try to get disentangled seems to lead to more entanglement.

- The way out is the way in
- Notice what you're looking at (seeing, feeling, witnessing)
- Look at it sufficiently until you know whether it's what you're looking for
  - ◊ *This generates detachment from the view*
- Remember that you're what's looking
  - ◊ Not the instrument
  - ◊ Not the digit
  - ◊ Not the outward-looking or backward-looking attention

Toughen up or soften up?

Where we come from, the place of eternal harmony, lies within. If it weren't "there" we wouldn't be "here" for even a nanosecond. It's the source of all, the void from which the cosmos depends (hangs pendulum-like) ... with you at the center of the cosmos (maybe not in quite the way you think).

Void is a seemingly cold, colorless word. Home could also be labeled Love, Truth, or Being. The return path — climbing the pendulum's cord — could be described as a path of, or to, Love, Truth, or Being.

How do you get there? Consider a flock of sheep. The individual sheep is going to die. If it knows that, it can run around in circles, catastrophizing, dying of hunger and thirst. Or it can curl up into depression, dying of hunger/thirst. Or it can believe (pretend) that everything's going to be okay and it won't really die.

What if an angel (messenger) appears to the sheep and says to it, in sheep's language: "Fear not" (which is how angels are supposed to open their messages). *"Fear not. The Lord is thy shepherd, thou shall not want...."* Will the sheep make room for (i.e., allow guidance from) the shepherd? Or will pride or fear prevent it from following the shepherd?

Is there room in your tent (your heart) for the Lord (the inner self) to guide you back to Love-Truth-Being? Do you need to toughen up (face fears) or soften up (face prides) in order to make room for the Lord in your tent? [Break into pairs; discuss; each person record "toughen" or "soften" on the LZC.]

Normal vs. power-law distribution

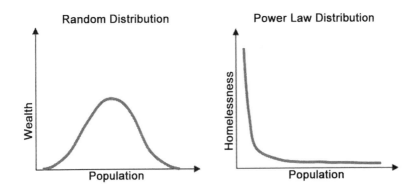

In Gladwell's *What the Dog Saw*, he cites research on social problems like homelessness, excess force of cops, and polluting vehicles. All exhibit power-law distributions, where a small number of the population is an exponentially large part of the problem. Studies show that providing apartments for the chronically homeless lowers the overall cost to society. And police captains not reading files of officers before giving them performance reviews keeps the offenders—a small minority that gives entire forces a bad reputation—in the system. But power-law solutions don't appeal to the political right (special treatment for the undeserving) or the left (efficiency vs. fairness).

We don't continue treating these power law distributions as normal distributions (like the height of adult US males, which clusters around the 70″ mean) because we don't know better. We don't want to know better.

Is ignorance of what we really are a power-law distribution problem? What do we see/know about what we really are that we don't want to admit to ourselves?

Simplicity

Let's wind up with a simple breath-counting exercise: Breathe normally. Count breaths (in/out = 1) silently. Try this for, say, 100 breaths.

If you were able to count your breaths, you were watching the mind. You were turning your head away from irrelevant activity.

When you "remember," you can do this head turning without the breath-counting *japa* (repetition).

Set aside at least one period every day to remind yourself what you're looking for … then watch the mind.

PS: Review the four answers you wrote down [1. puzzle vs. mystery; 2. advice re. fear; 3. advice re. competing desires; 4. toughen vs. soften]. Do they tie together and apply to you?

❧

A Direct Path?

"When the man is ripe for receiving the instruction and his mind is about to sink into the Heart, the instruction imparted works in a flash and he realises the Self all right." ~ *Talks with Sri Ramana Maharshi*, 5 November 1936, Talk 275

*T*he final act in the play of life will be the mind sinking into the Heart of All, its source. There, only, is total freedom, unalloyed peace, and never-beginning, never-ending satisfaction.

We, the mind-limited self, get a taste of the mind's sinking into the Heart whenever we fall asleep. But we awake none the wiser. The unripe mind closes its eye when it sinks into its source. The sun disappears below the western horizon when night falls.

The seeker of Self asks: "Who am I?" or "What am I?" in worded thought or emotional longing. As that mind-self is battered by life experience, resistance to seeing or admitting the truth about its status burns out ... slower or faster depending on the erosive or traumatic effects of experience. Faulty beliefs about I-amness come into view and thus loosen their hypnotic hold.

The seeker may discover the mental umbilical cord that connects the mind with its source and which, unlike the maternal umbilical cord, is never detached from the child. The vibration of that umbilical cord is picked up as a nostalgic longing for Home. The mind-self then has a conscious connection with its source, although its conviction of individual-being status, of being or having a separate awareness, prevents it from seeing its source as anything but Other.

The Guru or Teacher may appear, either externally or internally, when the mind-self is able to see the Truth as reflected in another apparently individual being. This form of conscious connection allows Self to suggest directed action to the self: "What you're looking for is *within*. Come Home."

The mind-self overcomplicates, procrastinates, and forgets. It gets caught up in the drama of life then gets hit with shocks to its self-sense or individuality sense. In a resulting deflated or depressive state life may seem pointless, and attaining true satisfaction may seem hopeless. The feeling of purpose, which is intuited by the quiet mind, is lost behind the focus on foreground noise.

The point or purpose of life is death; the lesson of living is dying. Life is effortful: the doer has to "do" it; dying is effortless. Life after the "death" of the doer-sense enjoys intervals of effortless "being in the zone." Life after the death of the individuality sense is simultaneously effortful and effortless.

❧

Meditation Is Simple

1. Notice what you're seeing
2. Everything else takes care of itself

The mind-self feels what it wants (i.e., what it lacks) and is constructed to satisfy the want:
- Food, shelter, etc. (biological)
- Companionship, etc. (psychological)
- Absolute/permanent X (love, certainty, life, peace, etc.)

It watches/looks for what it wants,
Often getting distracted by what it sees
But eventually goaded again to find what it's looking for …
By turning away from attention-getting distractions.

By "remembering" what you feel as your deep wanting
& noticing (consciously, effortfully as needed) what you're seeing,
The mind more productively turns away from the "100 other good ideas that are there."[5]

---

5   "People think that focus means saying yes to the thing you've got to focus on. But that's not what it means at all. It means saying no to the 100 other good ideas that there are. You have to pick carefully…. Life is brief, and then you die, you know?" Steve Jobs, Apple CEO, in a 3/17/08 *Fortune* magazine interview

Set aside some time each day to *notice.*

At the same time every day is best.

Doing so the first thing in your day sends a message to the inner self.

Conserve energy to aide in the process of conscious noticing.

Watch the mind calibrate the probability of relevance of what it's seeing

& watch it turn away from low-probability content.

At some point the mind's intuition-feeling sense will tell it that what it's looking for is *within*—where finding is becoming.

❄

Realization or Mind-Trick?

W *hat if the experience you had was just a bunch of neurons firing that had not fired before? What if your perceived end to the search was just the mind manufacturing some sort of experience (or non-experience), and that this too will die with the body? How are you able to judge that something Real happened that wasn't just a clever trick by your mind to convince itself the search was over?*

This is a ticklish question. It asks for absolute proof in the non-absolute mind dimension. What would you find to be satisfactory proof? (Think about it.)

Regarding another person's perspective, I don't think we'll ever know that for sure. Regarding our own perspective, the answer comes when the angle of the mirror adjusts to the critical degree where the questioner is blinded by his reflection, where a straight line bends back upon itself and infinity equals zero. Art Ticknor will fade away. J.M. (the dream of J.M.) will fade away. The dreamer of the dream will fade away. All that remains is That Which Is.

Here's another way to think about it: End of Phase One, the mind cannot accept what it sees when looking back at its source. The mind sees that its source is Self-aware and yet carries the conviction that it (i.e., the mind) is observing this Self and therefore is apart from it. "That is me, and yet it can't be." Phase Two, there is a discontinuity, which filters back into the mind in various ways depending on the mind's database (memories, including patterns of reaction). From outside the mind, the view is that the "separate observer" is a mental construct. The way this was apprehended by Art's mind was I (at the center) saw that I had created the 6 billion animations, including specifically Art T., with a belief that they were alive. Phase Three, back in the mind, the reaction is "I could be nuts." Better not mention this to any psychiatrists, or I might get a vacation in the nuthouse....

It's a great help to have schooled the mind in truthfulness before self-realization occurs. Also a great help to have had contact with real teaching from a living teacher.

Outside Is Inside

Outside your head
is inside your heart.
Outside your self
is inside you.

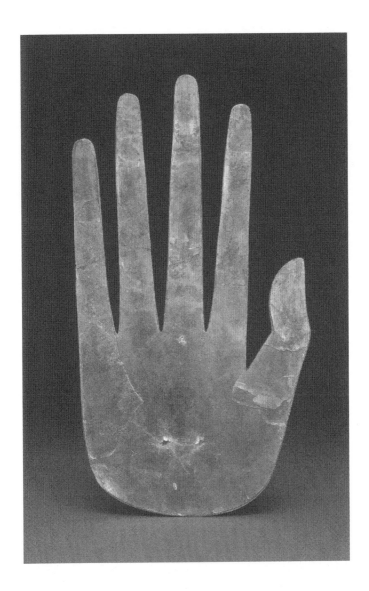

Mica found in mound 25 of the Hopewell culture (100 BC-AD 500) site in Ohio was cut into various shapes including this hand effigy with elongated fingers.

The Impulse to Observe

I want to ask you a question, but I don't know what specifically to ask… How does one increase the frequency or strength of the impulse to observe rather than judge?

We're always asking ourselves a question even if we aren't verbalizing it. It forms the backdrop of all our mental processes. It may be something along these lines: "How can I get rid of this feeling of loneliness and purposelessness?" Whatever forms the question takes, there's only one answer that completely satisfies. It undercuts all the assumptions that produce mental angst.

The melody that's coming into the mind from our source draws us back home. We begin by trying to find perfect happiness in the outside world. If fortunate, we graduate to trying to find it inside. When we see that we're enslaved by thoughts and feelings, positive and negative, we endeavor to get free by observing them without getting lost in them. Trying to do so is a reaction to the intuition that it's helpful in finding the perfect happiness we're longing to return to.

I looked for happiness in the world
And found that it wouldn't stand still,
That it was always coming and going.

I looked for happiness inside
And found that it was as transitory
As the outside world.

When all else failed,
I looked at looking …
And found what I'd been looking for.

Appendix I:
Common-Sense Meditation

E veryone has a built-in longing for ... well, check your own feeling and fill in the word or phrase that describes it best for you. I would say *completion*. Or I might borrow Franklin Merrell-Wolff's phrase, "full Satisfaction."[1]

When a person realizes that no external pursuit or acquisition is going to provide true satisfaction, there's only one remaining possibility, and that's going within to find what one's searching for. Meditation is the process of going within, which ultimately leads to discovery of our real self—our true state of being—and the end of the feeling of being incomplete.

Going-within meditation involves backing away from faulty beliefs about one's identity. This requires becoming conscious of what you believe yourself to be and then looking for evidence that supports or denies those beliefs. The crux of the distinction between self and other, or self and not self, is the distinction between subject and object, between viewer and view. You're looking to know the knower, the subject—and anything that becomes an object of consciousness can immediately be disqualified. Since we're looking to know the knower, there's an obvious paradox here that can only be transcended if it's possible to go beyond relative knowing to a state of absolute being.

Rest and relaxation are necessary ingredients for a healthy life, but to be a process of self-inquiry, meditation needs to be *confrontational* not restful. It also needs to be *observational*. Consider what a person may say when first asked what they believe themselves to be. They're likely to begin with something relational (I'm my parents' child, my spouse's partner, my child's

---

1   From his magnificent poem "Nirvana" in the autobiographical *Pathways Through to Space.*

parent, and so forth) or something they do (I'm a student, an employee, an employer, and so on). When reminded that those aren't self-definitions, they're likely to zero in on some variation of "I'm this body with its consciousness and memories." If they say: "I'm a soul" or "I'm a collection of molecules," it's going to be a long row for them to hoe, since they're afraid to face the facts of life and death and have buried their heads in the sands of wishful thinking.

Nobody wants to do the necessary work involved with self-definition, and everyone tries to find a way to skip directly to the expected reward. It doesn't come that way, though. Conceptually the going-within process is simple but ultimately unexplainable, since it relies on seeming accidents. Like learning algebra, for example, we struggle to comprehend what x, the unknown, represents. Sometimes the answer comes in a flash, sometimes it just becomes intuitively obvious, and sometimes the aspirant never gets it.

When we "get" the algebra[2] of self-inquiry, we realize that we're looking for the self—and anything in the view is not the self. Therefore self-inquiry becomes a process of looking. Or, to use a more neutral term, observing. But it's a looking by going within. We're constructed to look outward, and the farthest out we generally identify as our self is the body. Our common sense tells us that even without our fingers or toes we'd still be here, and that agrees with the self-inquiry algebra law that what's in the view is not our essential self. But if we consider the part of the body from the neck up, doubt comes into play. Doubt, by the way, is our greatest ally in self-inquiry. Would I still be here if my head were lopped off? We may not be ready to test that observation yet. But why does that question arise? Because we're thinking about thinking. In other words, when observation moves inward a bit—like retracting the zoomed-out lens

---

2   The word comes from the Arabic *al-jabr*, (the science of) reuniting.

on our camera—we become identified with thoughts. If some-one asks us if we can observe our thoughts, we may say no. But since we can remember some of our thoughts, that's a clue that thoughts are being observed and recorded even though we're not conscious of it.

Becoming aware that we're able to watch thoughts may come as an accident—as when we're caught up watching a film and suddenly remember we're sitting in a theater watching the film. When it occurs, the lens of our camera has receded back a step. We know then that we're not our thoughts.

Feelings are entangled with what we generally refer to as thoughts, and since they're often sensed as occurring in various body locations, we may need to go through a separate process of detachment from identification with them. A little investiga-tion into the basic description of how the nervous system func-tions will show us that we perceive a feeling in much the same fashion as we perceive a tree: something affects a nerve ending near the surface of the body, which causes a series of electro-chemical reactions to travel up the nerve pathway to the brain, where a picture of a tree or the sensation of a feeling mysteri-ously appears in consciousness. When we're talking about an emotion type of feeling, some stimulus had produced a reaction that may then be felt as located in some area of the body, but again the feeling appears mysteriously in consciousness. In any case, since they're observable, we're not our feelings. What then are we if not our thoughts or feelings and not our body (at least not parts that aren't essential to support consciousness)?

An irritation that keeps us looking for what we are, or a con-scious strategy that fills in the gaps when irritation isn't pres-ent, is necessary to maintain the self-inquiry as it becomes more abstract. We may try to skip to consciousness itself as our self-definition, but if we do so we'll need to come back to something not as far within—and that's the belief in being the decider in charge of doing. Symptoms of this belief are statements we tell ourselves such as: "If I don't make the right decision, there will be a price to pay," and: "If I stopped making decisions, all action would come to a halt."

Generally we don't become aware of decisions unless there's prolonged conflict between various desires and fears. But if someone asks us, or we ask ourselves, why we did or didn't do something, we can often remember parts of a decision-making process that led to the witnessed results. The fact that we remember some of the details indicates that they're being observed and recorded even when we're not particularly conscious of it. But this indirect evidence may not be sufficient to convince our self-inquiry algebra that we're not doing it, that we're not the decision-making process. It may require an accidental retraction of the camera lens so that we consciously view decision-making as it's occurring in order for the fact to sink in that the process is observable and, therefore, not us. What does that leave then in our bag of beliefs about what we are? Are we ready to tackle consciousness itself?

If we define ourselves as consciousness, then we're faced with saying that we're something that comes and goes with the waking state and the dreaming state. This is liable to lead us back to our belief that we're the body, with its waking, dreaming and non-dreaming sleep states. But to believe that requires that we take somebody else's word for the body's existence during sleep. And other people, with their testimony, are appearances in our consciousness. Since we know nothing directly about their existence, they have the same merits as any other objects of consciousness—our thoughts, for example. No matter how believable it is, their testimony is not acceptable evidence in the court of self-inquiry algebra.

To find what we're looking for, which could also be described as ultimate certainty about what we are, we cannot rely on any external authority, no matter how much value we place on it. We must become our own authority. When we have peeled away the outer layers of what we once believed ourselves to be and are left with a belief in "this individual consciousness," we seem to come up against an impenetrable barrier. Is it possible to go any further within?

I can see that I'm not my thoughts or feelings and that I'm not the decision-maker or causal agent of my body's actions (since I can observe thoughts, feelings, and decision-making). If I'm my body with its consciousness, then I'm something that was born and is going to die. I have a feeling, which might be wishful thinking or it might be intuition, that I'm not going to cease existing—although I have to admit that I can't actually conceive of nonexistence. The closest I can come is to imagine a bodiless awareness with no sensation, perhaps limited to end-less memory replay or even witnessing a blank screen. Even the state of dreamless sleep is beyond my conscious imagination.

So let me come back to consciousness as the only object of continued self-inquiry. What can I observe of consciousness?

Since consciousness appears to come and go, I can deduce that it's similar to a kitchen appliance. I can also inductively reason that something switches it on and off, and it has a power source that energizes it. Self-inquiry then might lead me to ask myself what is the source of consciousness. That very question latched onto my mind one time when I was on a solitary retreat. It stayed with me for a couple days, being the first thought on my mind when I awoke in the morning, the last thought as I went to sleep at night, and a recurring thought throughout the day. And an answer came to me one afternoon as I sat down on a tree stump in the woods. It came in the form of a simple vision or picture in my mind, where I saw that I was connected to something bigger than myself at the end of a long string. The picture satisfied the question, which then evaporated.[3]

Another clue about consciousness didn't occur to me until years later. The reason I was identified with the body and its consciousness, both in its dreaming and waking states, was that in addition to being conscious, I knew that I was conscious. That self-consciousness, with its associated fears as well as prides, didn't appear until a few years after the body's birth. So there are two observable facts: I feel or believe that I'm what's conscious—what's looking outward and is aware of the cosmos, the exterior of this body, its thoughts, feelings, decision-making, and so on—and I'm also what's aware of that outward-looking awareness. This second me is inward looking. I can say that I'm a composite of the outward looking and the inward looking, but that's at the conceptual level. At the level of observation, I'm one or the other at any moment. Either I'm aware of being what's looking outward or I'm aware of being what's looking inward (or remember it just occurred). Thus I firmly

---

3   A friend asked me why it was a long string that separated me from my source. My response was that I wasn't ready at the time to see how *closer than close* that source-self is.

believe, although it may be hard to admit to myself, that there are two me's. Yet I also believe that to be nonsense, that there's only one me.

If you persist with self-inquiry, you'll arrive at a final opposition or contradiction in your beliefs about what you are. Continued persistence in the face of the seemingly insoluble final opposition will burn out or blow out the resistance circuitry that prevents individual consciousness of awareness. The power source—what you really are—has always been self-aware, and now by some mysterious discontinuity, the appliance becomes a conscious mirror of self-awareness.

A Practical Guide

Establish a daily meditation time. Establishing and maintaining a daily meditation habit may be your biggest battle. "How much time?" you may be thinking. How important to you is knowing what you are, of finding completion, of transcending life and death? An hour, for example, is 6% of a day in your waking life. What investment is pursuit of life's highest goal—with no guarantee of success—worth to you?

Self-inquiry meditation can be done sitting or walking. Lying down generally leads to sleep. It works best to find a place where there's no distraction. It may take some time before you build a reservoir of mental energy to make productive use of the time without becoming lost in thought for extended periods. As for any worthwhile goal, energy needs to be conserved from other activities and channeled into self-inquiry. Meditating after a meal is generally tough because brain activity is being affected by digestion. These are a few of the factors that you'll need to experiment with to find out what helps and what hinders self-inquiry.

When you begin each meditation period, remind yourself why you're doing it. If you don't remember your worded goal (to know the Self, become the Truth, or however your phrase it), feel the feeling that propels the search—the hole in the chest, the longing. Then recall where you ended up the previous day. A journal helps greatly so that you're not dependent on a memory that's subject to painting the past erroneously. The journal should document what beliefs you have about what you are, which ones you've worked on and have seen through, and which one you're currently investigating.

Beliefs about what we are aren't all that unique, but typically we haven't tried to put them into definite form. Working with others can be tremendously useful in bringing the beliefs into view and in questioning them. The basic operation during meditation is one of *looking.* We look (or whatever sensory analogy makes sense to you) until the belief is verified or invalidated. Thinking about what you see and your feelings about it are more material for observation.

Finding the real self is looking until what's looking is known.

Work diligently for the beauty of working, but don't strain. It's a fascinating mystery to solve. Look with light-hearted curiosity. Look for insights into your behavior. Look (feel, listen, etc.) then relax. It's the most natural thing in the world.

Appendix II:
The Diamond Sutra, Simplified

$\mathcal{T}$he following discourse is attributed to Siddhartha Gautama, later called the Buddha Shakyamuni (the holy sage of the Shakya clan), passed on by word of mouth throughout the centuries from around 500 BC until the second century AD, when it was written down by Nagarjuna. Hui-neng, the sixth Patriarch of Ch'an, identified Nagarjuna as being about halfway in the line of *dharma*-succession from Siddhartha to Bodhidharma, who carried the Great Jewel from India to China.

I read the *Diamond Sutra* in the A.F. Price and Wong Mou-Lam translation, and I found that the stylistic conventions interfered with my absorbing the message, so I reworded it into a simplified form that was easier for me to read and consider. I'm including my version here in hopes that it might be a useful introduction if you're not already familiar with the *sutra*.

1. The Convocation of the Assembly
In Jeta Grove, the park of Anatha-pindika near the once-great city of Shravasti, the "city of wonders" in northern India close to the border of Nepal, twelve hundred and fifty wandering monks broke their fast then gathered round to hear the words of the Buddha.

2. Subhuti Makes a Request
The disciple Subhuti arose and, raising his hands with palms joined in respect, said: World-Honored One, if good men and women seek enlightenment, how should they then conduct themselves?

3. The Real Teaching of the Great Way
They should discipline their thoughts as follows, Buddha replied. All living creatures are caused by me to attain unbounded liberation. Yet when vast numbers of beings have thus been

liberated, in truth no being has been liberated. And why is this? Because no enlightened being cherishes the idea of a separate individuality. [My comment: You could stop here and get the entire teaching.]

4. Even the Most Beneficent Practices are Relative

Furthermore, the Buddha said, a *bodhisattva* [aspirant] should practice good acts without regard to appearances, without attachment to sight, sound or any other quality.

Thus is merit gained, as Krishna instructed Arjuna in *The Song of the Blessed One [Bhagavad Gita]*, when action is performed with detachment.

5. Understanding the Ultimate Principle of Reality

Do you think that Reality is to be recognized by some material characteristic? [Is Reality perceivable by the senses?]

No, World-Honored One.

That's right, Subhuti. Wherever there are material characteristics, there is delusion. But whoever perceives that all characteristics are in fact no-characteristics, perceives Reality.

6. Rare is True Faith

Will there always be men who truly believe after hearing this teaching? Subhuti asked.

Twenty-five hundred years after the passing of the Buddha [i.e., circa 2000], men hearing this teaching will have an uprising of pure faith, and the Buddha will recognize them, Siddhartha answered.

Yes, he will clearly perceive all those of pure heart. And why is that? It is because such men will not cherish the idea of individuality, of a separate being. Neither will they cherish the idea that things [e.g., bodies] have intrinsic qualities, which includes the idea of an ego or individuality, nor even that things are devoid of intrinsic qualities. For the latter ideas imply the former.

My teaching of the dharma, the good law, is like a raft that has carried one safely across a flood. One does not continue the journey carrying the raft upon his head. Thus even the buddha-teaching must be relinquished.

7. *Great Ones, Perfect beyond Learning, Utter No Words of Teaching*

Has the Buddha attained enlightenment, Subhuti? Has he a teaching to enunciate?

As I understand Buddha's meaning there is no formulation of truth called enlightenment, he answered. Moreover there is no teaching to enunciate. The Buddha has said that truth is uncontainable and inexpressible. It neither is nor is not.

This *unformulated principle* is the foundation of the different systems of all true sages, Subhuti.

8. *The Fruits of Meritorious Actions*

If anyone filled three thousand galaxies with all the treasures of the universe and gave it all away in alms, would he gain great merit? Buddha asked.

Great indeed World-Honored One.

On the other hand, Buddha said, if anyone received and retained even four lines of this discourse and taught them to others, his merit would be the greater. From this discourse issue forth all the buddhas and the enlightenment teachings of all the buddhas.

[This seems like a device for ensuring that the teaching would be carried on to succeeding generations verbatim, which was probably a major concern before the advent of widespread recording media. On the other hand, Buddha has just said that there is no teaching to enunciate and that truth is inexpressible. Apparently he didn't assume there would be an unbroken chain of enlightened teachers to keep the lamp burning. Although words cannot express Truth, they can be catalysts for the advent of awakening, as Hui-neng describes his first hearing of the Diamond Sutra—and as two friends and fellow students of Richard Rose found out in 1999, one upon reading something written by Alfred Pulyan, the other when reading something said by Franklin Merrell-Wolff.]

9. Real Designation is Undesignate

Does a venerable one who will never more be reborn as a mortal say to himself, "I obtain the fruit of a nonreturner"?

No, World-Honored One. "Nonreturner" is just a name. There is no nonreturning; hence the designation "nonreturner."

Does a holy one say to himself, "I have obtained perfect enlightenment"?

No, World-Honored One, for that would partake of the idea of an ego or individual self. Claiming spiritual superiority is separative and enhances the illusory personality.

10. Setting forth Pure Lands

[The reference is to a bodhisattva who has attained complete enlightenment and who may preside as a king over a world of beings whom he never ceases to help until they are free and perfected.]

Does a buddha set forth any majestic buddha-lands?

No, Subhuti answered, because such "setting forth" is not a majestic setting forth but merely a name.

Therefore, Buddha said, all bodhisattvas should develop a pure, lucid mind that alights upon nothing whatsoever.

11. The Superiority of Unformulated Truth

If a good man or woman filled three thousand galaxies with all the treasures in the universe as many times over as there are grains of sand in all their great rivers and gave all away in gifts to the needy, would he gain great merit?

Great indeed, World-Honored One.

Nevertheless, if a good man or woman studies this discourse only so far as to receive and retain four lines, and teaches and explains them to others, the consequent merit would be far greater.

[Richard Rose felt strongly that a person's path is accelerated by a vow to help others. He remarked that while few have ears to hear Truth, even fewer can act—pointing out that while Jesus had about seventy disciples, there were only twelve apostles. Following this proportion as a guide, every seeker should be helping six other seekers on the rung of the ladder below his own.]

12. Veneration of the True Doctrine

Furthermore, you should know that wherever this discourse is proclaimed, by even so little as four lines, that place should be venerated by all the realms of sentient beings.

How much more is this so in the case of one who is able to receive and retain the whole. Such a one attains the highest and most wonderful truth.

13. How this Teaching Should Be Received and Retained

By what name should this discourse be known, World-Honored One, and how should we receive and retain it?

It should be known as the Diamond Cutter of Perfect Wisdom. But according to the buddha-teaching, the perfection of transcendental wisdom is not really such, but just the name given to it.

Would there be many molecules in three thousand galaxies, Subhuti?

Many, indeed, Subhuti said.

The *Tathagata* [a way Gautama referred to himself; "thus come" or "thus gone," maybe implying "beyond all coming and going"] declares that all these molecules are not really such; they are merely called molecules. Furthermore, a world is not really a world; it is merely called such.

If on the one hand a good man or woman sacrifices as many lives as sand grains on the Ganges, and on the other hand anyone receives and retains only four lines of this discourse, and teaches it to others, the merit of the latter will be greater.

14. Perfect Peace Lies in Freedom from Characteristic Distinctions

Upon hearing the discourse Subhuti had an interior realization and was moved to tears. It is a most precious thing, World-Honored One, that you should deliver this supremely profound discourse, he said. Never have I heard such an exposition since my eye of wisdom first opened. If anyone listens to this discourse in faith with a pure, lucid mind, he will thereupon conceive an idea of fundamental reality.

Just as you say, Buddha replied. If anyone listens to this discourse and is filled with neither alarm nor awe nor dread, be it known that such a one is of remarkable achievement.

The first perfection, the perfection of charity, is not, in fact, the first perfection; it is merely a name. Likewise the perfection of patience is not such. Therefore bodhisattvas should leave behind all phenomenal distinctions and awaken the thought of enlightenment by not allowing the mind to depend upon notions evoked by the sensible world.

The mind should be kept independent of any thoughts that arise within it, or it has no sure haven. As bodhisattvas practice charity for the welfare of all living beings, they should do it in this manner. Just as the Tathagata declares that characteristics are not characteristics, so he declares that all living beings are not, in fact, living beings.

The Tathagata is he who declares that which is true, he who declares that which is fundamental, he who declares that which is ultimate. The truth to which the Tathagata has attained is neither real nor unreal.

If there be good men and women in future ages able to receive, read and recite this discourse in its entirety, the Tathagata will clearly perceive and recognize them by means of his buddha-knowledge; and each one of them will bring immeasurable and incalculable merit to fruition.

15. The Incomparable Value of this Teaching

If on the one hand a good man or woman performs in the morning as many charitable acts of self-denial as the sand grains of the Ganges, and performs as many again in the noonday and as many again in the evening, and continues so doing throughout numberless ages, and, on the other hand, anyone listens to this discourse with heart of faith and without contention, the latter would be the more blessed. But how can any comparison be made with one who writes it down, receives it, retains it, and explains it to others! *[Propaganda :-]*

The full value of this discourse can be neither conceived nor estimated, nor can any limit be set to it. The Tathagata has declared this teaching for the benefit of the initiates of the great way; he has declared it for the benefit of the initiates of the supreme way.

16. Purgation through Suffering the Retribution for Past Sins

If good men and women who receive and retain this discourse are downtrodden, their evil destiny is the inevitable retributive result of sins committed in their past mortal lives. By virtue of their present misfortunes the reacting effects of their past will be thereby worked out, and they will be in a position to attain the consummation of incomparable enlightenment.

If I fully detailed the merit gained by good men and women coming to receive, retain, study and recite this discourse, my hearers would be filled with doubt and might become disordered in mind, suspicious and unbelieving. You should know, Subhuti, that the significance of this discourse is beyond conception; likewise the fruit of its rewards is beyond conception.

[The above remark is consistent with the teachings of the Ch'an masters, which is that reality cannot be conceived by the intellect but can only be realized through direct experience.]

17. No One Attains Transcendental Wisdom

World-Honored One, if good men and women seek enlightenment, how should they abide and how control their thoughts?

They must create this resolved attitude of mind, Buddha replied: "I must liberate all living beings; yet when all have been liberated, verily not anyone is liberated."

In reality there is no formula that gives rise to the consummation of incomparable enlightenment. Tathagata is a signification implying all formulas. The basis of the Tathagata's attainment of enlightenment is wholly BEYOND; it is neither real nor unreal.

If a bodhisattva announces: "I will liberate all living creatures," he is not rightly called a bodhisattva. There is really no such condition as bodhisattvaship, because all things are devoid of separate individuality. Bodhisattvas who are truly devoid of any conception of separate selfhood are truthfully called bodhisattvas.

18. All Modes of Mind Are Really Only Mind

If there were as many Ganges rivers as the sand grains of the Ganges and there was a buddha-land for each sand grain in all those rivers, would those buddha-lands be many?

Many, indeed.

However many living beings there are in all those buddha-lands, though they have manifold modes of mind, the Tathagata understands them all. All these are not mind; they are merely called mind. It is impossible to retain past mind, impossible to hold on to present mind, and impossible to grasp future mind.

19. Absolute Reality Is the Only Foundation

If anyone filled three thousand galaxies with treasure and gave it all away, would he gain great merit?

Indeed, World-Honored One, he would gain great merit.

If such merit were real, the Tathagata would not have declared it to be great, but because it is without a foundation the Tathagata characterized it as "great."

20. The Unreality of Phenomenal Distinctions

Can the Buddha be perceived by his perfectly formed body?

No, World-Honored One. A perfectly formed body is not really such; it is merely called that.

Can the Absolute be perceived by means of any phenomenal characteristics [that is, perceptible by the senses]?

No, Subhuti replied, because phenomenal characteristics are not really such but are merely called so.

21. Words Cannot Express Truth; That which Words Express Is not Truth

If anyone says that the Tathagata sets forth a teaching he really slanders Buddha and is unable to explain what I teach. As to any truth-declaring system, truth is undeclarable; so an "enunciation of truth" is just the name given to it.

In future ages, Subhuti asked, will there be men coming to hear a declaration of this teaching who will be inspired with belief?

Those to whom you refer are neither living beings nor not-living beings. "Living beings" are not really such; they are just called that.

22. It Cannot Be Said that Anything Is Attainable

Subhuti asked: In the attainment of enlightenment did the Buddha make no acquisition whatever?

Just so, Buddha replied. Through the consummation of incomparable enlightenment I acquired not the least thing.

23. The Cultivation of Goodness Purifies the Mind

Furthermore, THIS is altogether everywhere, without differentiation or degree. It is straightly attained by freedom from separate selfhood and by cultivating all kinds of goodness. But, though we speak of "goodness," the Tathagata declares that there is no goodness.

24. The Incomparable Merit of this Teaching

If one gives the needy a mass of treasures equal in extent to as many mighty Mount Sumerus as there would be in three thousand galaxies, and if another selects even four lines from this discourse upon the perfection of the transcendental wisdom, receiving and retaining them, and clearly expounding them to others, the merit of the latter will be so far greater than that of the former that no conceivable comparison can be made between them.

25. The Illusion of the Ego

Let no one say the Tathagata cherishes the idea "I must liberate all living beings." In reality there are no living beings to be liberated by the Tathagata. If there were living beings for the Tathagata to liberate, he would partake of the idea of selfhood, personality, ego entity and separate individuality.

26. The Body of Truth Has No Mark

May the Tathagata be perceived by the thirty-two marks of a great man? Buddha asked.

As I understand the meaning of Buddha's words, the Tathagata may not be perceived by the thirty-two marks, Subhuti replied.

Whereupon the World-Honored One uttered this verse:

> Who seeks me by form,
> Who seeks me in sound,
> Perverted are his footsteps upon the way;
> For he cannot perceive the Absolute.

27. It Is Erroneous to Affirm that All Things Are Ever Extinguished

The Tathagata's attainment of enlightenment was not by reason of his perfected form [I believe he's referring to the entire organism, physical and mental, as well as its manifested actions]. On the other hand, do not believe that anyone in whom dawns the consummation of incomparable enlightenment would declare that all manifest standards are ended and extinguished. Such a man does not affirm concerning any formula that it is finally extinguished.

28. Attachment to Rewards of Merit

If one bodhisattva bestows in charity sufficient treasures to fill as many worlds as there are sand grains in the Ganges, and another, realizing that all things are egoless, attains perfection through patient forbearance, the merit of the latter will far exceed that of the former.

What is the saying, World-Honored One, that bodhisattvas are insentient as to rewards of merit?

Bodhisattvas who achieve merit should not be fettered with desire for rewards. Thus it is said that the rewards of merit are not received.

[From the Bhagavad-Gita: Thy right is to work, but never to its fruits; let not the fruit of thy work be thy motive, nor take refuge in *abstinence from works. Standing in union with the Soul, carry out thy work, putting away attachment, O conqueror of wealth; equal in success and failure, for equalness is called union with the Soul.]*

29. Perfect Tranquility

If anyone should say that the Tathagata comes or goes or sits or reclines, he fails to understand my teaching. Why? Because the Tathagata has neither whence or whither.

30. The Integral Principle

If a good man or woman ground an infinite number of worlds to dust, would the resulting minute particles be many, Subhuti?

Many, indeed! Because if such were really minute particles Buddha would not have spoken of them as minute particles. "Minute particles" is just the name given to them. Also, when the Tathagata speaks of worlds, these are not worlds; for if reality could be predicated of a world it would be a self-existent cosmos, and the Tathagata teaches that there is really no such thing.

Words cannot explain the real nature of a cosmos, Buddha agreed. Only common people fettered with desire make use of this arbitrary method.

31. Conventional Truth Should Be Cut Off

If anyone should say that Buddha declares any conception of egoity, would he understand my teaching?

No, Subhuti replied, because the World-Honored One declares that notions of selfhood, personality, entity and separate individuality are erroneous; these terms are merely figures of speech.

Those who aspire to the consummation of incomparable enlightenment should recognize and understand all the varieties of things in the same way and cut off the arising of aspects, Buddha said.

32. The Delusion of Appearances

Someone might fill innumerable worlds with treasure and give all away in gifts of alms, but if any good man or woman awakens the thought of enlightenment and takes even four lines from this discourse, reciting, using, receiving, retaining and spreading them abroad and explaining them for the benefit of others, it will be far more meritorious.

In what manner may he explain them to others? By detachment from appearances—abiding in real truth.

Appendix III:
Douglas Harding & Richard Rose

*D*ouglas Harding wrote an essay in *Look for Yourself* titled "Ramana Maharshi and J. Krishnamurti"[4] in which he distinguished two general camps of spiritual warfare. One, represented by the approach of Jiddu Krishnamurti, strives to know the mind:

> It is essential, says Krishnamurti, to understand ourselves, how we think, what we think, why we think that way, the nature of our conditioning. "To follow oneself, to see how one's thought operates, one has to be extraordinarily alert, so that as one begins to be more and more alert to the intricacies of one's own thinking and responses and feelings, one begins to have a greater awareness, not only of oneself but of another with whom one is in relationship." Everywhere Krishnamurti insists that we must get to know the processes of the mind.

The other, represented by Ramana Maharshi's teaching, eschews knowing the mind:

> Ramana Maharshi flatly denies that there is a mind to get to know. In investigation "it will be found that the mind does not exist." "There is nothing but the Self. To inhere in the Self is the thing. Never mind the mind. If its source is sought, it will vanish."

Harding says you could label the first type spiritual-psychological and the second spiritual-religious and admits that he lands in the spiritual-religious camp. He also expresses his conviction that "to follow a spiritual path to its conclusion, you have to be careful not to be diverted along other paths."

---

4   See Harding's essay in the May 2003 *TAT Forum*

What does the seeker of truth need to do—roll the dice to determine which of the two camps to join? An open-ended commitment to either path means a possibly life-long commitment with no guaranteed results. If you pursue it for years or decades without ultimate realization and then quit it for the other camp, you may have been one day away from success and may have slid some or all the way back toward where you started. Or should the seeker attempt to walk both paths simultaneously? Either way's a crapshoot. So what's the best way to proceed?

I have read some of the Krishnamurti books (and seen him in public talks at Ojai) and Ramana's dialogues, and I don't find much of a path laid out by either teacher. I do think Ramana's advice to "Dive within … sink within and seek"[5] points the way, but it doesn't offer much guidance. As more directive examples of teachings that represent the two camps, let's consider the paths outlined by Douglas Harding and by Richard Rose.

Meetings with Remarkable Men

I met Richard Rose in 1978 after a decade of growing frustration at not being able to find the missing purpose or meaning in my life. I have written about that meeting in more detail[6] and will skip to the bottom line: he inspired me to the roots by pointing out that all answers lie within. His "Threefold Path" article[7] outlines the spiritual path that he recommended and that I attempted to implement over a period of 25 years.

Rose advised meditation on the mind in order to become detached from our hypnotic identification with it. For example, in *Psychology of the Observer* he wrote:

If there is a greater Reality than the Mind-dimension, then those who are in search of it cannot ignore the need to

5   No. 196, *Talks with Sri Ramana Maharshi*
6   See *Meeting Richard Rose: 1978* in the May 2006 *TAT Forum*
7   See *Threefold Path* in the January 2005 *TAT Forum*

thoroughly understand the Mind, from the somatic mind to the most intricate functionings of the higher mind in its direct-mind experiences.

In searching for the Self or ultimate Truth, we examine the dividing line between inside and outside ... between self and not self. By introspecting the mind, the line—or our view of it—shifts, as more and more of what we once identified as our self moves into the view. To accelerate that process, we employ "the law of the ladder":

> We do not advance without helping or being helped. The LAW OF THE LADDER is the formula by which the group or Sangha is able to find for all someone to help and someone who can use help. [From the "Threefold Path."]

More specifically, Rose described the structure of the mind that we retraverse in the search for our source as a "Jacob's Ladder"[8] and felt that we get pushed up the ladder by those we reach down to help more so than we climb it by our own efforts.

Sometime before the end of the 25 years I had climbed or been pushed most of the way up Jacob's Ladder, paring away my self-definition to that of being an individual observer with no qualities or qualifiers other than that of coming and going with consciousness. And I was seemingly stuck there, not being able to go beyond that limitation.

Then in 2003 I met Douglas Harding.[9] Douglas was strongly convinced that the best route to self-discovery was a relentless practice of looking back at what we're looking out from, which

---

8   Rose described and diagrammed the climb from earth to heaven, the ascension from the mundane to the sublime, in *Psychology of the Observer*, labeling it as Jacob's Ladder from the story of Jacob's dream in the biblical book of *Genesis*.

9   See *Douglas Harding in Memoriam* in the February 2007 *TAT Forum* for some details of our meeting.

he referred to as practicing headlessness. I knew from my years of introspecting the mind what he meant by that and had also done some of his experiments, which he had developed over the years to assist people in getting those glimpses. On the last day of my first visit with him, he assembled a few friends and put on a mini-workshop. When he did his "tube" experiment[10] with me, it established a new and contradictory paradigm through which I could view the world and myself.

Whereas I had been viewing the world—i.e., everything other than myself—as outside and my undefined self as inside, in the Harding model it was apparent that everything was in-side me. As with the optical illusion of the Necker cube that flips 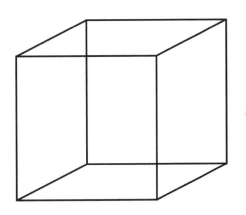 in and out as you stare at it, after doing the tube experiment with Douglas my mind was able to flip back and forth between the two contradictory paradigms of "everything is outside me" and "everything is inside me"—without being able to conclude that one was more valid than the other. That led to my personal demise six months later.[11]

Two Paths or Two Paradigms?

Let's go back to the question of whether the Harding and Rose teachings are best pursued separately or whether they can be

---

10   See "The Tube" at www.headless.org/experiments for details.

11   That statement may sound odd. Some people have described their transition to recognition of their true nature as an awakening; others as a dying-while-living. Both descriptions are accurate reflections of finding what we really are.

mined for joined benefit. Here's one line of thinking on the issue:

- There's something that we need to see or hear or feel (I'm attempting to use a sense analogy for the more abstract "intuit") to awaken us to the possibility of finding the permanent satisfaction of our heart's desire and to get the ball rolling in that direction—in other words, starting us on an intentional path of action. For me, it was this troika: all the answers are within; nothing can be known until the knower is known; and the self is never that which is known. Hui-neng tells us for him it was hearing a wandering monk reciting the Diamond Sutra.[12]

- That catalyst will propel us to look for a permanent state of wholeness by going within.

- No paradigm or way of looking at the self and world is going to take us beyond the self-other duality to our unitary state of being.

- We take that paradigm we're working with as far as it can go. This can't be done by agreement or mere intellectual comprehension. We have to see (feel, hear, intuit) for ourself, becoming our own authority rather than taking someone else's word as the authority.

- What will then take us the next step? An opposing paradigm, which appears equally valid.

- Every paradigm has an equal and contradictory opposite. For example, are your feet up or down? The worldview most if not all of us are conditioned into tells us that if we're standing or sitting, we're up—i.e., we're in our head (a meatball parked atop our torso)—and our feet are below us, or down. But if we go with our first-person view rather

---

12   In the autobiographical sketch he gave during his first public talk circa 670-680 AD. See *The Diamond Sutra & The Sutra of Hui-Neng* translated by Price & Wong, or *The Sutra of Hui-Neng* translated by Thomas Cleary.

than the interpretation we've been taught to parrot, we may "see" that our feet are up from the headless point of view.[13]

- Every pair of equal and opposite paradigms can be transcended.
- When the opposition is big enough, transcending it will take you beyond all paradigms to Recognition of what you really are.

I think you can probably see what I'm leading up to, which is that Harding's teaching and Rose's teaching, while seemingly incompatible and contradictory, can provide an opposition that would propel you beyond oppositions. The important thing is to develop a system of work and persist with it, letting intuition guide you. For intuition to do that effectively, you need to cultivate clarity of mind, which is an integral part of your system of work.

Spiritual progress occurs by dispelling illusory beliefs and is thus a subtractive business. The end result of spiritual investigation is knowing what we are at the core of our being. This knowing is not a type of knowing we're familiar with since it goes beyond the knower-known split. We recognize our essential nature by becoming one with it. The drop of rain loses its boundaries, its individuality, when it hits the ocean.

By practicing headless exercises, or by other means, we see that we're what's aware—and that awareness is void of characteristics. By climbing the Jacob's Ladder of self-definition we become viewers of all the characteristics we were previously identified with. This is a collision course of the raindrop falling toward the ocean.

Addendum

In 1947, a month after his self-realization, Richard Rose wrote to a friend:

13   See The Bottom Line experiment at www.headless.org/experiments

I am glad that you are in accord with the idea of forming a circle.
Let us at least call it a circle ... something without a head or tail ...
a ring of equality.

That was Rose's ideal for a group of people working together on the grand project of knowing the self, which became the basis for the TAT Foundation he formed in 1973.

Douglas Harding embodied the "no-head circle" concept into an experiment.[14] Try this sometime with a few friends:

◊ Stand in a circle with some friends—between say 3 and 10 of you. Put your arms round each other so that you are close, and look down.

◊ There you see a circle of bodies. Obviously they are distinct from one another, each taking their own space. They do not merge into some kind of 'oneness'. Each body there has a name, a background and history, an age, a nationality and so on. Down there we are separate from one another.

◊ Notice your own body—it disappears above the chest into No-thingness.

◊ Notice that from this point of view the other bodies also disappear above their chests—into the same No-thingness that your body disappears into.

◊ Here at the top there are not many No-things—just one. Here in this edgeless space are no dividing lines, no name tags, no bit of the No-thing that is mine or yours. Here we are indivisibly one.

---

14   See the "No-Head Circle" at www.headless.org/experiments

◊ The nameless awareness here at the top includes all those different bodies. They all disappear into, or emerge out of, this One who has no name.

◊ Looking down, each of us has our own unique point of view, our own thoughts and feelings. I don't know what you are thinking, or what your past is. I might not even know your name. But I can see who you really are—here at the top of the circle.

◊ Here at the top all our differences dissolve, all separation is overcome—without destroying those differences down there. The space at the top has room for every point of view.

◊ The No-Head Circle is like a circular temple. The bodies form the walls, like columns. But this temple is ruined—the roof has been blown clear off. The temple lies wide-open to the sky—a sky that is totally clear. A sky that is boundless. You are that infinite sky—the sky of Being.

◊ Who is it that now looks down?

◊ Looking at the Looker I come home to who I really am, the One who has no boundaries, and I find that this One includes everyone. Down there in the circle I am one amongst many—others stand either side of me, apart from me, with me, perhaps even against me. But here, above the line of chests, there are no others. All divisions are healed, all separation overcome.

◊ Here, looking down, including us all, is the One within all beings. You are that One.

Dear reader: Please note that reading about this experiment doesn't do the trick. Try it, and see if it causes a shift in your paradigm. The same caveat applies to all spiritual reading. To be helpful it must inspire action, which ultimately means looking for yourself.

In friendship,
Art Ticknor

About the Author

I found that:
There's an antidote for dissatisfaction.

Intuition awoke to guide me.

It took me 26 years to "get there."

Along the way there was an opening of the faith center—where I saw intuitively that, unlike my previous conviction that whatever had created me had kicked me out and left me to fend for myself, I was still attached to my source by a mental umbilical cord.

You'll never know how close you are until you complete your task. Keep with it. Persevere.

ALONG THE WAY I also found that there's no joy in life like doing something for others. Albert Schweitzer must have made a similar discovery. He told an audience: "I don't know what your destiny will be, but one thing I know: the only ones among you who will be really happy are those who will have sought and found how to serve."

❧

Memorable one-liners from helpers along the way:

- *I think you'll make it.* In a letter from Richard Rose following my first solitary retreat, responding to a question about whether I was too old at 33 to pursue self-definition.

- *Pass it on.* When I was leaving for California, I said goodbye to Richard Rose and told him I wished there was some way I could repay him for all his help. He said, "That's not the way it works. Pass it on."

- *I'm always right behind you.* Someone behind me had called my name when I was carrying a bowl of hot soup. Richard Rose warned me about turning around abruptly, saying, "I'm right behind you." Then he added, sotto voce, "I'm always right behind you."

- *Don't you realize you're always backed into a corner?* I was telling my good friend Bob Fergeson that pride got in the way of my praying for help, saying that the only time I could pray was when I felt I was backed into a corner. He responded with the above rhetorical question.

- *God has no interest in your perfection or imperfection.* I was complaining about some trait or other in a message to my good friend Shawn Nevins. Shawn replied with the above head-straightener.

- *If you can't inspire yourself, find someone else to inspire.* From Richard Rose.

- *Your job is not to be Douglas Harding or someone else. Your job is to become yourself—your real self.* First words from Douglas upon meeting him for the first time.

Check out my website at *www.SelfDiscoveryPortal.com*. You can find an email address there to contact me if you're interested.

"For Art"
By Corina Bardasuc

*Y*ou are my evening star in the summer sky who
Can dissipate my ignorance all thru
Within you I can see that which I lack
Not just another cloud shape
But a brilliant fact.
For you my evening star I traveled land and sea
So I can rest my soul at your feet
And let it, softly, be.

Within my heart so many things have grown to rot
Tied with invisible strings that keep me
Getting caught
Up in myself.
But you, my constant, even, ever balanced star,
So near within my reach, and yet so far,
You have spoken to me through many nights and dreams
And called out to my soul to look thru all that seems.

From my window tonight I turn to you my face,
Within the purple night you reverberate your grace
And I feel the soft rays of your celestial embrace.
The night is no longer a stranger, nor a foe,
Within your light all things are revealed
To form the great below
The counter part to your snow white brilliance
No longer a dark threat, but a sweet countenance
Of the opposite of grace.
Instead of fear, I only now feel
Reverence.

Your brilliance the darkness in my heart dispels
And wakes me from the deep slumber
Of many jaded spells.
Within your shade my soul can grow
Like a lily flower,
The harsh heat of the sun is no match
For your gentle power.

I was inspired to write a poem about you, since you have been a constant companion in my thoughts and dreams during the past months (I find when I don't see you for a while, at the meetings or whatnot, I dream about you more), and your words of wisdom and insight my constant companions during hard times. This poem I just wrote one night after a long walk out and admiring the starry night sky ... and the thought came to mind that I wanted to write about the evening star and how it's a guiding star reaching down to earth and all that imagery, and then it ended up being all about you, haha.   It's the closest thing I've written to a love poem :-)

I think Corina nailed the function that the projected guru serves—allowing us to see, hear and feel the radiance of our essential being before we're ready to accept it as what we truly are.

From Readers of Solid Ground of Being

"It definitely plucks the heart strings." - Wyatt W.

"It is a joy. You have a natural sto-
rytellers voice and conversational
style that draws the reader in and
pulls us gently along. You also
get right to the point in each piece
with no wasted words, which is
excellent, and unfortunately not
the case with most writers. I also
like how you've mixed up the visual style with bullets, lists, etc.,
and how you've integrated your
poems into the flow of the book.
In a way it reminds me of *Gödel,*
Escher, Bach in this regard—lots of different elements...." - Bart
M.

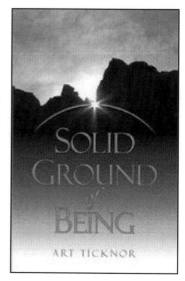

"The book was very confrontational, and I could see getting a
lot out of reading it, or sections of it, several times." - Ben R.

"I've read 20ish pages, and it's like sitting and talking with
you; your presence comes through clearly and most comfort-
ably. For some reason, the idea of giving up one's individuality
struck a chord with me and is staying with me. I am feeling re-
inspired and even on the verge of 'getting serious.' Funny how
one word can get through like that." - Judy M.

"I have to tell you I'm enjoying your book immensely. It is exactly the type of read I've been looking for. Despite a week in
Aruba, (I read a lot on the beach) and both plane rides, I could
not get through more than chapter 8 due to having to stop and
actually run the work you suggest.

"Right off the bat, I especially liked the One and the Same essay [Ch. 1]. Bang, right up against my head. I laughed out loud when I realized, yes, it is...it's aloneness.

"I do recognize my need to reach out to other seekers at this point. You're so right, the minutes are just clicking away."
- Mike M.

"I'm really enjoying your book Art - it is so you :)" - Heather S.

"Then, Sunday morning, I read your passage on Elton John and the piano on stage [Breathe In, Breath Out; Ch. 9].

"I ran the exercise and was pretty much awed when I let go of my truck, my wife, kids, dogs, the house, and finally my birth/self. Emptiness is the only way I can describe it, and that doesn't do it justice." - Mike M.

"BTW, I am reading *Solid Ground of Being* now. It's really great. I love the way it's broken into 1-page chunks. I'm going through something in my life now that made me see first-hand the pain of separation. The pain of being separate from others. The one you always talked about before when I was in Pittsburgh. Now I understand..." - Jon T.

"You know your book was a kick in the teeth for me on the falseness of the sense of individuality, which I have been absorbing for a couple of weeks. I realize now that I was feeling that this was some final understanding, though I never saw or thought that. Tonight I picked it up again and was again kicked in the teeth, this time by seeing that not only did I have a false belief in my own individuality, but I believe that this individual is who/what is aware. Once again, even though I had seen before the concept that awareness is universal, this is a new understanding or seeing. I suppose it will be a couple of weeks before I absorb this, too. So add one more to your list of those who have been truly affected by your book." - Judy M.

"I still feel like your book was the impetus for the self-inquiry that came over me in isolation. Thank you so much for that." - Heather S.

"Over the course of the last few months, your book Solid Ground of Being has become the 'standard' against which I've been comparing all of my introspective findings. Thank you for writing that book." - Rashed A.

"I just started reading Solid Ground of Being today—it's got some great pointers! I'm enjoying it." - Jenny T.

"I recently enjoyed reading *Solid Ground of Being* and got a lot out of it. I spread out the reading by just covering a couple entries of it every night before I went to bed and found that to work well.... Another way Solid Ground of Being impacted me was how I got a deeper sense of how the 'What am I?' question is the crux of the spiritual search and how direct inquiry is important."
- Tim S.

"I read Art's book. It is the best book on the topic that I have ever read. It has it all, it's just complete. I take my hat off to him. It's my new 'the one book to give to someone interested.' My only criticism is the 'it's so simple' tone that is sometimes there, sometimes I wanted to strangle him or something similarly vile. In truth, it's wanting to strangle myself." - Mario P. [from an email group report. The mind loves complexity :-]

"Solid Ground of Being—the perfect book for any level seeker. Chapter brevity allows time to attack the offending problem, before wordiness has a chance to become obsessive thought." - Dan A.

"I think you wrote a great book with a humble and simple presentation of big ideas with the reader and potential seeker in mind." - Paul S.

Graphics Credits

Cover photo: Reflective Morn, Bob Fergeson, www.nostalgiawest.com/.
Treasure map (p. 2): Thanks to Bob Fergeson (design by author).
Child looking thru door (p. 4): Photo courtesy of Maggie Raptis.
I-64 E. to Dulce, NM (p. 10): Photo by author.
Path thru woods (p. 13): Photo by author.
Ohio River (p. 17): Photo by author.
Richard Rose (p. 22): Photo by Bob Cergol.
Bonsai garden (p. 26): Dawes Arboretum. Photo by author.
Alabama Hills (p. 29): Outside Lone Pine, CA. Photo by author.
US-550 S. to Ouray, CO (p. 36): Photo by author.
Grass & flowers (p. 41): Photo by author.
Girls under umbrella (p. 44): Daughters Jen and Meg, 1970s.
Star magnolia (p. 48): Photo by author.
I.M. Pei museum (p. 56): Doha, Qatar. Photo by B. Erne.
Snowy walk in Galway (p. 59): Photo by Tess www.TessHughes.com/.
Truth-beauty-freedom-love (p. 62): Chinese calligraphy.
Sand river (p. 66): Dawes Arboretum. Photo by author.
RR tracks (p. 71): Photo by author.
Peegee hydrangea (p. 78): Photo by author.
Miami Metrorail 1984 (82): sites.google.com/site/transitmiami/.
Abbeyknockmoy cloister (p. 87): Photo by Tess www.TessHughes.com/.
1686 Marshall Street, Benwood, WV (p.99): Richard Rose home.
Sequoia corpse (p. 104): Yosemite. Photo by Chris Ticknor.
Byodo-In, O'ahu, Hawaii (p. 107): Photo by author (1983).
Rose (p. 110): Photo by Bob Fergeson, www.NostalgiaWest.com/.
Mesa Verde sun temple (p. 114): Photo by author.
Mexican Hat formation (p. 117): Monument Valley, AZ. Author photo.
Mussoorie, India (p. 124): Photo by Anima Pundeer.
Wild morning glory (p. 129): Photo by author.
Salisbury Cathedral (p. 132): Photo by Tess www.TessHughes.com/.
Canyon de Chelly rim (p. 138): Arizona. Photo by author.
Shadows (p. 141): Photo by author.
Callery pear flower (p. 144): Photo by author.
Hua Shan boardwalk (p. 149): Wikimedia Commons.
Philosopher in meditation (p. 156): Rembrandt; Wikimedia Commons.
Last of the Fostoria smokestacks (p. 160): Photo by author.

Wild flower (p. 166): Beach pea? Photo by author.

Cathedral of Learning (p. 173): U. of Pittsburgh; Wikimedia Commons.

Hookers, Féile Mhic Dara (p. 178): By Tess, www.TessHughes.com/.

Great Sand Dunes National Park (p. 182): Photo by author.

Abandonned house, De Beque, CO (p. 187): Photo by author.

Coole Park, Galway (p. 191): Photo by Tess, www.TessHughes.com/.

Pot-o-gold (p. 196): Chaffee County, CO wildfire protection plan.

Profusion crabapple buds (p. 201): Photo by author.

Tatev monastery (p. 206): Armenia. By Tess, www.TessHughes.com/.

Benwood, WV railroad (p. 210): Edge-detected photo by author.

Fruita, CO schoolhouse (p. 219): Bob Fergeson, NostalgiaWest.com/.

Hua Shan gazebo (p. 222): Wikimedia Commons.

La Sal Mountains (p. 231): Bob Fergeson, NostalgiaWest.com/.

Abbeyknockmoy gate (p. 235): Photo by Tess, www.TessHughes.com/.

Standardbred horse (p. 239): Photo by author.

Moundsville, WV bridge (p. 244): Photo by author.

Shadow man (p. 251): Photo by B. Erne.

Mesa Verde steps (p.256): Photo by author.

Aten sun disc (p. 261): Wikimedia Commons.

Monarch emerging from chrysalis (p. 266): Wikimedia Commons.

McCreary cemetery (p. 273): Marshall Co, WV. Photo by author.

Eyeglasses on table (p. 278): Photo by author.

Retreat cabin in woods (p. 285): Photo by author.

Bench on bike path (p. 290): Photo by author.

Another cabin in the woods (p. 294): Photo by author.

Self-portrait 2003 (p. 296): Drawing by author.

Arranmore Island beach (p. 302): Photo by Tess, www.TessHughes.com/.

Quiet life (p. 307): Photo by author.

Afternoon shade on the deck (p. 312): Photo by author.

Random vs. power law (p. 317): By Bob Fergeson (design by author).

Hopewell mound mica hand (p. 323): Wikimedia Commons.

Contemplation (p. 329): Photo by author.

Sadhus (p. 339): Photo by Anima Pundeer.

Necker cube (p. 349): Wikimedia Commons.

No-head circle (p. 352): Courtesy of Richard Lang; www.headless.org/.

Author (p. 354): 2010 photo by Phil Franta.

Solid Ground of Being cover (p. 358): Artwork by Luke Roberts.

Wingstem? (p. 363): Photo by author.

Clew Bay, County Mayo (p. 367): By Tess, www.TessHughes.com/.

Index

A Direct Path?, 318

A Special Case?, 51

A Suggestion?, 198

Additional TAT Press Books, 369

Advice?, 108

Afflictions to the Sense of Self, 19

Afraid to Commit, 14

Always Right Behind You, 19

Ambrosia Dialogue, 300

Another Way, 133

Anxiety, 143

Are You Sure?, 235

Are You the Thinker?, 24

Ask Yourself, 305

Aspiration, 257

Attitude?, 233

Author Info, 354

Being Is, 84

Between-ness, 155

Beyond Experience: How?, 280

Blindsight & Group Efforts, 43

Bottom Line, 367

Can't Do's, 141

Casting off Illusion, 73

Catalyst, The, 21

Center Cannot Hold, The, 308

Common-Sense Meditation, 325

Conciliatory Path, 89

Confused About Self-Realization, 200

Conventional Practice, 229

Conviction State Revealed, 250

Convictions About Knowing, 308

Crisis of Hope, 95

Decalogue, 89

Determination, 33

Diamond Sutra, 333

Dissatisfaction, 3

Doing Zen, 233

Douglas Harding & Richard Rose, 346

Dream of Grace, 166

Dreamless Sleep, 279

Egoless Action for Others, 216

Energy, 240

Eyeglasses on a Table, 278

Failure to Thrive, 289

Fear Mode, 276

Fear of Worthlessness, 273

Flower Sermon, The, 162

For Art, by Corina Bardasuc, 356

Frustration, 198

Generic Advice, 287

Grace, Simply, 167

Graphics Credits, 362

Group Retreat, 94

Guessing vs. Looking, 231

Hear, Say, 84

High Definition TV, 30

Holding On or Letting Go, 305

Home Base, 203

I May Be Wrong, 241

Impulse to Observe, 324

Indestructible, 160

Interview Questionnaire, 244

Introduction
  Aim, 2
  Ready, 1

Irreconcilable?, 227

Knot Untied, The, 168

Ladderwork, 86

Last Straw, The, 289

Limbo, 199

Liquidity Trap of Self-Ignorance, 39

Little Bird, 302

Living on Borrowed Time, 10

Lo-Cal Snacks, 25
  II, 69
  III, 112
  IV, 164
  V, 274

Longing, 202

Looking & Questioning, 47

Looking All the Way Through, 63

Looking vs. Thinking, 135

Love, 111

Love & Friendship, 17

Man to God, 205

Marshmallow Test, 85

Mechanics, 302

Meditation & Celibacy, 287

Meditation Is Simple, 320

Meeting of the Minds, 272

Middle Way, 51

Mood Is a Message, A, 14

No Question?, 305

Observing the Observer, 105

Opening Your Heart, 61

Outside Is Inside, 322

Pardon Me, But…, 51

Physical Dying Process, 306

Productive Self-Inquiry, 156

Purity of Intent, 70

Q & A, 127
  II, 135
  III, 205

Realization or Mind-Trick?, 321

Resolving Personal Crap, 201

Richard Rose, 88

Right Action, 201

Salt Doll, 72

Seek Me First, 157

Self-Definition, 20

Self-Perspective, 131

Sense of Self, 195

Separation, 18
Settled Your Soul?, 132
Signposts of Progress, 54
Silence & Stillness, 50
Sitting in Rapport with Yourself, 48
Solid Ground reader feedback, 358
Solitary Retreat, A, 158
Stark, Alone, 202
State of Simply 'Being'?, 115
Status Quo Trajectory, 196
Struggling, 304
Struggling to Move, 145
Struggling to Open, 30
Stuck Between, 280
Stuck in Despair, 119
Stuckness, 139
'This Self Won't Die'?, 116
To & Fro, 11
To Know the Truth, 163
Triangulation, 90
Turn Around?, 205
Two Awarenesses?, 15
Two of Me?, 27
Umbilical Cord, 52
Unhappiness, 13
Unknown Goal, The, 259
Untenable?, 308
Waiting for Revelation, 25
Way Out Is the Way In, 66
We Succeed by Failing, 49
What Is Aware?, 130
When the Body Dies, 199
When You're Ready, 368
Who Are You Trying to Please?, 271
Winter Intensive 1982, 281
With or Without, 161
Your Relationship to Awareness, 11
Zero, 303

*G*od (a problematic word) is not a being.
God is Absolute Being = Total Freedom.
Becoming one with God = transcending all enslavements.
A self-inquiry practice is the ultimate form of prayer.

When you know all, you know nothing.
When you do all, you do nothing.
When you love all, you love nothing.
When you are all, you are nothing.

YOU ARE MORE THAN YOU THINK … AND LESS.

The Bottom Line

A summing up of advice for your consideration:

- Feel the longing, and respond.
- Establish a daily inward practice.
- Find others to work with.
- Question your beliefs, and help others do the same.
  ◊ Conserve and channel sex energy toward your goal.
- Keep daily exigencies from sidetracking your focus.
- All depends on looking within.
- Become aware of that which is self-aware.

When You're Ready

Come unto Me
   When you're ready to lay your burden down,
When your work is done
   And you recognize it as your innermost desire.

I am the Home that you long for,
The surcease of your suffering
And of the world's suffering.

I am the Sanctuary that you've never left
During your long dream of expatriation.
I am the Perfection that you've been seeking.

When you're ready, my beloved,
To awaken from your dream of separation,
You will find that You and I
Have never parted.

Additional TAT Press Books

A Handyman's Common Sense Guide to Spiritual Seeking. David Weimer's "Common Sense Guide" is a compendium of his years of spiritual search. This Army veteran, surveyor, reporter, and jack-of-all-trades handyman offers an unwavering portrait of the determination and single-mindedness that led him to experience what he calls completion.  Alternating between practical advice and heartfelt exhortations, he inspires readers to pursue their own understanding of existence. *ISBN: 9780979963087.*

 **At Home with the Inner Self.** Jim Burns was the only living person that Richard Rose spoke of as having "made the trip." *At Home with the Inner Self* consists of transcripts from informal talks recorded in 1984 and 1985. New to the third edition is an interview conducted in 2006 as well as the photographs that evoke the graceful dissolution of the urban landscape that Jim calls home. *ISBN: 9780979963070.*

Beyond Mind, Beyond Death. An anthology of the best essays, poems, and humor from the TAT *Forum* online magazine. Many are the voices in this volume, from classic to contemporary, yet all point toward a greater reality than that of which we are typically aware—a Reality that can only be hinted at with words; that must and can be discovered  by you rather than described by an author. *ISBN: 9780979963001.*

 **The Celibate Seeker: An Exploration of Celibacy as a Modern Spiritual Practice** by Shawn Nevins. A survey of people's experiences with celibacy as a spiritual practice. Examines the effect of celibacy on intuition and energy level as well as other benefits and difficulties of this practice. Offers a wealth of practical advice and insight. *ISBN: 9780979963032.*

The Listening Attention by Bob Fergeson. How can we re-connect, open the Gateway to Within, and once more gain the Peace and Understanding of our Inner Self? The Listen ing Attention is our innate ability to observe the world and ourselves without identification. Separate from the world of the mind and action, it points the way home. *ISBN: 9780979963063.*

The Perennial Way by Bart Marshall. New English versions of Yoga Sutras, Dhammapada, Heart Sutra, Ashtavakra Gita, Faith Mind Sutra, and Tao Te Ching. These insightful new versions are presented without commentary ... clear and poetic, yet intensely faithful to the language and nuance of the originals, they invite direct communication with the masters, and vibrate with a revelatory self-evidence that resonates in the mind and heart long after reading. *ISBN: 9780979963049.*

Solid Ground of Being. In sharing the simple facts of his life experience, Art Ticknor takes us on an extraordinary journey, which hopes "to inspire another with a possibly unimagined possibility, and to encourage another to persevere." *ISBN: 9780979963056.*

These books are available at *Amazon.com* and other booksellers. See the TAT Foundation website at *www.tatfoundation.org* for books, audio files and DVDs published by TAT.

Made in the USA
Columbia, SC
19 September 2020